Media and Crisis Communication

This volume centers on the relationship between media and crisis communication, the need to address which has only been heightened by the recent experience of COVID-19 and the needs for public health crisis communication.

With multiple voices and multiple fields engaging simultaneously with crisis communication, this book illuminates the role of media in crisis communication within this complex environment. Both traditional and digital media, including social media platforms, respond to an array of crisis contexts including political crises, public health crises, disasters, and organizational crises. The book presents original research that approaches the effects of media in any of the possible crisis contexts.

This collection will interest scholars and students of crisis communication, public relations, risk communication, digital media, and political communication.

W. Timothy Coombs (PhD Purdue University) is a former university professor and currently is on the Advisory Board for the Centre for Crisis & Risk Communications and is the Editor-in-Chief of the *Journal of Contingencies and Crisis Management*. He has been researching crisis communication for the past 30 years and develop the situational crisis communication theory. His crisis communication research has won multiple awards from professional organizations including the Jackson, Jackson & Wagner Behavioral Science Prize from the Public Relations Society of America and the Pathfinder Award from the Institute of Public Relations in recognition of his research contributions to the field and to the practice. He is the author of *Communicating in Extreme Crises: Lessons from the Edge*. Coombs is also an ICA Fellow and *an Academic Core member of the University of Georgia Crisis Communication Think Tank.*

Electronic Media Research Series
Sponsored by the Broadcast Education Association
Michel M. Haigh, Series Editor

Risk and Health Communication in an Evolving Media Environment
Edited by H. Dan O'Hair

Race and Gender in Electronic Media
Content, Context, Culture
Edited by Rebecca Ann Lind

Digital Technology and the Future of Broadcasting
Edited by John V. Pavlik

Media and Social life
Edited by Mary Beth Oliver and Arthur A. Raney

Media Management and the Economics Research in a Transmedia Environment
Edited by Alan B. Albarran

Media and the Moral Mind
Edited by Ron Tamborini

Media Literacy in a Disruptive Media Environment
Edited by Dr. William G. Christ and Dr. Belinha S. De Abreu

Political Communication, Culture and Society
Edited by Patricia Moy and Rico Neumann

Triaging the Streaming Wars
Edited by Robert Alan Brookey, Jason Phillips and Tim Pollard

US Media and Diversity
Representation, Dissemination, and Effects
Edited by Travis L. Dixon and Dana Mastro

Media and Crisis Communication
Edited by W. Timothy Coombs

Media and Crisis Communication

Edited by W. Timothy Coombs

Routledge
Taylor & Francis Group
NEW YORK AND LONDON

First published 2025
by Routledge
605 Third Avenue, New York, NY 10158

and by Routledge
4 Park Square, Milton Park, Abingdon, Oxon, OX14 4RN

Routledge is an imprint of the Taylor & Francis Group, an informa business

Library of Congress Cataloging-in-Publication Data
Names: Coombs, W. Timothy, editor.
Title: Media and crisis communication / edited by W. Timothy Coombs.
Description: New York : Routledge, 2025. | Series: Electronic media research | Includes bibliographical references and index.
Identifiers: LCCN 2024028230 (print) | LCCN 2024028231 (ebook) | ISBN 9781032619064 (hardback) | ISBN 9781032619149 (paperback) | ISBN 9781032619187 (ebook)
Subjects: LCSH: Communication in crisis management. | Mass media. | Crisis management.
Classification: LCC HD49.3 .M43 2025 (print) | LCC HD49.3 (ebook) | DDC 658.4/5--dc23/eng/20240722
LC record available at https://lccn.loc.gov/2024028230
LC ebook record available at https://lccn.loc.gov/2024028231

ISBN: 978-1-032-61906-4 (hbk)
ISBN: 978-1-032-61914-9 (pbk)
ISBN: 978-1-032-61918-7 (ebk)

DOI: 10.4324/9781032619187

Typeset in Sabon
by SPi Technologies India Pvt Ltd (Straive)

Contents

List of Figures *vii*
List of Tables *viii*
List of Contributors *ix*
Acknowledgments *xii*
Series Editor's Foreword *xiii*

Introduction 1

1 Black Press Videos as Crisis Communication Tools for Social Amplification of Risk in a Global Pandemic 7
CHALISE MACKLIN AND GEORGE DANIELS

2 Examining How Medium, Message, and Apology Used in Crises Responses Impact Stakeholders 33
MICHEL M. HAIGH AND PRISCA S. NGONDO

3 Arab Spring Conflict Visuals: A Content Analysis of Crisis Coverage on Pan-Arab TV News 52
MICHAEL D. BRUCE

4 Differentiation Versus Denial: Impact of Messaging about Player Transactions on Team Reputation, Ticket Sales, and Sports Channel Subscriptions 68
JOSEPH R. BLANEY AND STEPHEN K. HUNT

5 Media Framing, Sports Activism Failure, and Crisis Communication: European Football Teams and the *One Love* Campaign at the World Cup 2022 81
KAROLINE KOKHOLM, MARIT LOTT, AND WINNI JOHANSEN

6 Lessons Learned from the Early Days of the COVID-19 Pandemic: Communicating about Public Health Risks on Social Media 124
ELINA R. TACHKOVA AND GRACE ELLEN BRANNON

7 The Effectiveness of Converging Alert Messages from Multiple Weather Communicators 141
SAYMIN LEE, JIYOUN KIM, ANITA ATWELL SEATE, AND BROOKE F. LIU

8 Crisis Communication in the Age of AI: Navigating Opportunities, Challenges, and Future Horizons 172
YANG CHENG, JAEKUK LEE, AND JINZHE QIAO

9 Checking the Pulse of Stakeholders through the Eyes of the Media: Examining Publics' Emotions in COVID-19 Management and Communication 195
AUGUSTINE PANG, JERENA C. K. NG, AND RYAN LIM

10 Cloaking through Crisis Communication: Hiding Uncomfortable Information 222
W. TIMOTHY COOMBS

Index *241*

Figures

1.1 Social stations 10
1.2 The COVID-19 coronavirus Crisis March 2020–December 2021 20
3.1 Frequency of conflict and violent imagery of Arab Spring coverage by network as represented in RQ2 63
7.1 Model for communicative preparatory action (RQ2-1) 153
7.2 Model for sheltering preparatory action (RQ2-1) 154
7.3 Model for sharing information with others (RQ2-2) 156
7.4 Models for social media engagement (RQ3) 157
A.1 Convergence on the threat 164
A.2 Convergence on the threat and communicative preparatory action 165
A.3 Convergence on the threat, communicative preparatory action, and sheltering preparatory action 166
8.1 Key functions of AI tools across crisis stages 177

Tables

1.1 COVID-19 Videos by News Outlet 19
2.1 Means and Standard Deviations for Dependent Variables and Print/Video 42
2.2 Means and Standard Deviations for Dependent Variables and Medium/Message 44
2.3 Image Repair Strategy Employed by Organization as Identified by Stakeholders 45
3.1 Frequency and Percentages of Arab Spring Conflict by Network Taxonomy 60
3.2 Standardized Pearson Residuals for Arab Spring Conflict Visuals on Western and Liberal Commercial Networks 60
3.3 Frequency and Percentages of Arab Spring Conflict by Network 62
3.4 Standardized Pearson Residuals for Arab Spring Conflict Visuals by Network 63
4.1 Bivariate Correlations for All Dependent Variables (N = 321) 75
4.2 Descriptive Statistics for Dependent Variables by Condition 75
4.3 Descriptive Statistics for Sex by Condition 76
4.4 Descriptive Statistics for Income by Condition 76
5.1 Overview of Newspaper Articles and Characteristics 93
5.2 Frames Used by Danish and German News Media in the One Love Controversy 103
6.1 Counties Selected for Inclusion in the Study 129
6.2 List of Generic Frames 130
7.1 Message Credibility across Three Convergence Types 152
7.2 Indirect Effects of Convergence Type on Communicative Preparatory Action 153
7.3 Indirect Effects of Convergence Type on Sheltering Preparatory Action 154
7.4 Indirect Effects of Convergence Type on Sharing Information with Others 155
7.5 Indirect Effects of Convergence Type on Social Media Engagement 157

Contributors

Joseph R. Blaney (PhD, University of Missouri) is a professor of Communication and interim director of the School of Social Work at Illinois State University. His research interests include image repair of persons and organizations across corporate, religious, political, and other contexts.

Grace Ellen Brannon, PhD, is an assistant professor in the Department of Communication at the University of Texas at Arlington. Her research focuses on patient-provider(-family) experiences and health outcomes for marginalized populations with chronic or long-term health issues using mixed methods. Much of her work focuses on developing pilot-tested materials leading toward larger-scale intervention implementation.

Michael D. Bruce has a PhD in Communication from the University of Oklahoma. He is a member of the faculty in the Journalism and Creative Media Department at the University of Alabama where he primarily teaches sports media courses. His scholarly research focuses on risk/crisis communication, visual communication, and Middle Eastern media. Most of his publications focus on visuals of conflict and violence on Arab satellite television. In addition to traditional academic research, he is an award-winning creative scholar.

Yang Cheng, PhD, is an associate professor at North Carolina State University, USA. She teaches research methods, public relations, crisis communication, and global communication. Her research interests include artificial intelligence, relationship management, and crisis communication.

W. Timothy Coombs (PhD Purdue University) (USA) is an advisor for the Centre for Crisis and Risk Communications. His primary area of research and consulting is crisis communication and his research has won multiple awards from professional organizations including the Jackson, Jackson & Wagner Behavioral Science Prize. He is a fellow in the International Communication Association.

George Daniels, PhD, is an associate professor of journalism and creative media in the College of Communication and Information Sciences at the University of Alabama. Since 2003, he's taught courses in cross-platform reporting, electronic news reporting, media management, and diversity. Before beginning his academic career, he worked as a local television news producer.

Michel M. Haigh (PhD, University of Oklahoma) is a professor in the School of Journalism and Mass Communication at Texas State University.

Stephen K. Hunt (PhD, Southern Illinois University) is a university professor and director of the School of Communication at Illinois State University. His research interests include civic engagement and pedagogy.

Winni Johansen, PhD, is a professor of Corporate Communication and Crisis Management in the Department of Management, Aarhus BSS, Aarhus University. Her research interests include crisis management and crisis communication, strategic listening, social media, crisis consulting, internal crisis communication, environmental communication, and strategic communication in organizations.

Jiyoun Kim is an assistant professor of communication at the University of Maryland. Her research is broadly concerned with science, risk, and crisis communication. Specifically, her research program focuses on how we can harness the power of communication to design and deliver effective messaging to help the public make more informed decisions.

Karoline Kokholm holds a MSc in Economics and Business Administration with specialization in Strategic Communication, Aarhus BSS, Aarhus University, Denmark from 2023.

Jaekuk Lee is a doctoral student of CRDM program at North Carolina State University.

Saymin Lee is a PhD candidate in communication at the University of Maryland. Her research explores the intersection of public relations and science communication. She is particularly interested in how various publics engage in communication in scientific contexts.

Ryan Lim, BSocSc, is a senior analyst at Edelman Global Advisory, a boutique public affairs advisory firm. A specialist in government affairs, policy communication as well as crisis and risk management, his work covers a variety of sectors including energy, healthcare, petrochemicals, and technology.

Brooke F. Liu is a professor of communication at the University of Maryland where she co-directs the Pandemic Preparedness Initiative.

Her research program focuses on how governments can harness the power of risk and crisis communication for prosocial outcomes.

Marit Lott is an MA student in communication and media at Augsburg University, Germany, who has worked as a research intern, in 2023, at the department of Management, Aarhus BSS, Aarhus University, Denmark.

Chalise Macklin is an assistant professor of journalism who teaches broadcast journalism and other undergraduate and graduate-level journalism courses. She is a former digital and print news reporter and broadcast news producer. Her research focuses on diversity and inclusivity in newsrooms and news coverage with a focus on cultural influence and potential risks to the public. Macklin seeks to explore ways to reduce risks to the public through media messages and improve diversity and inclusivity in media messages.

Jerena C.K. Ng, MMC, works as a research assistant at Singapore Management University (SMU). She is also a professional copy editor and an English instructor.

Prisca S. Ngondo (PhD, Texas Tech University) is an associate professor of public relations in the School of Journalism and Mass Communication at Texas State University. Ngondo's research interests are in strategic communication and international public relations.

Augustine Pang (PhD, University of Missouri) is a professor of Communication Management (Practice) at the Lee Kong Chian School of Business, Singapore Management University. At SMU, he is appointed as associate dean (Partnerships & Engagement). His research interests include crisis management, communication and leadership, image/reputation management and repair, media management, and communication management.

Jinzhe Qiao is a doctoral student of CRDM program at North Carolina State University.

Anita Atwell Seate is an associate professor of communication at the University of Maryland. Their research examines how potentially threatening information is communicated and how publics respond to threatening messages. They examine these issues in intergroup, crisis, and disaster contexts.

Elina R. Tachkova (PhD Texas A&M University) is an assistant professor at the Department of Communication Studies at Hong Kong Baptist University. Her research focuses on the role of emotion into crisis communication research specifically examining the intersection between organizational crises and scandals.

Acknowledgments

I would like to thank BEA and Routledge for their support throughout this longer-than-expected journey to completing this volume. COVID-19 created a variety of challenges for that journey. I want to give a special thanks to Michel Haigh for all her work to keep the project on track.

Series Editor's Foreword

Since its inception in 1948, the Broadcast Education Association has fostered a serious commitment to scholarly research, though that commitment became more formalized with the publication of its first scholarly journal, *Journal of Broadcasting* (later *Journal of Broadcasting & Electronic Media*), in 1957. Over the Association's rich intellectual history, BEA's annual meetings have afforded both academics and professionals a wide range of opportunities for the presentation of important scholarship focusing on broadcasting and the electronic media.

In 2008, BEA launched a series of programs designed to advance original research initiatives under the direction of the Association's Research Committee. For over a decade, the BEA Research Symposium Series, a scholarly venture within the framework of the annual conference, has served to advance the research agendas of our discipline and provide a forum for some of the leading scholars and latest ground-breaking research in our field. The first research symposium in 2008 was orchestrated by Jennings Bryant with a focus on media effects. This was followed in 2009 with a research symposium about technopolitics, under the direction of Lynda Lee Kaid.

In response to these two highly successful symposia, BEA entered discussions in 2010 with the Taylor and Francis Group of Routledge to form a partnership. The goal of this partnership? To publish an annual volume resulting from the yearly BEA Research Symposium—the Electronic Media Research Series, a cutting-edge publication on a broad swath of significant topics. The expansive list of volumes includes: *Sports Media: Transformation, Integration, Consumption* (Andrew C. Billings); *Media and the Moral Mind* (Ron Tamborini); *Media Management and Economics Research in a Transmedia Environment* (Alan B. Albarran); *Media and Social Life* (Arthur A. Raney and Mary Beth Oliver); *Digital Technology and the Future of Broadcasting: Global Perspectives* (John V. Pavlik); *Race and Gender in Electronic Media: Content, Context, Culture* (Rebecca Ann Lind); *Risk and Health Communication in an Evolving Media Environment* (H. Dan O'Hair); *Video Games: A Medium That Demands Our Attention* (Nicholas

Bowman); *The Golden Age of Data* (Don A. Grady); *Media Literacy in a Disruptive Media Environment* (William G. Christ, Belinha S. De Abreu, and Michelle Ciulla Lipkin); *Communication, Culture, and Society* (Patricia Moy and Rico Neumann); and *Triaging the Streaming Wars: Investigations and Analyses* (Robert Alan Brookey, Jason Phillips, and Timothy Pollard). The most recent edition is *U.S. Media and Diversity: Representation, Dissemination, and Effects* (Travis Dixon and Dana Mastro).

This edition to the series, *Media and Crisis Communication: An Exploration of Intersections*, is edited by Timothy Coombs. The volume includes work presented at the 2021 BEA research symposium, Media and Crisis Communication, as well as studies conducted just for this volume. Coombs states, "of the many threads used to weave crisis communication tapestry, media is the most intricate and delicate." The growth of crisis communication continues partly because of the presence of social media. The role of the media in crisis communication is unique because it is a tool organizations use for crisis management, and the types of media used in the crisis response is key. Journalists are also using various media formats to explain the crisis to the public. The authors of the chapters provide empirical evidence and theoretical analyses to reflect on crisis and the media.

This volume enhances our understanding of the crisis communication and media. Authors investigate the role media played in disseminating COVID-19 information at the start of the pandemic. Crisis also occurs in sports. Authors examine how sports teams build for future years as well as the backlash from the media when soccer teams from Germany and Denmark did not have protests before the 2022 World Cup in Qatar.

Crisis communication research examines the role of paid, earned, shared, and owned media in disseminating crisis messages, and one chapter in this volume examines the differences between those formats. And two areas where crisis communication happens on a regular basis—war and weather—are also examined more closely by researchers in this volume. The book explores crisis communication from a variety of theoretical frameworks and a variety of research methods looking at a variety of topics. It is an eclectic volume—much like crisis communication is at its core. Everyone is impacted by crisis on a personal, professional, or societal level. This volume shows how expansive the area of crisis communication is as a field of research. Crisis communication continues to be an area that interests scholars because of the various types of crises occurring in society. This volume of work shines a light on the areas researchers focus their time and talents.

The Broadcast Education Association and Routledge are proud to make this important volume available to scholars and teachers across the communication discipline and beyond.

Michel M. Haigh
Texas State University

Introduction

The 2021 research symposium theme for BEA was the relationship between media and crisis communication. As the call stated:

> Crisis communication are the interventions (words and actions) taken by those seeking to manage the crisis in some way. Crisis communication is complex because it is multi-vocal. There can be multiple voices engaging in crisis communication. At times, those voice work in concert while at other times they can be in conflict. Moreover, research in a number of fields has begun to explore the various effects of the media in crisis formation and crisis communication. The goal of the symposium is to illuminate the role of media in crises communication within this complex environment. Media include both traditional and digital, including social media platforms.

BEA 2021 was remote, a consequence of the COVID-19 pandemic. Everyone was becoming familiar with the disruptive nature of crises. Crisis communication represents the interventions used to address the disruption by providing new directions for those impacted by crises. Crisis communication is a multi-vocal phenomenon. Many parties will be engaged in crisis communication and seek to influence how the crisis is resolved (Frandsen & Johansen, 2017).

The symposium upon which this volume is based focused on the role media, both tradition and digital, within the crisis communication process. Of the many threads used to weave the crisis communication tapestry, media is the most intricate and delicate. The media threat is intricate because it touches so many facets of crisis communication and the crisis management process. It is intricate because media use or misuse in crisis communication can result in decreased or increased suffering for those touched by a crisis.

Initially, crisis communication was a rather niche research area in the 1980s with just a small number of researchers deciding to specialize in it

DOI: 10.4324/9781032619187-1

(Benson, 1988). Those early researchers were beginning to develop and to publish crisis communication theories in the 1990s. Among those early theories were corporate apologia (Dionisopolous & Vibbert, 1988; Hearit, 1994), image repair theory (Benoit, 1995), and situational crisis communication theory (Coombs, 1995; Coombs & Holladay. 2002). The research experienced a "big bang" in the 2000s with stealing thunder (Arpan & Pompper, 2003; Claeys & Cauberghe, 2012), integrated crisis mapping (Jin et al., 2007), and threat appraisal (Jin & Cameron, 2007; Pang et al., 2006). The growth of crisis communication continues on a trajectory of expansion to this day fueled in part by the presence of social media.

The symposium sessions included examinations of crisis communication theory and research, race, and journalism through the lens of the media. This volume builds upon those diverse crisis communication and media topics in an effort to capture the variety of research topics and methods that comprise the rapidly growing field of crisis communication research and influence of media on that development. The PESO distinction for media is useful as part of the introduction to this volume. PESO divides media into four categories: paid, earned, shared, and owned. Paid is typified by advertising and digital platforms where an entity pays to place a message. Earned is traditional publicity and digital publicity such as bloggers where others decide to carry an entity's message. Shared are the use of social media platforms to present messages. Owned are materials (actual and digital) created by an entity. An entity's own web site is owned. Social media does not count as owned because the entity does not control the social media platform (Macnamara et al., 2016). This volume explores a range of media and crisis contexts.

Chapters 1, 6, and 9 all involve COVID-19, a public health crisis. These chapters each explore different facets of media within the COVID-19 public health crisis. Chapter 1 used the videos created by African American-owned media (aka the Black press) as its data. The research explores the emotions associated with the videos and how the messages being presented address the skepticism and concerns Black people have with the COVID-19 vaccine. Renn et al.'s (1992) social amplification of risk (SARF) is the guiding theoretical lens in the chapter. The media was owned, digital, video, and the content created by news outlets.

Chapter 6 explores the communication disseminated by public health organizations during COVID-19. County public health offices from the three largest states in the US. Press releases and tweets from the public health offices were the data from the study. Tweets are social media while press releases are owned when presented in the organization's web site. Witte's (1992) extended parallel process model (EPPM) and framing (Entman, 1993) were the theoretical lens used in the study. The media was owned and the content created by public health organizations.

Chapter 9 also examined the government as crisis communications but how those messages were covered by traditional news media. Stories appearing in the primary traditional news outlets in Singapore provide the data for the study. The integrated crisis model (ICM) provides the theoretical lens for the chapter. The authors unpack the emotions associated with news stories about COVID-19 and how those emotions were exhibited behaviorally. The media was earned and the content created by both the traditional media and the government because earned is a mix of the original source and how it is interpreted by the gatekeeper.

Chapters 4 and 5 explore crises within the sports context. Chapter 4 uses an experimental approach to test the effects of differentiation and denial when a sports team takes actions that indicate they are about to rebuild for the future rather than to contend for that year. Benoit's (1995) image repair theory provides the theoretical lens. Media are the stimuli for the experiment. More specifically news stories using quotations from the team were used. The study found differentiating the current effort from past rebuilds was superior to denying a rebuild. The differentiation strategy produced stronger, positive outcomes than the denial strategy. The media was earned and owned and the content created by the team and the news media.

Chapter 5 explored how the news media in Germany and Denmark covered the failure of their football teams to launched planned protests at the 2022 World Cup in Qatar. The news media coverage of the failed sports activism was the data for the study. Both situational crisis communication theory (Coombs, 2007) and the rhetorical arena theory (Frandsen and Johansen, 2017) were used as theoretical lens. The study found the German media was harsher on the German football federation than the Danish press was on the Danish football federation. The media was owned and content created by the news media (how it portrayed the failed activism).

Chapter 3 explored news coverage of the Arab Spring with a focus on transnational satellite news channels. Framing theory (Entman, 1993) provides the theoretical lens for the chapter. The framing compared the conflict and visual frames used by Western media and by liberal commercial media. The liberal commercial media showed more conflict visuals than the Western media. The media was owned and the content created by the news outlets themselves.

Chapter 2 is an experimental study that tests the effects of media channels on how people react to product recall messages. SCCT was the theoretical lens for the chapter. The message was an apology and it was delivered either by print (written state or print ad) or video statement. The study found the written statement produced more positive outcomes such as trust, commitment, and food safety involvement. Hence, there was a channel effect for crisis responses in the study. The media was owned and the organization-in-crisis was the source of the message.

Chapter 7 explores the critical topic of warning messages during severe weather by considering the concerns that arise when multiple warnings are coming from various actors including the government and the news media. The rhetorical arena theory provides the dominant theoretical lens for the chapter. Using an experiment that includes weather warnings from the government, broadcast meteorologist, and social media meteorologists, the chapter examines what happens when messages are consistent or inconsistent with one another in regard to threats and recommended actions. The study found people are more likely to act safely when messages are consistent with one another. The results support established views in crisis communication that consistency in messages/voices is important to effective crisis communication. The media was owned and both the government and news media were the sources of the messages.

Chapter 10 unpacks a potential negative consequence of crisis communication called cloaking. Cloaking is a possible negative outcome from attempts to dominate the crisis narrative. Organizations-in-crisis can push a dominant narrative that hides uncomfortable crisis-related information from future stakeholders. Collective memory and terminsitic screens are the dominant theoretical lens in the chapter. A case using the Texas A&M University Bonfire crisis is used to illustrate how pushing a dominant narrative allows TAMU to hide its responsibility for the crisis from future stakeholders. TAMU's dominant narrative emphasizes an unavoidable tragedy and the need to focus on a better future to avoid discussing its responsibility for the death. The media was both owned (web site, speech, and memorial) and earned with the organization-in-crisis the primary source of the messages but some news media content as well.

Chapter 8 is much more conceptual because it considers the present and future role of AI in crisis communication. AI can influence the complete array of media that used in crisis communication. Of special note is how social media provided data for crisis managers for both detecting crises and understanding how people react to their crisis messaging. The chapter explains natural language processing (NLP) and its relevance to AI. AI applications in crisis communication include real-time information dissemination, sentiment analysis, and public engagement. The chapter ends by speculating on future trends and how to mitigate the potential negative effects of AI on crisis communication.

On a final note, the disruptive nature of the COVID-19 was one force contributing to the delay of this volume's completion. COVID-19's disruption spread through various aspects of society, including the operation of academic institutions (a topic covered in one symposium session) and people's connections to those institutions. At the time of the BEA research symposium, I was still an academic. Since then, I have left academics, but still involved in research, and moved to another state. All of these actions resulted in disruption in my research life, including the sudden loss of access to my old academic email system. But we have navigated those disruption to chart a new course for the production of this volume. Crises can make those who live through them stronger. This volume is stronger for having survived the disruptions to craft a strong collection that reflects the great diversity that is the field of crisis communication. I hope you find reading the chapters insightful and helpful.

References

Arpan, L. M., & Pompper, D. (2003). Stormy weather: Testing "stealing thunder" as a crisis communication strategy to improve communication flow between organizations and journalists. *Public Relations Review*, *29*(3), 291–308.

Benoit, W. L. (1995). *Accounts, excuses, and apologies: A theory of image restoration*. Albany: State University of New York Press.

Benson, J. A. (1988). Crisis revisited: An analysis of strategies used by Tylenol in the second tampering episode. *Communication Studies*, *39*(1), 49–66.

Claeys, A. S., & Cauberghe, V. (2012). Crisis response and crisis timing strategies, two sides of the same coin. *Public Relations Review*, *38*(1), 83–88.

Coombs, W. T. (1995). Choosing the Right Words: The Development of Guidelines for the Selection of the "Appropriate" Crisis-Response Strategies. *Management Communication Quarterly*, *8*(4), 447–476. https://doi.org/10.1177/0893318995008004003

Coombs, W. T. (2007). Protecting organization reputations during a crisis: The development and application of a situational crisis communication theory. *Corporate Reputation Review*, *10*(3), 163–176. http://dx.doi.org/10.1057/palgrave.crr.1550049

Coombs, W. T., & Holladay, S. J. (2002). Helping crisis managers protect reputational assets: Initial tests of the situational crisis communication theory. *Management Communication Quarterly*, *16*(2), 165–186.

Dionisopolous, G. N., & Vibbert, S. L. (1988). CBS vs Mobil oil: Charges of creative bookkeeping. In H. R. Ryan (Ed.), *Oratorical encounters: Selected studies and sources of 20th century political accusations and apologies* (pp. 214–252). Westport, CT: Greenwood Press.

Entman, R. M. (1993). Framing: Toward clarification of a fractured paradigm. *Journal of Communication*, *43*(4), 51–58.

Frandsen, F., & Johansen, W. (2017). *Organizational Crisis Communication*. London: SAGE.

Hearit, K. M. (1994). Apologies and public relations crises at Chrysler, Toshiba, and Volvo. *Public Relations Review*, *20*(2), 113–125.

Jin, Y., & Cameron, G. T. (2007). The effects of threat type and duration on public relations practitioner's cognitive, affective, and conative responses in crisis situations. *Journal of Public Relations Research*, *19*(3), 255–281.

Jin, Y., Pang, A., & Cameron, G. T. (2007). Integrated crisis mapping: Toward a publics-based, emotion-driven conceptualization in crisis communication. *Sphera Publica*, (7), 81–95.

Macnamara, J., Lwin, M., Adi, A., & Zerfass, A. (2016). 'PESO'media strategy shifts to 'SOEP': Opportunities and ethical dilemmas. *Public Relations Review*, *42*(3), 377–385.

Pang, A., Jin, Y., & Cameron, G. T. (2006). Do we stand on common ground? A threat appraisal model for terror alerts issued by the Department of Homeland Security. *Journal of Contingencies and Crisis Management*, *14*(2), 82–96.
Renn, O., Burns, W.J., Kasperson, J.X., Kasperson, R.E. & Slovic, P. (1992). The social amplification of risk: Theoretical foundations and empirical applications. *Journal of Social Issues*, 48 (4), 137–160.
Witte, K. (1992). Putting the fear back into fear appeals: The extended parallel process model. *Communications Monographs*, *59*(4), 329–349.

1 Black Press Videos as Crisis Communication Tools for Social Amplification of Risk in a Global Pandemic

Chalise Macklin and George Daniels

The biggest global health crisis in more than a century has been an ideal time to generate new knowledge not only about crisis communication but also its inter-relationship with risk communication. In 2020, when the COVID-19 pandemic began to sweep across the globe, warnings, reassurances, predictions, threats, disclaimers, explanations, excuses—all part of the practice of risk communication (Lichtenberg & MacLean, 1991)—were issued. But, in addition to being a practice, risk communication is also an area of research. Risk managers need to know how to communicate the often technical data and the uncertainties surrounding them so that ordinary people can play an appropriate role in the decision-making process.

During the last pandemic—the Spanish flu in 1918, the failures of mainstream media outlets to document Black life led to reports that African American were somehow "immune" to the flu (West, 2020). It was Black-owned news outlets known as the Black press that resisted those notions. In doing so, they were continuing the Black press' historic mission as an important disseminator of public health information to Black communities.

Weeks after the COVID-19 pandemic begin, Kim Gallon, creator of the Black Press Collaborative, started a new website—COVID Black in April 2020 (Greer, 2021). Two years later, the site is more than a gathering place of data. It is a location to honor and value each Black life lost to COVID-19. One of those lives lost to the coronavirus was Mel Reeves, a longtime community editor at the *Minnesota Spokesman Recorder*, the state's largest Black-owned business. Just days before his death on January 6, 2022, Reeves was reporting on COVID-19 protocols in his last article for the *Spokesman Recorder*, from his Minneapolis hospital bed. His work as a member of the Black press exemplified the crucial role Black-owned outlets have played in distributing potentially life-saving information to the Black community.

While the role of the media in risk communication has been studied for decades (Lichtenberg & MacLean, 1991; Murdock et. al., 2003) and the

DOI: 10.4324/9781032619187-2

role of the Black press in communicating life-saving health information has been documented in the literature (Cohen et al., 2008; Lumpkins et al., 2010; Mastin & Campo, 2006; Rasmussen, 2014; Wang & Rodgers, 2013), little has been written about the Black press' role in communicating risk.

Given the fact that the management of and communication about risks has become a major question of public policy and intellectual debate, the social amplification of risk framework (SARF) since it was first introduced in 1988 prompted much scholarly research. The idea of SARF arose out of an attempt to overcome the fragmented nature of risk perception and risk communication research by developing an integrative theoretical framework that would account from findings in a wide range of studies, including those from media research (Kasperson et al., 2003). To date, virtually none of that research using SARF has involved examining the role of the Black press. The information in this chapter aims to fill this gap in the literature on SARF that has evolved since 1988.

In addition to the dearth of scholarship on SARF and the Black press, few studies have looked at the Black press as video outlets. Since their inception in 1827, the Black press have largely been seen as print media. This study turns the technological page by focusing exclusively on video offerings. Even though the majority of the more than 200 members of the National Newspaper Publishers Association (NNPA), the trade association for the Black press are print media, a host of largely digital and nimble outlets known as the "The New Black Press," have come online (Douglas, 2020). For them, video is a central platform for conveying information.

Culture, Risk, and Emotions

At its core, risk communication is a dialogue between organizations that create risks and stakeholders that must bear the risk (Coombs, 2012). Furthermore, risk communication is relevant to both instructing and adjusting information (p. 57). Instructing information helps victims protect themselves physically from a crisis while adjusting information helps them cope psychologically with the crisis. That adjusting information includes explaining what happened in the crisis. In offering their theories of communication and risk management, Sellnow and Seeger (2013) noted that all crises are preceded by risks. Some of these risks are known but are mismanaged or ignored. Other go completely undetected until a crisis erupts (p. 188). One of the theories they offer to explain the risk communication process is cultural theory. In a nutshell, cultural theory explains how institutions moralize, politicize, and prioritize risks with a given culture (p. 205). Sellnow and Seeger (2013) explain the primary assumption of cultural theory is that cultural biases play a role in how risks are perceived. Cultural theory allows us to observe predictable patterns of how risks are moralized, politicized, and prioritized (p. 208).

Given what cultural theory tells us about risk communication in a crisis, the purpose of this study is to elaborate and provide examples of the importance of diverse media coverage regarding a specific topic. "Clarifying the role of culture in risk communication has become a main concern in recent efforts to bridge risk perception research and social context" (Masuda & Garvin, 2006, p. 437).

As part of the Centers for Disease Control and Prevention's guidance for *Crisis and Emergency Risk Communication* (CERC), a separate guide on "Messages and Audiences" notes that as a complex set of values, ideas, attitudes, and symbols that shape behavior, culture is very relevant in how one communicates, understands, and reacts in emergencies. The agency notes:

> you may need to turn to cultural agents, people who belong to a certain cultural group, who can help you understand how a particular culture will view an issue. Cultural gatekeepers can take this a step further and help introduce communicators and responders to their community, making members more receptive to unfamiliar people and message. (p. 5)

Social Amplification of Risk Framework

SARF was established by professor and risk analyst, Roger Kasperson. He established SARF as a tool for "understanding how risks are perceived, interpreted, and amplified or attenuated as they are communicated throughout a society" (Mase, Cho, & Prokopy, 2015, p. 167). SARF's foundation includes people's personal experiences surrounding risk information. Because of this, SARF is poignant to this qualitative research study. Several disciplines have used SARF for research, particularly media scholars regarding health-related risk issues. SARF has been applied to a variety of health and technological risks (Frewer, Miles, & Marsh, 2002) as well as public health emergencies (Barnett & Breakwell, 2003; Busby & Duckett, 2012; Chong & Choy, 2018; Kasperson et al., 1988; Kasperson & Kasperson, 1996; Petts & Niemeyer, 2004; Rickard et al., 2013; Strekalova & Krieger, 2017; Wirz et al., 2018). The lived experiences of the public vary especially concerning what type of health risks members of the public may face during a pandemic. Because the lived experiences have a key role in risk perception and its manifestation, SARF aids in monitoring message distribution and interpretation.

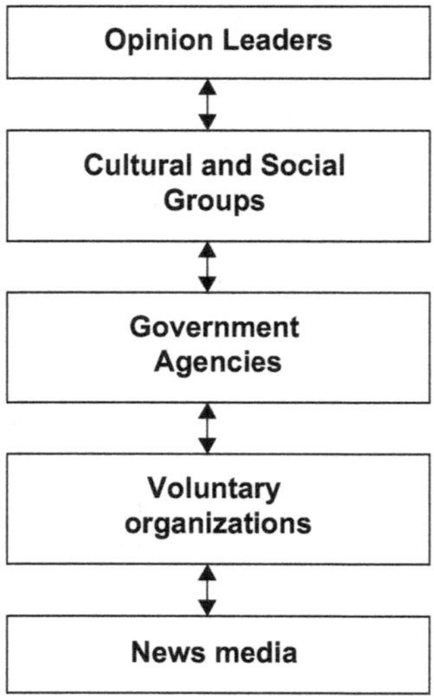

Figure 1.1 Social Stations.

The social amplification of risk framework has two key functions: the monitoring of how risk messages are transferred and how society responds to those messages. The public's subjective view of risk has a major impact on risk judgment, action, and assessment, according to Gutteling and Wiegman (2013). SARF provides a starting point for contextualizing and creating a path for the concept of public concern (Fellenor, Barnett, Potter, Urquhart, Mumford, & Quine, 2020, p. 5) and the amplification process starts with either a physical event or the recognition of an adverse effects (Renn, 1991).

In the framework, risk, risk events, and the characteristics of both are portrayed through various risk signals (images, signs, and symbols), which in turn interact with a wide range of psychological, social, institutional, or cultural processes in ways they intensify or attenuate perceptions of risk and its manageability (see Figure 1.1). The framework's developers adopted the metaphor of amplification from classical communications theory and use it to analyze the ways in which various social agents generate, receive, interpret, and pass on risk signals (Kasperson et al., 2003).

For this study, rather than utilize the full framework, the focus is on the *social stations of amplification* (opinion leaders, cultural and social groups, government agencies, voluntary organizations, and the news media). Figure 1.1 depicts these five groups that perceive the risks, those who manage the risks, and the risk "problem" according to cultural biases and values of their organization or group (Kasperson et al., 2003).

From Risk to Crisis Communication

Once an issue or event transitions from risk to crisis mode, communication and the disbursement of information becomes much more critical. Crisis can be defined "as a risk manifested" (Waymer & Heath, 2007, p. 90). Falkheimer and Heide (2006) defined a crisis as a very unusual situation that may threaten an organization's business, reputation, image, and relation, or in any way harm its publics (p. 181). Since it deals with the COVID-19 coronavirus, this study is focused on a public health crisis in which the health of people is affected across a range of areas, often more than a health-care system can manage (Coombs, 2023).

Crisis management represents a set of factors designed to combat crises by lessening damage the crisis inflicts and making the organization or unit resilient. More than just emergency preparedness, crisis manage includes prevention, preparation, response, and revision (Coombs, 2023). In the crisis management literature, many scholars have taken the life cycle approach where the crisis is conceptualized as a process. Depending on the conceptualization, that process can have anywhere from three to five stages. For example, Coombs (2023) identifies three stages: precrisis, crisis event, and postcrisis. There are three phases in George's (2012) crisis communication procedure: prevention, which includes planning and preparing before the crisis occurs; managing, which occurs during the crisis; and recovery, which occurs postcrisis.

In describing the nature of a crisis, Fearn-Banks and Kawamoto (2024) lays out five stages. *Detection* is the first stage of the crisis and involves a system within an organization in which key personnel are immediately notified of a crisis. The second stage, *Crisis preparation* is necessary for dealing with crises that cannot be prevented. From a public relations perspective, regular two-way communications build relationships with key publics and thereby prevent crises lessen the blows or limit the duration. In the third stage, *Containment* refers to the effort to limit the duration of the crisis or to keep it from spreading to other areas affecting the organization. Stage four, *Recovery* involves efforts to return the company to business as usual, while *Learning* is the fifth and final stage with a process of examining the crisis and determining what was lost.

Coombs (2023) also suggests a more advanced model of crisis—the regenerative model of crisis—that may help explain how crises can become reframed and produce significant communicative shifts for crisis managers. In the regenerative model, there are only two phases, *precrisis* and *postcrisis*. The precrisis stage involves signal detection, prevention, and crisis preparation, while in the postcrises stage, actions are taken to help organizations better prepare for the next crisis and ensure stakeholders have a positive impression of the organization's crisis management efforts. This means the crisis is simply a point in time marked by a turning point where a new crisis emerges because various factors led people involved with the crisis to view it as a new crisis type (p. 12). (See Coombs's [2023] for a visual depiction of the regenerative model.)

Regardless of the stage model, all have to do with the larger area of crisis communication.

> Crisis communication aims at preventing or lessening the negative outcomes resulting from a crisis, often crisis communication has an informative function. Such messages encourage the receiver to take some action to avoid a possible threat or harmful effect and to create a rational understanding of the risk, a persuasive function. The crisis message makes clear directions on the current state regarding the crises and what actions should now be taken.
>
> (Spence, Lachlan, & Griffin, 2007, p. 541)

Daily, new information, statistics and opinions about coronavirus are released by media outlets, but arguably. the information leaves much to be desired and tends to tell one-sided stories. "Crisis communication literature is largely void of the other voices and views present, in particular, situations and the possible ways that these voices can influence public discourse and opinion" (Waymer & Heath, 2007, p. 95). Often varying cultures' needs are not considered when media outlets, journalists, and PR practitioners craft risk and crisis messages.

The Case: COVID-19 Coronavirus

COVID-19 qualifies as a crisis by the Waymer and Heath's (2007) definition and has caused harm to the American public and beyond. In fact, in the sixth edition of *Ongoing Crisis Communication*, Coombs (2023) cited how the health-care system in New York City was overwhelmed during the early stages of the COVID-19 pandemic as an example of a public health crisis. The virus did not remain in the risk phase for long. It was just a few weeks past March 13, 2020, the day when President Donald Trump announced that COVID-19 was a national emergency, that it moved into full crisis mode. Coronavirus reportedly transitioned from risk to crisis mode around late April. Media outlets began to report more on the growing number of cases and emphasized the need to stay at home and wear masks. The messaging began to also focus more on the number of cases and deaths rising to emphasize the severity of the illness, a critical change in the messaging from the initial first stage.

During the summer of 2020, there were close to 4,000,000 cases of coronavirus in the United States and more than 140,000 deaths according to the Centers for Disease Control and Prevention (CDC). By late January 2021, there were close to 26,000,000 cases and nearly 440,000 deaths. The CDC also stated of those numbers, about 19 percent of those cases are Black, non-Hispanic people and of those who died from the disease approximately 22 percent were Black, non-Hispanic. When the pandemic first hit, African Americans received conflicting and false information, such as African Americans cannot contract coronavirus, the sun protects you from the virus, or drinking bleach could help prevent people from getting the virus. All those allegations are untrue but were spread by media outlets and word of mouth causing a great deal of confusion for countless Americans, including Black people. Media outlets serve as an information hub for the public and have a responsibility to make sure all information distributed is accurate and doesn't aid in misinforming the public. "In risk (or other) communication, the damage can be irreversible—if relations with one's communicants are poisoned. A shadow of a doubt can be difficult to erase" (Fischhoff, 1995, p. 137).

Some reporters at *The New York Times* have published stories suggesting a timeline that offers insights on the progression of the stages through Fearn-Banks and Kawamoto (2024) stages. While Yong (2018) in *The Atlantic* published "When the Next Plague Hits" in 2018 portraying an American government that was "negligent and unprepared" for the coronavirus pandemic, *The New York Times'* reported on how the National Security Council was disbanded in 2018 leaving the management of the coronavirus response to Health and Human Services Secretary Alex Azar (Haberman & Weiland, 2020). This suggests Stage 1 *Detection* dates back prior to 2018. Best-selling author and journalist Bob Woodward wrote in his book *Rage* about how President Donald Trump was told in January 2020 that the pandemic could reach the scale of the 1918 Spanish Flu that killed 675,000 Americans. The first stage of detection did not shift to Stage 2 *Preparation and Prevention* until after January 2020. A 12-person task force began daily meetings in late January (Haberman & Weiland, 2020). This was the beginning of Stage 2. One PBS "Frontline" documentary reported on months of inaction by the US government (Hale, 2020). Most states began putting in place stay-at-home orders in mid- to late March, signifying the beginning of Stage 3 *Containment*.

In the epilogue, Woodward (2020) wrote how the virus was "out of control" with "no end in sight, and certainly no clear path to get there" (p. 386). This would suggest that even as late as September 15, 2020, when the book was released, the country was still in the middle of Stage 3 *Containment*. In early December 2020, coronavirus cases were reported to be rising again in most states, many fearing a spike in the wake of those who ignored Centers for Disease Control warnings not to travel for the

Thanksgiving holiday. In 2021, not only did the pandemic reach new heights with the spread of the more contagious and deadly Delta variant, but also with the discovery of a third strain, the Omicron variant in late fall 2021.

There is a high level of misinformation surrounding coronavirus and that is very dangerous and could lead to consequences that cannot be undone. Originally, coronavirus was looked at as a small risk to America, but as of April 2020 catapulted into a full-blown crisis and remains that way currently. The goal of reviewing different periods of time is to define how and when the pandemic went from risk to crisis mode and how Black media outlets aided in providing vital information to its audience. Back in March 2020, COVID-19 was still in the risk stage. The main messages from health officials, the government and media outlets were for people to wear a mask in public at all times, wash their hands often and thoroughly, refrain from public gatherings and meetings, and to remain home as much as possible as a safety measure.

Depending on what media outlet the public tuned into or viewed determined the level of members of the public reaction and ultimately actions to potentially being exposed to coronavirus. For example, if a news outlet continuously reported that African Americans can't get coronavirus or are less likely to contract it, then Black people would less likely take preventative measures due to a false sense of security.

Black-owned and Targeted Media as Area of Research on Risk Communication

Even though the 20th century brought significant improvement in the health and longevity of the American public, some segments of the American public had not benefitted fully from that progress (Atrash & Hunter, 2006). In particular, for Blacks or African Americans, life expectancy was 72.2 years compared to 77.7 years for whites (p. 3). Blacks have worse health outcomes than any other race or ethnic group in the United States (p. 10). They experienced the highest rates of mortality from heart disease, cancers (including breast and lung cancer), influence, and pneumonia, cerebrovascular disease (including stroke), HIV and AIDS, diabetes, and homicide (p. 12). One barrier to positive health outcomes is the largely segregated medical profession. In the 1966 edition of *The Negro Handbook*, the editors of *Ebony* magazine reported that there was an increasing demand for physicians and the supply of what were then known as Negro MDs is not sufficient to take advantage of the number of internships, residencies, and staff appointments that were becoming available (Ebony Magazine, 1966). David Satcher (2006), who served five years as director of the Centers for

Disease Control and Prevention and four years as the surgeon general, argued for the role of government in eliminating health disparities. Still, Foster (2007) points out in her report on HIV/AIDS in the African American community, the government is giving African American limited support for addressing the disparities in that area. Broussard's (2019) research on Western Civil Rights since 1970 reports how Black westerners had the shortest life span of any racial or ethnic group in the western United States and had greater numbers than any other group in the West.

When it comes to addressing these health disparities and differences in health outcomes, Black media play an important role. For example, Mastin and Campo (2006) conducted a content analysis of 20 years of beverage ads and related articles on preventing and overcoming obesity, one of the health disparities. Their analysis of advertisements in *Jet*, *Ebony* and *Essence* found the vast majority of ads in all three magazines consistently advertised foods and nonalcoholic beverages high in empty calories and low in nutritional value (p. 279). This study focused on magazines, which were a small part of the Black press, defined by Wolseley (1990) three qualifications: (1) Blacks must own and manage the publication, (2) the publication must be intended for Black consumers, and (3) the paper or magazine must serve, speak, and fight for the Black minority.

While they drew little attention before World War II, by the time of the Civil Rights Movement in 1950s and 1960s, these largely Black weeklies ridiculed white hypocrisy, spoke out bitterly against racial injustice, and covered social and religious organizations in detail (Roberts & Klibanoff, 2006). In 1932, *The Atlanta World* became a daily after first publishing twice and then three times a week, it was the flagship publication of the Scott Newspaper Syndicate (SNS) that included the *Birmingham World* and *Memphis World* (Aiello, 2018). *The Chicago Defender* went daily in 1956 and competed with white-owned newspapers and broadcast outlets in covering the "race beat" just as Civil Rights leaders like Martin Luther King, Jr. came on the scene (Michaeli, 2016). More recently, however, the *Defender* ceased publication in July 2019 and shifted to a digital-only publication. It joined sister publication *Michigan Chronicle* in a conversion to digital-only outlets as a growing number of digital-only start-ups, some of which were not Black-owned and operated, were taking up roles once played by the Black press.

In 2021, a study released by the City University of New York's Craig Newmark Graduate School of Journalism found that Black media published as much as six times more coverage than mainstream outlets on issues of importance to Black communities, including racism, health disparities, and voting access (Brown, 2021). Results from the "Why Black Media Matters Now" study found that within coronavirus coverage, Black media wrote four times more on the disproportionate racial impact of the pandemic and nearly twice as much on frontline and essential workers.

Research Questions

If McLuhan's notion that "the medium is the message" applies, one ought to place as much emphasis on where risk is communicated as what the message is that is delivered. It is in this vein that the study presented here operates. In the context of cultural theory, which as Sellnow and Seeger (2013) explained assumes some cultural biases in the way risk is moralized, politicized, and prioritized, this study first sought to identify cultural gatekeepers in the Black press videos produced and transmitted during the COVID-19 pandemic (RQ1). In terms of the social amplification of risk, what role, if any, do Black press videos play in the cultural processes that heighten or attenuate individual and social perceptions of risk and shape risk behavior (RQ2)? In particular, among the social stations outlined in the SARF, which were most frequently present in videos posted by Black-owned media outlets? (RQ3)

Because news outlets are arguably the strongest vehicle for transporting risk communication, it is imperative to analyze how African American media build trust with the public and provide vital and overlooked information to their core audience and other marginalized people. The expert accounts, visuals, story angles, and also the emotion of the public was all considered and analyzed through SARF for this research. African American media outlets serve as an alternative information hub or "amplification station" for African Americans seeking information about the risks of COVID-19 tailored toward their needs and interests and providing different coverage than mainstream media outlets. SARF is as a "framework that, like a net, is useful for catching the accumulated empirical findings, and that, like a beacon, can point the way to disciplined inquiry" (Renn et al., 1992, p. 143).

Method

To answer the aforementioned three research questions, a convenience sample of video messages was drawn from websites and YouTube channels of Black-owned and Black-targeted media outlets. Some newspapers have embraced the video platform while others have virtually ignored it. A listing of videos was developed from the following Black press outlets: *The St. Louis American*, *The Philadelphia Tribune*, *The Atlanta Voice*, *The Michigan Chronicle*, *The Washington Informer*, and *the Minnesota Spokesman Recorder*. Among the digital-only outlets were *TheRoot.com*, *TheGrio.com*, *Fox Soul: The Black Report*, and *Black Enterprise.com*.

Given what cultural theory tells us about risk communication in a crisis, the purpose of this study is to elaborate and provide examples of the importance of diverse media coverage regarding a specific topic. Here, the topic is COVID-19 and the messages crafted for African American people. Today, there are more than 200 Black-owned or targeted media outlets, known as the Black Press that transmit video messages. Those messages regarding coronavirus were analyzed. To answer the research questions, the video content was reviewed to offer an opportunity for "clarifying the role of culture in risk communication has become a main concern in recent efforts to bridge risk perception research and social context" (Masuda & Garvin, 2006, p. 437).

The Internet has opened up the possibility for developing multimedia texts where video plays a big role. And there are several studies that have been done just on this medium. For example, Cha and Chan-Olmsted (2012) designed a study to compare consumers' perceptions of television and online video platforms in terms of content, technology, and cost-related attributes. They also identified the specific attributes of online video platforms that contribute to the overall relative advantage of this new video alternative. They found the most important attribute that contributes to improving the overall relative advantage of online video platforms is the quality of the video content. Elsewhere, Leon and Bourk (2018) conducted an international research project that involved the analysis of more than 800 videos on key scientific disciplines—climate change, vaccines, and nanotechnology. Their research included a series of interviews with experts in the field that provide keys for the production of online videos.

Most recently, Soni and Puthawala (2020) went beyond just online videos but the video streaming apps to examine millennials' preferences toward online video streaming in Ahmedabad, Gujarat. They found convenience/flexibility and choice-related content were among the factors that moved the 150 respondents ages 35 and under toward online video streaming apps. Most spent two to three hours daily online video streaming app, such as Netflix or Amazon Prime (Soni & Puthawala, 2020).

Video selection based on a listing of Black-owned newspapers and stories that were appearing in their print or online editions, the newspapers' websites, and YouTube channels were visited to check for evidence of coverage of COVID-19-related issues. Some videos focused on other non-health pandemic-related issues (i.e., cancellation of athletic events, impact on businesses) were not included in the convenience sample. Efforts were made to locate videos from different points on the pandemic timeline such as the initial announcements of the national emergency in 2020 and in 2021 when emphasis was initially on increasing vaccination rates.

Video analysis: Once the videos in the sample were identified, a textual analysis was used to catalog and compile the video messages directed at Black audiences related to COVID-19 coronavirus. According to McKee's (2003) guide to the method, textual analysis is a data-gathering process for those researchers who want to understand the ways in which members of various cultures and subcultures make sense of who they are and how they fit into the world in which they live.

Textual analysis has already been used in research on crisis communication. In a study of South Korean response to events surrounding the April 16, 2007, shooting at Virginia Polytechnic and State University, Elmasry and Chaudhri (2012) analyzed 25 staff-written news articles in *Korea Times* and *Chosun Ilbo*, which claimed the lives of 32 faculty and students.

Borrowing techniques from Tompkins et al. (2020), this study proceeded with a two-stage strategy. In stage one, each author independently searched for videos focused on the COVID-19 virus visiting the individual outlets' webpage and YouTube channel. A master list was compiled. Then, in stage two, both authors screened videos to identify specific patterns that would be the focus of the analysis. The result was the following list of categories of information gathered from each Black press COVID-19 video message: date of video posted, news outlet, title of the video, name of the major speakers/presenters, strategy/focus of message, and length. A tally of videos from each outlet and average times by outlet were calculated.

Findings

A total of 62 videos were a part of this research, 20 of which were associated with seven Black-owned media outlets that have a printed newspaper as its core product (*The Philadelphia Tribune*, *The Washington Informer*, *St. Louis American*, *The Atlanta Voice*, *Charlotte Observer*, *Philadelphia Tribune*, and the *Minnesota Spokesman Recorder*). The remaining 42 videos were posted by digital-only platforms, which target Black audiences but are not necessarily Black-owned and operated (*TheRoot.com*, *TheGrio.com*, *Black Enterprise*, and *Fox Soul: The Black Report*). As shown in Table 1.1, The Grio.com had the most videos, 18, in the sample selected with TheRoot.com coming a close second with 13 videos. Our search turned up only one video from Detroit-based *The Michigan Chronicle*, *The Philadelphia Tribune*, and *The Charlotte Post*. The videos range in length from just 30 seconds to one that ran nearly 63 minutes. With the exception of *Black Enterprise*, the digital platform associated with the former 50-year-old Black-oriented business magazine, the longest videos were ones posted by print newspapers. Some were news clips from other news organization while others were highly produced montages of

Table 1.1 COVID-19 Videos by News Outlet

News Outlet	*Number of Videos*	*Average Length*
The Grio.com	18	7:14
The Root.com	13	6:09
Fox Soul-*The Black Report*	8	5:56
St. Louis American	7	5:51
Minnesota Spokesman Recorder	5	10:45
The Atlanta Voice	3	17:26
Black Enterprise	3	51:14
Washington (DC) *Informer*	2	15:15
The Michigan Chronicle	1	:30
Philadelphia Tribune	1	3:14
Charlotte Post	1	2:19
Total	62	

multimedia elements (maps, graphics, video, and audio clips). The style of production differed sometimes within the video offerings of a single news organization.

With the most videos of any of the traditional printed newspapers, the *St. Louis American* featured multiple videos by Dr. Rebeccah Bennett, founder and principal of InPower Institute. In "Black Folks and Corona," Bennett, who was part of the Prepare STL, a St. Louis-based initiative, focused on the city's most vulnerable stop the spread of coronavirus and survive the shutdown. Bennett said, "I need you to take this as seriously as you can." A similar but shorter message featured Dr. Denise Hooks-Anderson, the newspaper's medical accuracy editor admonishing viewers to observe stay-at-home orders, maintain social distancing, and wash your hands. Hooks-Anderson also included a demonstration of how to make a home-made face mask with a bandana, rubber bands, and coffee filter. In a second video, Hooks-Anderson recaps the same health messages about social distancing and hand-washing, ending with a reminder that the *St. Louis American* is here with you, praying for you, and that "we can get through this crisis together." A fourth video showed 58-year-old Maurice Cooley, the 100th COVID-19 patient being discharged from St. Mary's Hospital as dozens of nurses gave him a round of applause and cheered. The 52-second video presented an African American man who just three days earlier had been admitted with severe COVID-19 symptoms. His survival from the illness was a message to counter to what had been reported about the large number of African Americans who were dying from the disease. In 2020, the newspaper produced an interview video with Mark Adrian Richardson (aka "Spanky"), a disabled man, who explained how

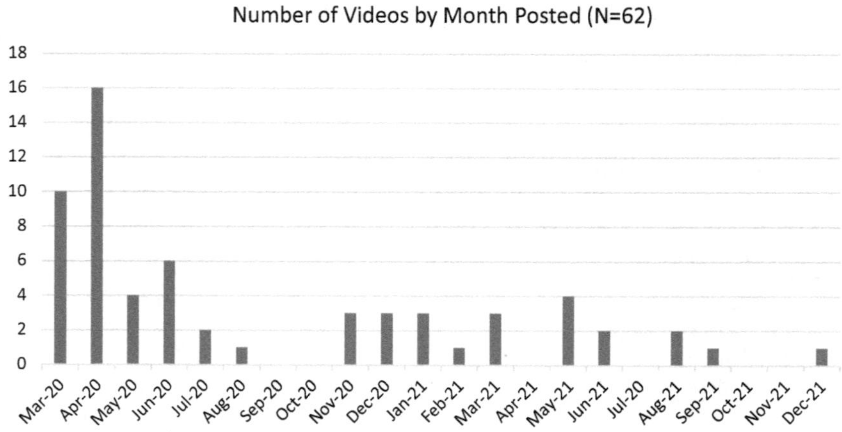

Figure 1.2 The COVID-19 Coronavirus Crisis March 2020–December 2021.

despite his disability, he was able to be tested for COVID-19 and results were negative.

Over the 22-month monitoring period between March 2020 and December 2021, the greatest number of videos containing COVID-19 risk information in our sample were posted in the months of April 2020 (16) and June 2020 (6). As Figure 1.2 shows, the Black press whose outlets were reviewed posted far more videos in 2020 than in 2021.

In 2020, two Black-owned newspapers—The *Atlanta Voice* and The *Washington Informer*—posted long-form interviewed with COVID-19 survivors who gave detailed accounts of becoming infected with the virus and going through extended hospital stays where they were on a ventilator. The *Washington Informer* included video footage of Therrien Clark and Mary Myles-Clark being released from Johns Hopkins University Medical Center before the two appeared on camera in matching red t-shirts saying "Praying Wife" and "Healed Husband." The *Atlanta Voice* video featured Alethea Brown was joined by her mother, Wendy Bonhart, a retired nurse who described her role as her daughter's caretaker.

The Philadelphia Tribune posted a three-minute video feature on the Black Doctors COVID-19 Consortium as they conducted coronavirus testing. The group's Dr. Ala Stanford is featured as she gave a statement to a large bank of television cameras from Philadelphia area television stations telling the story of this consortium. Stanford noted, "It needed to be black doctors because I wanted people to know that we are claiming responsibility for you and your loved ones." At least three other Black female doctors were interviewed in the *Philadelphia Tribune* feature.

The segment closes with footage of a $4,000 check presentation from the DeSean Jackson Foundation.

While that video was produced in-house by the team at *The Philadelphia Tribune*, the *Minnesota Spokesman Recorder* posted videos on its YouTube channel that were produced by the Rae Mackenzie Group, a minority-owned, female-owned marketing consulting company in Minneapolis. Each video closes on Black graphic with red-and-white writing—COVID In Black? Stay Smart, Stay Safe, Stay Alive. In another video, singer/songwriter Ashley DuBose introduces herself as a contestant on the Voice and a Mother who lives right here in Minneapolis. DuBose spoke into the camera saying, "We need you to understand that African American people are disproportionately dying and being affected by this COVID-19 pandemic." Another video in the COVID In Black series featured social epidemiologist Sharrell Barber speaking about racial bias involved in how hospitals respond to COVID-19 patients and the racism involved in the algorithms in place for rationing health equipment. Barber's comments are followed by words on the screen saying, "Yall already know what it is ... we have to save ourselves" with the hashtag #COVIDINBLACK. In a separate video, Minnesota Attorney General Keith Ellison, an African American man, reflects on the loss of his mother from complications related to COVID-19. The video clip from MSNBC included Ellison saying, "We know from firsthand experience how absolutely serious coronavirus is. That if you are not observing social distancing you're putting your loved ones at risk no matter how strong or healthy you think you are, you could be asymptomatic carrier.

Research Question 1 asked about what cultural gatekeepers appeared in the Black press videos produced during the COVID-19 pandemic. There appeared to be at least three types of cultural gatekeepers in the videos analyzed: the African American opinion leader/government official, the African American celebrity journalist/TV personality, and the African American medical professional or expert.

Exemplifying the African American celebrity journalist, The *Root.com*'s producer Felice Leon notes, "With social media's ability to amplify coupled with the extreme uncertainty of the moment, it's no surprise there's a whole heap of outlandish conspiracy theories." Leon's comments in her ten-minute video are not just about reporting the present but providing historical context noting that for African American, conspiracy theories are a way to explain inequalities. Also on The *Root.com*, the "Black COVID-19 Experiences features firsthand accounts of three younger (under 40) African American COVID-19 survivors. Following an opening-animated graphic showing a computer user searching for information with Google search engine and the search terms "coronavirus deaths by race," Nicholas Ryan Gant, 39, Harlem, Geniece Ward, 27 of Queens, and

Celeste Demby, 36, from Long Island, all tested positive. Demby's cousin died from the disease. He admitted his own cynicism and dismissiveness about the virus initially.

The research generated more "hits" from TheGrio.com than any of the other sources. Of all of the outlets which had videos with risk-related messages, TheGrio.com was the most consistent in posting items throughout the pandemic. In 2020, early on, it explored the matter of how the COVID-19 pandemic impacted Black churches, who were forced to respond to stay-at-home orders that included restrictions of the size of gatherings. The nearly two-minute video with the provocative question "Is Coronavirus Destroying the Black Church?" included a montage of interview clips from pastors, some of whom had completely transitioned to a digital delivery platform for church services. An example of the cultural gatekeeper who is an African American government official, California Congresswoman Maxine Waters, appeared in one of the most provocative videos targeting young African Americans. At one point in the five-minute video, she references the fact that theGrio gets a lot of exposure and probably should not show this. But then she embraced the moniker "Auntie Maxine" and says, "I want Black people, my people to keep your a—at home and don't be out on the street and don't be socializing because you've got a lot of people out there who don't care about you."

Dr. Darien Sutton Ramsey, an emergency medicine physician in New York City, gives a brief overview of COVID-19 virus in a three-minute video that include brief clips from Black news reporters from CBS and graphics. It was mostly an informational background segment that did not include regular Grio.com personalities.

Calling it "Rona, our least favorite cousin," True Blue, a columnist on Grio.com, gives her list of five things Black people need to keep in mind: (1) pre-existing conditions, (2) Black people are immune from coronavirus, (3) testing, (4) working from home, (5) Black joy. Her less formal, colloquial style of presentation is noteworthy. For example, Blue said, "If Idris Elba, with his fine self can get it, nobody is immune," with a soundbite from Elba sharing his experience. Blue refers to her audience as her "Grio family" and herself as "your girl, Blue/" This relationship would appear to be a factor in way her crisis communication messages would be received.

In 2021, TheGrio.com posted videos featuring White House correspondent April Ryan interviews with opinion leaders such as Chief of Infectious Diseases Anthony Fauci and singer/actor and HIV/Billy Porter. The network's vice president of Digital Content Natasha Alford in addition to interviewing health authorities on the COVID-19 vaccine shared her own story of giving birth to a child during the pandemic and having to make the choice of interacting with her parents who wanted to see their grandchild.

Her father, Mr. Alford, was at first reluctant to get the COVID-19 vaccine, because of underlying health conditions.

Research Question 2 focused on the cultural processes that heighten or attenuate individual and social perceptions of risk. Because of the nature of this research, the "news media" are linked to all 62 videos as well as the "cultural and social group" social station. But government agencies were frequently exhibited as attenuating the risk. As noted earlier, government officials such as Dr. Anthony Fauci as well as local health department officials would reflect this attenuator. Least prevalent in the videos analyzed was the "voluntary organizations" attenuator.

The *Black Enterprise* video offerings were noticeably longer than any of the other outlets. One video featuring Sekou Kaalund, Head of JP Morgan Chase's Advancing Black Pathways initiative, ran 36 minutes. Kaalund spoke to *Black Enterprise* Digital Editor Selena Hill about how to protect your financial well-being during the coronavirus pandemic. In another video, *Black Enterprise* Senior V.P. and Executive Editor-at-Large Alfred Edmond interviewed BE100's CEO Randal Pinkett, the author of *Black Faces White Places*, in a 54-minute conversation on COVID-19, Donald Trump, and Crisis Leadership.

TheRoot.com Producer Felice Leon interviewed Dr. Yusef Salaam about COVID-19 and the conditions for those inside New York City's prisons. Titled "The Forgotten Population," the Root.com paired the video report with *The New York Times* that as of early April 2020, 167 inmates, 114 correction staff, and 23 health workers had tested positive for COVID-19. Salaam noted, "Whatever we're seeing in the world is going to magnified 10 times in the Prison Industrial Complex." Salaam is one of the "Exonerated Five," teens who were exonerated after their trial and conviction in the 1989 high-profile "Central Park jogger" rape case.

In terms of the social amplification of risk, Research Question 3 sought to determine what role, if any, do Black press videos play in the cultural processes that heighten or attenuate individual and social perceptions of risk and shape risk behavior (RQ3). One way that the videos attenuated the individual and social perceptions of risk was by using well-known, credible individuals to heighten awareness and dispel myths about the disease and its impact on the Black community. Two examples of this were videos by Drs. Denise Hooks-Anderson and Rebeccah Bennett, whose videos appeared on the *St. Louis American*'s YouTube channel. A second strategy to attenuate the risk was the use by the digital outlets *TheRoot.com* and *TheGrio.com* of highly emotional testimonials of those who were diagnosed as positive for COVID-19. A third strategy to attenuate risk was the "Public Service Announcement" strategy employed by Rae McKenzie Group in its "COVID In Black" series that featured individuals in the Minneapolis area to tell the story of the COVID-19 coronavirus as it impacted Black Minnesotans. *Fox Soul*, the African American-oriented digital channel launched on January 13, 2020, included in its "Black Report" panels discussing medical findings related to COVID-19 vaccines. The video discussions attenuated the risk of African Americans not taking the vaccine.

During 2021, the focus of African American and African American-focused media outlets was providing information on COVID-19 vaccines. Since the height of COVID-19, the coverage has gone through phases. The first phase of the coverage by both mainstream and African American media outlets was to provide safety information surrounding COVID-19 and defining the virus. As more information about the virus became available, the focus moved from preventive measures such as social distancing, wearing mask, and washing and sanitizing hands. Coverage began to focus on efforts of creating a vaccine. Once the vaccine was ready, many people had questions, especially African Americans. Naturally, African American media outlets tailored their coverage to provide information about the issues that their core audience was focused on and expressing concerns about.

Outlets such as theRoot and theGrio interviewed Dr. Fauci and other medical experts to speak directly to the African American community about their concerns regarding getting vaccinated. In 2021, there was a shift from using African American celebrities to credible medical professionals. Among those professionals, were African American medical doctors, PhD researchers and nurses, all of whom became the dominant choice for interview subjects. Many African Americans remain hesitant about whether or not to get vaccinated. Those reasons included limited information about the newly-created COVID-19 vaccines and the history of how African Americans have been improperly treated such as what happened in the Tuskegee Syphilis study. In that study, 600 African American males were recruited for the experiment with almost 400 having syphilis, according to the Centers for Disease Control. Penicillin could have been administered to cure the men of syphilis but was not although the men thought they were receiving treatment. Although this happened in the 1940s and the information about the study became available to the public in the 1970s, the distrust remains high among African Americans. There was also Henrietta Lacks, an African American woman, who died from cervical cancer when cells were taken from her body without her knowledge or consent for medical research. These are examples of why African Americans do not trust the medical community to have their best interest at heart.

Several African American doctors and medical experts have spoken directly to the public through digital media outlets such as theGrio and theRoot as well as with African American newspapers. The focus of most of the interviews were to debunk myths about getting the vaccine and to get the African American community to see the benefit of getting vaccinated for themselves and the community as a whole. Many of the messages published on the African American media outlets focused on lessening people's apprehension of getting vaccinated based on the impact of nostalgia surrounding prior mistreatment of African Americans by the medical industry and the government. Another goal of those media outlets was to reduce fear of adverse effects to the vaccine. Experts used statistics to point out how unlikely it was for African Americans to have a negative reaction or outcome from getting vaccinated. Information was also provided explaining why some people experienced negative side effects to the vaccine to aid in strengthening the overall benefits of the vaccine. Medical experts also explained the differences in the types of vaccines on how each works (Moderna, Pfizer, and Johnson & Johnson). Those media outlets worked to paint a message of hope that we could get back to our "normal" life sooner if everyone gets vaccinated.

All of the African American and African American-focused media outlets distributed messages with wording encouraging African Americans to take care of themselves and take charge of their own fate regarding their health. There was a distinct push in the messages those outlets distributed advising the African American community of helpful information about COVID-19 and how to protect themselves against it while reiterating to their core audience to not rely solely on the government and the medical community to have their best interest at heart but to rely on self and building a community among themselves to aid each other. The shift in the messages seem to be a direct result in maintaining awareness in what their core audience expressed they wanted and needed. The structure and angle of the stories these outlets distributed compared to mainstream outlets further iterates why it is imperative to not only consider but deliver multiple risks messages aimed at various subpopulations of the public. The use of SARF with the messages distributed from these outlets provided a roadmap to how messages were interpreted, received, and utilized by their core audience. The lived experience and daily unique circumstances of their core audience was woven into the media messages distributed by these outlets.

Because COVID-19 has gone through several stages, the media coverage has undergone shifts as well. Digital media outlet messages shifted from relying on well-known political figures such as Congresswoman Maxine Waters, high-profile people, and celebrities to validate COVID-19 vaccinations and preventive measures. During 2021, digital media outlets created content centralizing African American medical experts and medical doctors as well as Dr. Anthony Fauci, President Joe Biden's Chief Medical Advisor, who is one of the leading members of the White House Covid-19 Response Team to discuss and inform the public about the five stages of crisis. Digital media outlets coverage shifted to place medical experts front and center of their coverage area and allowed the opportunity for African Americans to receive vital information regarding COVID-19 from qualified medical personnel and for people who look like their core demographic to provide information in a way that resonated with them. African American medical experts not only have the medical knowledge to debunk myths about COVID-19 but provide valuable information and take into account what members of this community need from their personal experiences.

Digital media outlets placed significant emphasis on providing information with the intent on increasing their core audience's willingness to become vaccinated. With efforts to increase African Americans willingness to become vaccinated, digital media outlets such as *theGrio* included interviews of people who were initially against getting vaccinated but changed their minds. Personal accounts from members of the African American community paired with medical experts provided a more credible lens for the African American community to view and utilize in their decision-making process regarding COVID-19. *Fox Soul's: The Black Report* utilized traditional news coverage that morphs into a panel-style discussion during its coverage. This coverage format allows people to receive information in the form of traditional news coverage and gain commentary about the issue from the same coverage.

Both African American digital media outlets and traditional media outlets such as newspapers covered COVID-19 extensively. But newspapers dominated with follow-up messages in a way that digital outlets did not. In this research, the analysis of newspapers indicated that newspapers released multiple follow-up stories weekly about COVID-19. Each newspaper focused on varying angles of the topic, the same as digital outlets. Experts were included in their coverage as well, but the focal point of newspaper coverage remained about detailing the virus such as the various strains, types of vaccines, and impact on the African American community. Newspapers kept journalism predominantly in the role of storyteller in its coverage. Digital media outlets strategy on the other hand was to reduce the journalist's role as the storyteller into more of a moderator, thus allowing the medical experts and doctors to dominate the video messages released to their audience with the intent of increasing validity and believability.

Discussion

The National Newspaper Publishers Association, the trade association for African American-owned newspapers, announced in early April 2020 the formation of the NNPA Coronavirus Task Force and Resource Center (Brown, 2020). The task force included publishers, editors, physicians, nurses, corporate partners, and supporters of the Black Press of America. Among those reacting to the creation of the task force was Robert W. Bogle, the president and CEO of *The Philadelphia Tribune*, the nation's oldest newspaper serving the African American community and one of the few black-owned news outlets publishing three days a week. Bogle noted, "We became an independent voice to speak up and speak out deliberately embracing the telling of our story." Bogle's outlet has been one of those employing videos to tell the story of African Americans and the COVID-19 coronavirus.

Once the COVID-19 vaccine became available to the public, several Black media outlets including *theRoot*, *theGrio*, and *Fox Soul*'s new show *The Black Report* provided videos addressing Black people's concerns and skepticism to take the vaccine. TheRoot provided a detailed video with two medical experts (nurse and host as well as a medical and PhD doctor) to explain the benefits of taking the vaccine. *The Black Report* approached the topic with an experienced news reporter and panelists showcasing information provided by the Pfizer company and the government about the vaccine and discussed the viewpoints of Black people. The viewpoints ranged from the willingness to take the vaccine and the uncertainty due to the vaccine's newness and reported side effects. The unknown and the poor medical history of the past has many still on the fences of whether or not to take the vaccine. The videos also demonstrate that age (generation) plays a major role in which media outlets and content Black people pay attention to. Younger demographics prefer shorter clips that use youthful language along with graphics, memes, video, etc. While people aged 40 and over tend to prefer longer length clips with experts and verifiable information.

There seems to be a common thread among the coronavirus messages in each video viewed in this study. Each Black-owned media outlet either used an expert, prominent person, or celebrity such as Congresswoman Mrs. Maxine Waters, or testimonial from everyday citizens or college students to aid in driving home the seriousness of coronavirus and the preventive measures that must be taken to their target audience. Research has found that the public does not pay equal attention to all the information they are presented with, but instead "rely on sources that they most trust, internalizing information from reliable sources and rejecting information from sources they consider unreliable" (Mase, Cho, & Prokopy, 2015, p. 168). Those videos included intentional, detailed, and nuanced messages meant for specific communities that range from Generation Z and Millennials to Baby Boomers and beyond, as well the LGBTQIA community, low-income people, and more. McComas (2013) stated, "Risk-as-feelings hypothesis can explain gender and age-related differences in responses to risk, as well as why vivid language, narratives, or affective-laden imagery, often accompanying news stories, strongly influence people's reactions to risk" (p. 78).

The Black media outlets realized that although their main demographic is the Black community, it was imperative to create multiple messages that targeted subpopulation within the main demographic. By focusing on multiple subpopulations, the desired message can reach a wider range of people, come across more relatable, and connect with individuals in way that mainstream media messages do not. Waymer and Heath (2007) point out that most crisis communication focuses on the perspective of management trying to avoid lawsuits and damages and fail to place more attention to the needed response to the affected public (p. 88). This is a practice that mainstream media should adopt to widen its impact on a more diverse audience, thus ultimately the public may gain a better understanding of the message and take proper actions. "Phenomenological studies have shown that risk not only reflects social context, but that culture accounts for differences in the ways that risks are communicated, leading to unique outcomes from place to place" (Masuda & Garvin, 2006, p. 438).

This research indicated how important cultural sensitivity is to media coverage. African American journalists have an innate sense of what type of news coverage this sector of the public needs and wants because of shared heritage and membership in the community. Because of this, African American journalists' approach to news coverage will likely connect better with the African American sector of the public. Their coverage was tailored to provide more details about COVID-19 using wording and phrasing African Americans could understand and provided direct answers to their questions that mainstream media outlets did not while providing clarity to information originated from mainstream media outlets, press releases, and government and medical officials.

Trust and continued viewership have the potential to increase substantially, if subgroups of the public are addressed the same way the dominant group is catered to in news content and coverage. White males, well-educated people, and middle class to rich people can no longer be the bulk of the population considered and spoken to in mainstream news coverage. All sectors of the public should be addressed daily. In doing so, members of the public stand to be better informed, make better choices, risks to overall population may reduce significantly, and better relationships between the public and the media could be cultivated.

This research has the potential to aid mainstream media outlets in future coverage of not only crisis-related health stories but other topics as well for not just the African American community but other people of color and underrepresented groups. Mainstream media outlets should use this study as a way to gauge the usefulness of diverse coverage and diverse experts' interviews into storytelling efforts and practices. Cultural gatekeepers are vital to news coverage as they have the ability to balance news content and help all media outlets live up to fair and well-informed news coverage.

References

Aiello, T. (2018). *The grapevine of the Black South: The Scott newspaper syndicate in the generation before the Civil Rights Movement*. Athens, GA: University of Georgia Press.

Atrash, H.K. & Hunter, M.D. (2006). Health disparities in the United States: A continuing challenge. In D. Satcher, R.J. Pamies, N.N. Woelfl (Eds.) *Multicultural medicine and health disparities*. (pp. 3–31) New York: McGraw-Hill.

Barnett, J., & Breakwell, G. M. (2003). The social amplification of risk and the hazard sequence: the October 1995 oral contraceptive pill scare. *Health, risk & society*, *5*(3), 301–313.

Broussard, A.S. (2019). Western Civil Rights Since 1970. In B.A. Glasrud & C.D. Wintz (Eds.) *Black Americans and the Civil Rights Movement in the West*. (pp. 255–269). Norman: University of Oklahoma Press.

Brown, S.M. (2020, April 2–8). Black Press establishes coronavirus pandemic task force, resource center. *New Journal and Guide*, 2A.

Brown, S.M. (2021, October 13). CUNY study underscores the enduring vitality of the Black Press. *The Times Weekly.com* Retrieved January 15, 2022 from https://thetimesweekly.com/news/2021/oct/13/cuny-study-underscores-enduring-vitality-black-pre/

Busby, J., & Duckett, D. (2012). Social risk amplification as an attribution: The case of zoonotic disease outbreaks. *Journal of risk research*, *15*(9), 1049–1074.

Cha, J and Chan-Olmsted, S.M. (2012) Substitutability between online video platforms and television. *Journalism & Mass Communication Quarterly 89*(2), 261–278.

Chong, M., & Choy, M. (2018). The social amplification of haze-related risks on the internet. *Health Communication*, *33*(1), 14–21.

Cohen, E.L., Caburnay, C.A., Rodger, S., Cameron, G.T. & Kreuter, M.W. (2008). Cancer coverage in general-audience and black newspapers. *Health Communication*, 23, 427–435.

Coombs, W.T. (2012). Crisis communication and its allied fields. In W. T. Coombs & S.J. Holladay (Eds.) *The handbook of crisis communication*. (pp. 54–64) Malden, MA: Wiley-Blackwell.

Coombs, W.T. (2023). *Ongoing crisis communication: Planning, managing and responding*. (6th Ed.) Sage Publications.

Douglas, D. (2020, July 14) The new black press. *Nieman Reports*. Retrieved July 21, 2020 from https://niemanreports.org/articles/meet-the-new-black-press/

Ebony Magazine (1966). *The Negro Handbook*. Johnson Publishing.

Elmasry, M.H. & Chaudhri, V. (2012). The press as agent of cultural repair: A textual analysis of news coverage of the Virginia Tech shootings. In W. T. Coombs & S.J. Holladay (Eds.) *The handbook of crisis communication*. (pp. 142–158) Malden, MA: Wiley-Blackwell.

Falkheimer, J., & Heide, M. (2006). Multicultural crisis communication: Towards a social constructionist perspective. *Journal of Contingencies and Crisis Management*, *14*(4), 180–189.

Fearn-Banks, K. & Kawamoto, K. (2024). *Crisis Communications: A casebook approach*. (6th Ed) Mahwah, NJ: Routledge.
Fellenor, J., Barnett, J., Potter, C., Urquhart, J., Mumford, J. D., & Quine, C. P. (2020). 'Real without being concrete': the ontology of public concern and its significance for the Social Amplification of Risk Framework (SARF). *Journal of Risk Research*, *23*(1), 20–34.
Fischhoff, B. (1995). Risk perception and communication unplugged: twenty years of process 1. *Risk Analysis*, *15*(2), 137–145.
Foster, P. (2007) "Is There a Black in Black America?" Perspectives on HIV/AIDS in the African American Community. Montgomery, AL: AfAm South.
Frewer, L. J., Miles, S., & Marsh, R. (2002). The media and genetically modified foods: Evidence in support of social amplification of risk. *Risk Analysis: An International Journal*, 22(4), 701–711.
George, A. (2012). The phases of crisis communication. In A. M. George & C.B. Pratt (Eds.) *Case studies in crisis communication: International perspectives on hits and misses*. (pp. 31–50). Routledge.
Greer, C.M. (2021, February 24). COVID Black is using data and creating space to honor Black lives lost to virus. *The Grio.com* https://thegrio.com/2021/02/24/covid-black-data-kim-gallon/
Gutteling, J. M., & Wiegman, O. (2013). *Exploring risk communication* (Vol. 8). Springer Science & Business Media.
Jin, Y., Pang, A., & Cameron, G. T. (2007). Integrated crisis mapping: Toward a publics-based, emotion-driven conceptualization in crisis communication. *Sphera Publica*, (7), 81–95.
Haberman, M. & Weiland, N. (2020, March 17), Distrust, blame, and denial mar Trump's virus response. *The New York Times*, A10.
Hale, M. (2020, June 16) PBS's 'Frontline' explores COVID-19 missteps in U.S. *The New York Times*, C1.
Kasperson, R. E., Renn, O., Slovic, P., Brown, H. S., Emel, J., Goble, R., & Ratick, S. (1988). The social amplification of risk: A conceptual framework. *Risk Analysis*, *8*(2), 177–187.
Kasperson, R. E., & Kasperson, J. X. (1996). The social amplification and attenuation of risk. *The Annals of the American Academy of Political and Social Science*, *545*(1), 95–105.
Kasperson, J.X., Kasperson, R.E., Pidgeon, N. & Slovic, P. (2003). The social amplification of risk: Assessing fifteen years of research and theory. In N. Pidgeon, R.E. Kasperson, P. Slovic (Eds.) *The social amplification of risk*. (pp. 13–46). Cambridge University Press.
Leon, B. & Bourk, M. (2018). *Communicating science and technology through online video: Researching a new media phenomenon*. New York: Routledge.
Lichtenberg, J. & MacLean, D. (1991). The role of the media in risk communication. In R.E. Kasperson & P.J.M. Stallen (Eds.) *Communicating risks to the public* (pp. 157–173). Kluwer Academic Publishers.
Lumpkins, C.Y., Bae, J. & Cameron, G.T. (2010). Generating conflict for greater good: Utilizing contingency theory to assess Black and mainstream newspapers as public relations vehicles To promote better health among African Americans. *Public Relations Review*, 36, 73–77.
Mase, A. S., Cho, H., & Prokopy, L. S. (2015). Enhancing the Social Amplification of Risk Framework (SARF) by exploring trust, the availability heuristic, and agricultural advisors' belief in climate change. *Journal of Environmental Psychology*, *41*, 166–176.

Mastin, T. & Campo, S. (2006). Conflicting messages: Overweight and obesity advertisements and articles in Black magazines, *The Howard Journal of Communications*, 17 (4), 265–285.
Masuda, J. R., & Garvin, T. (2006). Place, culture, and the social amplification of risk. *Risk Analysis: An International Journal*, *26*(2), 437–454.
McKee, A (2003). *Textual Analysis: A Beginner's Guide*. Los Angeles: Sage Publications.
Michaeli, E. (2016). *The Defender: How the Legendary Black Newspaper Changed America From the Age of the Pullman Porters to the Age of Obama*. New York: Houghton Mifflin Harcourt.
Petts, J., & Niemeyer, S. (2004). Health risk communication and amplification: learning from the MMR vaccination controversy. *Health, Risk & Society*, *6*(1), 7–23.
Rasmussen, A.C. (2014). Causes and solutions: Mainstream and Black press framing of racial and ethnic health disparities. *Howard Journal of Communications*, 25, 257–280.
Renn, O. (1991). Risk communication and the social amplification of risk. In R. Kasperson & P. L. Stallen (&Is.), *Communicating risk to the public* (p. 287–324). K1uwer.
Renn, O., Burns, W.J., Kasperson, J.X., Kasperson, R.E. & Slovic, P. (1992). The social amplification of risk: Theoretical foundations and empirical applications. *Journal of Social Issues*, 48 (4), 137–160.
Renn, O., & Levine, D. (1991). Credibility and trust in risk communication. In *Communicating risks to the public* (pp. 175–217). Springer, Dordrecht.
Rickard, L. N., McComas, K. A., Clarke, C. E., Stedman, R. C., & Decker, D. J. (2013). Exploring risk attenuation and crisis communication after a plague death in Grand Canyon. *Journal of Risk Research*, *16*(2), 145–167.
Roberts, G. & Klibanoff, H. (2006). *The Race Beat: The Press, the Civil Rights Struggle, and the Awakening of a Nation*. New York: Alfred A. Knopf.
Satcher, D. (2006). Working in and With Communities to Eliminate Disparities in Health. *Health Promotion Practice* 7(3), 176S–178S.
Sellnow, T.L. & Seeger, M.W. (2013). *Theorizing crisis communication*. Malden, MA: Wiley-Blackwell.
Soni, A. & Puthawala, H. (2020). Factors affecting millennials' preference for online video streaming apps in Ahmedabad. *The IUP Journal of Marketing Management*, 19 (1), 23–54.
Spence, P. R., Lachlan, K. A., & Griffin, D. R. (2007). Crisis communication, race, and natural disasters. *Journal of Black Studies*, *37*(4), 539–554.
Strekalova, Y. A., & Krieger, J. L. (2017). Social Amplification of Risk in Health and Risk Messaging. In *Oxford Research Encyclopedia of Communication*.
Tompkins, J.E., Lynch, T., Van Driel, I.I. & Fritz, N. (2020). Kawaii killers and femme fatales: A textual analysis of female characters signifying benevolent and hostile. *Journal of Broadcasting & Electronic Media*. 64 (2), 236–254.
Wang, Y. & Rodgers, S. (2013). Reporting on Health to Ethnic Populations: A Content Analysis of Local Health News in Ethnic Versus Mainstream Newspapers. *Howard Journal of Communications*, 24, 257–274.
Waymer D. & Heath R. L. (2007). Emergent agents: the forgotten publics in crisis communication and issues management research, *Journal of Applied Communication Research*, 35(1), 88–108, doi.10.1080/00909880601065730
West, E.J. (2020, September 2). African American newspapers are a vital source of public health information. *The Washington Post*, Retrieved January 15, 2022 at

https://www.washingtonpost.com/outlook/2020/09/02/african-american-newspapers-are-vital-source-public-health-information/
Wirz, C. D., Xenos, M. A., Brossard, D., Scheufele, D., Chung, J. H., & Massarani, L. (2018). Rethinking social amplification of risk: Social media and Zika in three languages. *Risk Analysis*, *38*(12), 2599–2624.
Wolseley, R.E. (1990). *The Black Press USA*, (2nd Ed) Ames, IA: Iowa State University Press.
Woodward, B. (2020). *Rage*: New York: Simon and Schuster.
Yong, E. (2018, July/August) The Next Plague is Coming: Is America Ready? *The Atlantic* https://www.theatlantic.com/magazine/archive/2018/07/when-the-next-plague-hits/561734/

2 Examining How Medium, Message, and Apology Used in Crises Responses Impact Stakeholders

Michel M. Haigh[1] *and Prisca S. Ngondo*

Corporate reputation is one of the most important variables an organization tries to manage. It is defined as "the overall estimation in which a particular company is held by its various constituents" (Fombrun, 1996, p. 37). Maintaining a positive reputation ensures an organization has a competitive advantage (Roberts & Dowling, 2002) and bolsters goodwill with publics (Jones, Jones, & Little, 2000). However, an organization's reputation can be called into question during a crisis.

One type of crisis is a product recall. In 2015, there were more than 600 products recalled ranging from furniture to chocolates, black bean burgers, sour cream lemon pies, seatbelts, and motor homes (Consumer Affairs, 2015). There were roughly the same number of products recalled in 2020 (Consumer Affairs, 2020). Two organizations that faced crises in 2015 were Blue Bell and Chipotle.

Blue Bell, a Texas-based ice-cream manufacturer, had its first-ever recall in its 108-year history on March 13, 2015. Three listeria deaths were linked to a variety of Blue Bell products (Levin, 2015). By April 2015, the company announced a new worker training program and plant cleaning procedures. It also recalled all of its products on the market. The company started redistributing ice cream in August 2015 (Levin, 2015). In October 2020, Blue Bell agreed to pay a $19 million fine, and the president and CEO Paul Kruse was indicted on seven felony counts for concealing the outbreak (Keyser, 2020).

About the time Blue Bell was ramping up ice-cream production, Chipotle was suffering its own crisis. More than 20 people in Minnesota were infected with Salmonella, and more than a 100 were sickened with a norovirus in southern California. The restaurant then suffered an E. coli outbreak in October and November 2015 that impacted people in nine states (Smith & Garcia, 2016). After two additional outbreaks in December 2015, the company closed all of its stores on February 8, 2016, to host a food safety meeting. In 2020, the company agreed to pay $25 million to resolve criminal charges related to foodborne illness outbreaks

DOI: 10.4324/9781032619187-3

from 2015 to 2018. More than 1,100 people were sickened (Food Safety News, 2020).

Both cases are unique because it is not often a company shuts down. These two organizations followed the guidelines Liu, Shankar, and Yun (2017) provide on how to recover from product harm crises.

Liu et al. (2017) examine long-term effects of product harm crises. They suggest organizations recall the smallest volume of product possible when they discover the recall. The organizations can expand the recall when needed. This practice "mitigates the negative impact on long-term abnormal returns" (Liu et al., 2017, p. 44). They also recommend managers invest in brand advertising to create a buffer against crisis incidents, but pull the advertising during the actual crisis situation.

Liu et al. (2017) examine product harm crises from the impact they have on the organization's bottom-line. More important than an organization's bottom-line is its reputation. Organizations protect their reputations because they are intangible assets (Alsop, 2004; Dowling, 2001). Examining secondary data is important to determine patterns across product recalls regardless of industry (Liu et al., 2017). However, it is also important to understand how stakeholders perceive the crisis, and how the organization's response impacts stakeholders' perceptions of it. This type of understanding comes from experimental research (e.g., Dardis & Haigh, 2009; Haigh & Dardis, 2012; Haigh & Brubaker, 2010). A number of studies have examined different types of crisis response strategies such as apology, sympathy, or compensation (e.g., Coombs & Holladay, 2008). Coombs and Holladay (2009) point out the medium used to apologize is an important thing to consider. Their study found little "meaningful difference between print and video delivery… Additional research on channel differences is solely needed" (p. 5).

The current study addresses Coombs and Holladay's (2009) call for further research by examining the multiple channels an organization can use to disseminate crisis messages. Most research examines different types of crisis messages (e.g., Coombs & Holladay, 1996; Dardis & Haigh, 2009; Haigh & Dardis, 2012) rather than the medium used to deliver the messages. The current study examines how the medium impacts the message. It investigates if there are differences between releasing a crisis response message on an owned-channel (e.g., an organization's YouTube channel), an earned-channel (e.g., news story), or a paid channel (e.g., a paid ad in a newspaper). As media change, organizations no longer have to rely on traditional gate keeping media (e.g., newspapers, magazines, or traditional broadcast news) to disseminate their crisis response messages. Blue Bell and Chipotle crisis messages are employed to determine how the medium used to deliver the crisis message impacts stakeholders' perceptions of the organization-public relationship, corporate social responsibility, and purchase intent to see if the reputation of the organizations can be salvaged.

Literature Review

Situational Crisis Communication Theory

Traditionally, there were four crisis response strategies employed in product harm research. Denial is when the organization states the product offers no threat. Forced compliance is when the government forces an organization to recall a product. Voluntary compliance occurs when the organization takes corrective action on its own, and the support efforts strategy occurs when an organization takes corrective action, offers compensation, and uses a communications campaign to promote the organization's efforts. These types of crises impact the sales of the recalled product, stock prices, purchase intent, and other product sales (Siomkos & Kursbard, 1994).

There are several lines of research examining the messages organizations deliver after a crisis. One line of research employs Benoit's theory of Image Restoration (1995), later named Image Repair (2015). Another line of research employs the Situational Crisis Communication Theory (SCCT) (Coombs & Holladay, 2002). SCCT is composed of three core elements: the crisis situation, the crisis response strategy, and matching the crisis situation with the response strategy.

Coombs (2006) groups crises types into the victim cluster, accidental cluster, and preventable cluster. The crisis cluster examined in the current study is the *accidental cluster*. These types of crises (e.g., challenges, mega damage, technical breakdown accidents, and technical breakdown recalls) occur when the organization's actions lead to an unintentional outcome. Challenge crises occur when stakeholders claim an organization acted inappropriately. Megadamage crises happen when a technical accident occurs, and the organization focuses on the environmental damage. A technical breakdown accident occurs when technology or equipment fails and causes an accident. A technical breakdown recall is when technology or equipment failure causes a product to be recalled (Coombs, 2006). The current study examines the technical breakdown recall crisis situation.

The second aspect of SCCT is the crisis response strategy. Coombs (2006) states the initial crisis response needs to provide instructing information. Instructing information includes the basic information about what happened (crisis basics), information about what stakeholders should do to protect themselves (protection information), and information about what the organization is doing to correct the problem (correction information).

There are three basic options for crisis response strategies. The organization can state no crisis exists (deny). It can alter the attribution of the crisis event to be less negative (diminish), or it can alter how stakeholders perceive how the organization repairs its image (deal).

When an organization wants to deny the crisis exists, it can attack the person or group claiming the crisis occurred, deny there was a crisis, or blame a group outside the organization for the crisis (Coombs, 2006). The diminish response options include an organization making an excuse to say it was not able to control the events that triggered the crisis. The organization could also justify the crisis by stating the damage/injuries were minor (Coombs, 2006).

There are a number of strategies available when the organization chooses to deal with a crisis. An organization can remind stakeholders of past good works, such as corporate social responsibility efforts (known as ingratiation). Organizations can express concern for its victims. It can offer money or products as compensation to show a compassionate response. It can also express regret. The organization can apologize and take full responsibility for the crisis (Coombs, 2006).

The final aspect of SCCT is matching the strategy with the crisis situation. The severity of the crisis and the organization's responsibility should influence the strategy employed. In the case of a low responsibility and low-severity crisis, an organization should attack the accuser or deny the event. In the case of a low responsibility and high-severity crisis, the organization should offer an excuse. In the case of high responsibility and low-severity crisis, justification and ingratiation are two strategies that may be employed. When there is high severity and high responsibility, the organization should take corrective action and offer a full apology (Kim, 2002).

The repair strategy should be selected based on the organization-public relationship (OPR) or the transactions and exchanges between an organization and its stakeholders (Broom, Casey, & Ritchey, 2000). If there is not a positive or favorable relationship with stakeholders, the strategies employed will have little effect on attitudes toward the organization and there will be a negative perception of the crisis. The relationship history will influence how the public perceived the crisis and the restoration strategy used (i.e., attack accuser, denial, excuse, justification, ingratiation, corrective action, and full apology). The initial positive attitudes publics have based on the OPR will help deflect the negative damage a crisis may have on publics (Kim, 2002). "Stakeholders forgive a crisis because of the past good works of the organization" (Coombs, 2000, p. 82).

Research Questions

Research has applied Benoit's (1995, 2015) image restoration strategies to a product recall scenario for a fictitious company (Dardis & Haigh, 2009;

Haigh & Dardis, 2012; Kim & Sun, 2014). They found the most successful image restoration strategy to use during a product recall scenario was to reduce the offensiveness.

Reducing the offensiveness includes bolstering the reputation by discussing previous good deeds, minimizing the negative feelings toward the crisis thereby reducing negative feelings toward the organization, attack the accuser, or offering compensation (Benoit, 2015). Threat to the image is associated with the function of committing the act; therefore, reducing the offensiveness of the act should restore the reputation (Benoit, 2015). This strategy is a mixture of Coombs' (2006) deny option (specifically attacking the accuser), and the deal option (e.g., ingratiation, compassion).

Past research found crisis response messages employing this strategy protected stakeholders' attitudes toward the corporation, the reputation of the corporation, the credibility of the corporation, and perceptions of its corporate ability (Dardis & Haigh, 2009). The reduce offensiveness strategy was also the better strategy to protect the organization-public relationships and perceptions of corporate social responsibility (Haigh & Dardis, 2012). Corporate social responsibility is "the social responsibility of business encompasses the economic, legal, ethical, and discretionary expectations that society has of organizations at a given point in time" (Carroll, 1999, p. 283).

Haigh and Brubaker (2010) examined restoration strategies for an actual organization rather than the fictitious organization. To reduce the offensiveness strategy was most effective in protecting the trust and commitment dimensions of the OPR. It is also the most effective strategy in protecting stakeholders' perceptions of CSR efforts (Haigh & Brubaker, 2010).

In summary, the strategy organizations use to address the crisis situation impacts stakeholders' perceptions of the OPR and perceptions of CSR. Past experimental research has tested different crisis response strategy messages (e.g., Arpan & Roskos-Ewoldsen, 2005; Coombs & Holladay, 1996; Dean, 2004), but limited research has examined the medium used (e.g., Coombs & Holladay, 2009).

Past experimental research has employed print stimuli (e.g., Arpan & Roskos-Ewoldsen, 2005; Coombs & Holladay, 1996; Dardis & Haigh, 2009; Haigh & Brubaker, 2010). However, print content is processed differently than visual content. Visual content is processed using more of the right brain, which is more holistic and emotional (Barry, 1997). Paivio (1986) posits that "affective reactions would ordinarily occur more quickly to pictures than words because the former have more direct access to affect-mediating images" (p. 79). Visual content is processed quickly and heuristically, sometimes bypassing conscious thought (Zhou, 2005). Graber (1987) argues people process visual information "simultaneously rather than sequentially" (p. 76). Thus, visual content is absorbed quickly. Coombs and Holladay (2009) point out the medium used to apologize is an important thing to consider. Their study found little difference between print and video messages, but they also call for additional research in this area. Therefore, the following question is asked:

> RQ1: Does the medium used to apologize impact consumers' perceptions of: (a) food safety, (b) brand credibility, (c) the organization-public relationship, (d) corporate social responsibility, and (e) purchase intent?

The current study examines various forms of print messages and video messages. It examines who "owns" the medium on which the crisis message appears. For example, many organizations now have their own YouTube channels. If they release an apology video on their own YouTube channel does that alter stakeholders' perceptions differently than a print apology message issued in a newspaper? If the CEO makes an appearance on a morning news show, does that change perceptions more than a video on a company's YouTube channel?

> RQ2: How does the format used to apologize (paid, earned, owned) impact consumers' perceptions: (a) food safety, (b) brand credibility, (c) the organization-public relationship, (d) corporate social responsibility, and (e) purchase intent?

Past research shows the strategy used in the message (e.g., denial, reduce the offensiveness) impacts stakeholders' perceptions of the organization-public relationship as well as perceptions of corporate social responsibility. Image repair/restoration research has often tested experimental messages to see how the message strategy impacts the stakeholder (i.e., Cos, Worrell, & Blosenhauser, 2016; Gribas, Disanza, Legge, & Hartmann, 2018; Spence, Lachlan, & Omilion-Hodges, 2016; Twork & Blaney, 2013). However, none of those studies ask the stakeholders to identify the strategy they think the organization is employing in the crisis message. The current study asks stakeholders if they can identify the image repair strategies employed by the organization in order to understand if stakeholders can identify these message types. The current study asks the following:

> RQ3: Can stakeholders identify different image repair strategies in crisis messages?

Method

This study examines how different mediums employed during a crisis impacts stakeholders' perceptions of the OPR, past CSR efforts, and purchase intent.

Participants

The online experiment was conducted using Amazon Mechanical Turk. A "hit" was created with a link to the online questionnaire and specific instructions. Only participants with a US-based address, as registered through a Mechanical Turk profile, were eligible to participate. Participants earned $1.50 for completing the questionnaire. The research team excluded several participants' data based on failing a reading-check/fact test, response sets, and/or study completion times that were ostensibly too fast compared to the sample average, data from 518 total participants were fit for analysis.

The final sample (N = 518) included 277 females (53.9%,) with an average age of 35.78 (SD = 11.05), ranging from 18 to 78. More than 60% of participants had earned college credit (38.7% bachelor's degrees, 10.3% associate's degree, and 11.3% had a master's degrees). A majority of participants were Caucasian (73.9%), 7.8% were African-American, 8.6% were Asian/Pacific Islander, 7.6% were Hispanic/Latino, and 2.9% failed to report ethnicity.

Procedure

The study took the form of a 3 (written statement, video statement, or print ad) × 2 (Blue Bell/Chipotle) online experiment. The first page of the pre-questionnaire was the online implied consent form for the study. After reading the consent form, users were asked to click "proceed" and to answer questions measuring their attitude toward Blue Bell and Chipotle and how important food safety was to them. They were randomly assigned to one of the experimental conditions.

Following reading or watching the stimulus message, participants were directed to a post-test questionnaire that measured their attitudinal and behavioral intent measures about the organization they were assigned to and demographic information.

Stimuli

Each participant was randomly assigned to *one of the* stimulus conditions: Chipotle transcript (n = 91), Chipotle video (n = 75), Chipotle ad (n = 92), Blue Bell YouTube video (n = 89), Blue Bell written statement (n = 92), or Blue Bell transcript (n = 79). Message length was held relatively consistent across each condition by making some small edits.

The Chipotle transcript was the written transcript of the CEO appearing on the Today Show with Matt Lauer. The Chipotle news video condition exposed participants to the video of the CEO being interviewed by Matt Lauer. The Chipotle ad was the actual ad that appeared in *The New York*

Times. The Blue Bell YouTube video was a message posted to the Blue Bell YouTube channel. It shows the CEO apologizing for the product recall. The Blue Bell written statement was the printed statement Blue Bell released during the crisis, whereas the Blue Bell transcript was a written copy of the YouTube video.

Measures

Food Safety Involvement. Issue involvement was assessed using an abbreviated version of Zaichkowsky's (1985) Personal Involvement Inventory. Six adjective pairs were employed in this study including: insignificant/significant, doesn't/does matter to me, unimportant/important, of no concern/of much concern, means nothing/means a lot, and irrelevant/relevant ($\alpha = .97$, $M = 6.35$, $SD = .98$). Items were placed on 7-point scales.

Brand Credibility was measured using a shortened version of the Individualized Trust Scale (Wheeless & Grotz, 1977). Items were placed on 7-point semantic differential scales. Adjective pairs included: untrusting/trusting, deceptive/candid, insincere/sincere, dishonest/honest, inconsiderate/considerate, unreliable/reliable, and deceitful/not deceitful ($\alpha = .95$, $M = 5.66$, $SD = 1.21$).

Organization-Public Relationships (OPR). Three dimensions of the Ki and Hon's (2007) OPR scale were used in this study. The questions were placed on 7-point Likert scales. Questions were reworded slightly to fit the purpose of this study. Dimensions included: ***satisfaction*** (both the organization and the public benefit from their relationship; the public is dissatisfied with its interaction with the organization; the public is happy with the organization; generally speaking, the public is unhappy with the relationship the organization has established with them; the public enjoys dealing with the organization; the organization fails to satisfy the public's needs; the public feels it is important to the organization; and in general, and nothing of value has been accomplished by the organization for the public) ($\alpha = .90$, $M = 4.64$, $SD = 1.18$); ***trust*** (the organization treats the public fairly and justly; whenever the organization makes an important decision, the organization considers the decision's impact on the public; the organization can be relied on to keep its promises; the organization takes public opinion into account when making decisions; the public feels very confident about abilities of the organization; sound principles guide the organization's behavior; and the organization misleads the public) ($\alpha = .94$, $M = 4.90$, $SD = 1.25$); and ***commitment*** (the organization is trying to maintain a long-term commitment; the organization wants to maintain a positive relationship; compared to other organizations, the public values its relationship with this organization the most; the public would rather work with the organization than against it; and the public feels a sense of loyalty to the organization) ($\alpha = .89$, $M = 5.29$, $SD = 1.14$).

Corporate Social Responsibility (CSR). CSR was measured using five items on 7-point Likert scales (Lichtenstein et al., 2004). Questions included: the organization is committed to using a portion of its profits to help nonprofits; the organization gives back to the communities in which it does business; local nonprofits benefit from the organization's contributions; the organization integrates charitable contributions into its business activities; the organization is involved in corporate giving (α = .95, *M* = 4.32, *SD* = 1.14).

Purchase Intent. Purchase intent was measured by combining two scales from Gill et al. (1988) and Urbany et al. (1997). Questions were placed on 7-point, sematic differential scales. Adjective pairs included: unlikely/likely; nonexistent/existent; improbable/probable; impossible/possible; uncertain/certain; definitely would not/definitely would (α = .97, *M* = 5.05, *SD* = 1.82).

Crisis Strategy Employed. Participants were asked to select all strategies they thought the CEO/organization applied in the message they read/watched. Statements included: the CEO denied the crisis; the CEO tried to shift the blame to someone other than the organization; the CEO claimed he lacked information or ability to prevent the crisis; the CEO declared the crisis was an accident; the CEO tried to bolster the reputation of the company; the CEO offered compensation to those impacted by the crisis; the CEO has taken corrective action to prevent the crisis from happening again; the CEO offered a sincere apology. The strategies tie to Benoit's (2015) theory of Image Repair.

Open-Ended Responses. After watching/reading their message, participants were asked two, open-ended questions. One question asked participants, "Please reflect on the message. What is your overall perception of the organization?" Another question asked participants, "please list what came to mind while reading/watching the message from the organization." The first author trained a graduate student in the use of the categories of apology (Benoit, 2015). Categories included: mortification, reducing the offensiveness, corrective action, evading responsibility, and denial. To train, they discussed and coded 10% of the examples from the data. The coder could code the response into multiple categories if the participant listed several statements. The first author and the coder then coded independently for intercoder reliability. The intercoder reliabilities were more than 90% using Holsti (1969).

Results

The purpose of this study was to determine how the medium used to distribute crisis responses impacted stakeholders. To answer **Research Question 1**, a multivariate analysis of variance (MANOVA) was computed to assess the differences between the independent variable medium (print versus video) and the dependent variables: dimensions of the OPR (trust, commitment, satisfaction), CSR, purchase intent, food safety involvement, and brand credibility. The omnibus results found significant differences for the experimental condition Wilks' $\lambda = .97$, $F(7, 505) = 2.31$, $p = .02$, partial $\eta^2 = .03$.

The subsequent univariate tests revealed significant differences for the independent variable **experimental condition** (print or broadcast) on the dependent variables: *food safety involvement* $F(1, 512) = 6.24$, $p = .01$, $\eta^2 = .01$; *OPR* (satisfaction $F(1, 512) = 5.66$, $p = .02$, $\eta^2 = .01$; trust $F(1, 512) = 5.95$, $p = .02$, $\eta^2 = .01$; and commitment $F(1, 512) = 3.76$, $p = .05$, $\eta^2 = .01$). There were no statistically significant differences for *brand credibility* $F(1, 512) = 2.98$, $p = .08$, $\eta^2 = .01$; *CSR* $F(1, 512) = .07$, $p = .77$, $\eta^2 = .00$; and *purchase intent* $F(1, 512) = 2.36$, $p = .12$, $\eta^2 = .01$.

When examining the pattern of means, those in the print condition indicated higher scores on the dependent variables. Participants reading the transcript, written statement, or a print ad all indicated higher perceptions of the organization-public relationship ($M = 4.72$, $SD = 1.18_{OPRSatisfaction}$, $M = 4.98$, $SD = 1.24_{OPRTrust}$, $M = 5.35$, $SD = 1.14_{OPRCommitment}$) than those watching a video message ($M = 4.46$, $SD = 1.15_{OPRSatisfaction}$, $M = 4.69$, $SD = 1.25_{OPRTrust}$, $M = 5.14$, $SD = 1.13_{OPRCommitment}$). They also indicated more positive perceptions of brand credibility ($M = 5.75$, $SD = 1.20_{PRINT}$; $M = 5.56$, $SD = 1.22_{VIDEO}$) and purchase intent ($M = 5.13$, $SD = 1.84_{PRINT}$; $M = 4.88$, $SD = 1.76_{VIDEO}$). Please see Table 2.1 for a comparison of means and standard deviations of the condition and the dependent variables.

To address **Research Question 2**, a MANOVA was computed to assess the differences. Experimental condition (Chipotle transcript, Chipotle news video, Chipotle ad, Blue Bell YouTube video, Blue Bell written statement,

Table 2.1 Means and Standard Deviations for Dependent Variables and Print/Video

	Print	*Broadcast*
Food Safety	6.42(.92)	6.20(1.08)
Brand Credibility	5.75(1.20)	5.55(1.22)
OPR Satisfaction	4.72(1.18)	4.46(1.49)
OPR Trust	4.98(1.24)	4.69(1.25)
OPR Commitment	5.35(1.14)	5.14(1.13)
CSR	4.32(1.10)	4.32(1.22)
Purchase Intent	5.13(1.84)	4.88(1.76)

Notes: Means and standard deviations (shown in parentheses) for variables. Food safety involvement was measured using a 7-point semantic differential scale (Zaichkowsky, 1985). Brand credibility was measured using 7-point semantic differential scales from Wheeless and Grotz (1977). CSR was measured using a 7-point Likert scale from Lichtenstein et al. (2004). Perceptions of the OPR were measured using a 7-point scale from Ki and Hon (2007).

or Blue Bell transcript) was the independent variable and the dimensions of the OPR (trust, commitment, satisfaction), CSR, purchase intent, food safety involvement, and brand credibility were the dependent variables. The omnibus results found significant differences for the experimental condition Wilks' $\lambda = .90$, $F(35, 2109) = 1.46$, $p = .04$, partial $\eta^2 = .02$.

The subsequent univariate tests revealed significant differences for the independent variable **experimental condition** on the dependent variables: *brand credibility* $F(5, 512) = 3.33$, $p = .01$, $\eta^2 = .03$; *OPR dimensions* (satisfaction $F(5, 512) = 3.19$, $p = .01$, $\eta^2 = .03$; trust $F(5, 512) = 3.38$, $p = .01$, $\eta^2 = .03$; commitment $F(5, 512) = 2.23$, $p = .04$, $\eta^2 = .02$). There were no statistically significant differences for *food safety involvement* $F(5, 512) = 1.90$, $p = .09$, $\eta^2 = .02$; *CSR* $F(5, 512) = .50$, $p = .78$, $\eta^2 = .00$; and *purchase intent* $F(1, 512) = 1.50$, $p = .18$, $\eta^2 = .01$.

Tukey HSD post hoc tests were conducted. Only the statistically significant differences are reported. For the OPR dimension of *trust*, those reading the Blue Bell transcript ($M = 5.31$, $SD = 1.17$) had significantly more trust in the relationship than those viewing the Chipotle news story ($M = 4.66$, $SD = 1.25$). Those reading the Blue Bell transcript had more positive perceptions ($M = 5.31$, $M = 1.17$) compared to those watching the Blue Bell YouTube apology ($M = 4.72$, $SD = 1.26$). See Table 2.2 for a complete list of means and standard deviations.

Research Question 3. Participants were asked to identify all image repair strategies they thought the organization/CEO used in the message they watched/read. They selected yes/no for each of the following types of statements. When reviewing the strategies participants thought the CEOs employed, the most common was mortification ($n = 438$). They also thought the organizations took corrective action ($n = 405$), tried to bolster reputation ($n = 196$), and stated the crises were accidents ($n = 115$). See Table 2.3 for a breakdown of strategy type and organization.

Participants answered two, open-ended questions after they were exposed to the experimental stimuli. When reviewing the open-ended statements, there were differences. For the first statement asking participants to reflect on the overall message, most participants noted the organization was making a statement of apology (mortification, $n = 220$), followed by "other" statements (not going to eat there again, unsafe food, etc., $n = 149$), corrective action statements ($n = 126$), reducing the offensiveness statements ($n = 38$), and evading the responsibility ($n = 33$).

When reviewing the responses to the question "What is your overall perception of the apology." Most participants indicated the organization was employing mortification in the message they had seen/read ($n = 367$), the company took corrective action ($n = 100$), were trying to reduce the offensiveness ($n = 63$), evade responsibility (35), or "other" ($n = 22$).

Table 2.2 Means and Standard Deviations for Dependent Variables and Medium/Message

	Chipotle Transcript	*Chipotle News Story*	*Blue Bell YouTube*	*Blue Bell Written Statement*	*Blue Bell Transcript*	*Chipotle Ad*
Food Safety	6.51(.88)	6.10(1.10)	6.28(1.05)	6.36(.88)	6.49(.91)	6.34(.99)
Brand Credibility	5.54(1.28)	5.42(1.18)	5.67(1.25)	5.55(1.22)	6.07(.85)	5.88(1.30)
OPR Satisfaction	4.55(.12)	4.46(.14)	4.46(.12)	4.52(.12)	4.95(.13)	4.89(.12)
OPR Trust	4.79(.13)	4.66(.14)	4.72(.12)	5.27(.12)	5.59(.13)	5.43(.12)
OPR Commitment	5.15(.12)	5.12(.13)	5.16(.12)	5.27(.12)	5.59(.13)	5.43(.12)
CSR	4.22(.12)	4.34(.13)	4.31(12)	4.26(.12)	4.50(.13)	4.29(.12)
Purchase Intent	4.80(.19)	4.80(.21)	4.93(.19)	5.15(.19)	5.38(.21)	5.24(.19)

Notes: Means and standard deviations (shown in parentheses) for variables. Food safety involvement was measured using a 7-point semantic differential scale (Zaichkowsky, 1985). Brand credibility was measured using 7-point semantic differential scales from Wheeless and Grotz (1977). CSR was measured using a 7-point Likert scale from Lichtenstein et al. (2004). Perceptions of the OPR were measured using a 7-point scale from Ki and Hon (2007).

Table 2.3 Image Repair Strategy Employed by Organization as Identified by Stakeholders

	Blue Bell	*Chipotle*
Denied	1	5
Shifted the blame	0	18
Lacked information	10	13
Accident	52	63
Bolster	88	108
Offered compensation	23	10
Corrective action	183	222
Apology	229	209

Note: Participants were shown the following statements. They selected all that they thought applied. Only the "yes" responses are shown. Statements included: the CEO denied the crisis; the CEO tried to shift the blame to someone other than the organization; the CEO claimed he lacked information or ability to prevent the crisis; the CEO declared the crisis was an accident; the CEO tried to bolster the reputation of the company; the CEO offered compensation to those impacted by the crisis; the CEO has taken corrective action to prevent the crisis from happening again; The CEO offered a sincere apology. The strategies are tied to Benoit's (2015) theory.

Discussion

The current study analyzed whether the medium used to apologize impacted consumers' perceptions of the organization-public relationship, corporate social responsibility efforts, and future purchase intent. The answer is sometimes. The effect sizes were small, but the medium the message appeared on did impact stakeholders' perceptions. Yes. The medium the message appeared on (print or video) significantly impacted stakeholders' perceptions of the dimensions of organization-public relationships (satisfaction, trust, commitment) and food safety involvement. The medium did not impact stakeholders' perceptions of corporate social responsibility or purchase intent.

Contrary to Coombs and Holladay (2009), who found no meaningful difference between the use of video and print. This study used different dependent variables and employed additional types of messages. Once again, the effect sizes in this study were small. So though there were significant results, there are still a number of things to learn about mediums used to apologize.

The print messages (print ads, transcripts, or written statements) all performed better than the video (interview or video statement). Those in the print message condition indicated significantly higher perceptions of the organization-public relationship. They also rated the organizations higher for brand credibility and food safety after reading a print message. This study indicates the print and video messages were processed differently. The video messages may have been processed more quickly, so the participants did not reflect on what was being (Zhou, 2005) said but rather concentrated more on the nonverbal components—including how the CEO looked. When examining the pattern of means, in most cases print messages work better than video apologies and this could be related to the nonverbal communication present from the person in the video and how sincere the person comes across. As Pfau and Wan (2006) pointed out, viewers tend to focus on the message source in a video message as compared to print readers who focus on the message content.

When reviewing some of the open-ended comments, participants did not find the CEO of Chipotle believable. A number of participants commented he looked "insincere," was appearing on the show "for business interests," and "I felt like he was trying to cover-up something much bigger, like the real reason why they messed up." Another stated, "At first I did not feel his feelings were very sincere. I felt he was more worried about stock value, profits, and corporate image rather than caring for consumers...." Those who saw video of the Blue Bell CEO commented how he looked "humble," "seemed like the CEO really cared and was upset and just wanted to help out," and "the CEO sounded very remorseful and upset and sincere about his apology." One participant even commented on the Blue Bell CEO not having a fancy office. The Blue Bell CEO was not wearing a suit jacket or a tie, but just sitting at a small desk with windows behind him. There is a difference there since the Chipotle CEO was wearing a suit coat, had more fashionable eye glasses, and was dressed to be on a morning show.

This study also examined if where the message was placed impacted the stakeholder. More and more organizations rely on owned forms of communication (e.g., social media platforms, and websites) to disseminate their message rather than disseminating it through the traditional forms of media with gate keepers. There were significant differences found for the perceptions of the organization-public relationship and brand credibility.

Regardless of the platform used to apologize or if the message was print or broadcast, participants indicated the food produced by both organizations was safe. The means displayed in Table 2.2 indicate the participants were highly involved in the topic of food safety. A vast majority of the open-ended comments reviewed also indicated people felt both organizations had addressed the issues that led to the shutdown of the organizations.

The Blue Bell transcript of the YouTube apology had the highest score for brand credibility. The video apology was very direct since it was on the owned medium. However, it had more impact on brand credibility when the visuals were removed. It also scored higher than the written statement. People prepare different types of messages for different types of platforms. The findings here indicate the tone and content of the video apology had more impact when people read it instead of saw it. The type of message prepared for broadcast also performed better than the message prepared for print (written statement).

The pattern of means for organization-public relationship were somewhat neutral and approaching positive because the means were 4.0 to almost 5.0 on the 7.0 scale.

There were no interesting findings for the organization-public relationship dimension of satisfaction. The mean scores were neutral leaning toward positive on the scale. Commitment scored highest in the Blue Bell transcript condition. Two Blue Bell conditions (written statement and transcript) scored the highest for trust. The Chipotle ad in *The New York Times* also scored higher on trust. The findings here indicate once again the type of message prepared for video but delivered in a print format performs the best. These findings have implications for the type of crisis communication plan management can develop. The current findings would suggest taking out a full-page ad (paid channel) apologizing in *The New York Times* may be as impactful as recording a video apology and playing it on an organization's YouTube channel (owned channel). But if an organization wants to create the most impactful message, it should blend the casual writing style of broadcast and deliver the message in a print format rather than a video format.

Coombs and Holladay (2009) noted they had a small effect size, where the print condition produced slightly more positive reputation scores than the video condition. However, the authors note this result should be taken cautiously as it accounted for a small percentage of the variance. The current study provides additional evidence for the print versus video debate in relation to OPR (satisfaction, trust, and commitment). Ultimately, if maintaining and building trust is important to an organization, a focus on print messages is recommended based on these findings.

As communication continues to evolve in the digital era, traditional forms of delivery may still play a crucial role in crisis communication. Practitioners should consider using a mixed-media approach depending on the crisis criteria. As noted by Coombs and Holladay (2009), "…it is still solid advice for organizations to deliver their messages in a variety of media as a means of reaching more people and to not worry about the specific type of media being used" (p. 5).

The current study is one of the first studies to have stakeholders identify apology types. Most research crafts messages employing an apology strategy and then compares how the strategies impact stakeholders (i.e., Cos, Worrell, & Blosenhauser, 2016; Gribas, Disanza, Legge, & Hartmann, 2018; Spence, Lachlan, & Omilion-Hodges, 2016; Twork & Blaney, 2013). This study tried to determine if stakeholders could identify crisis response types. It was interesting when examining the open-ended results how many would use terms like "apology," "bolstering," and "reducing the offensiveness." Stakeholders are able to identify different strategies employed in crisis messages.

Limitations and Future Research

This study is not without limitations. One weakness is that participants were not assigned to each condition based on previous attitudes toward the company. Another limitation is the stimuli. Chipotle did not release an apology on their owned medium channel, and Blue Bell was not interviewed on the national news. Haigh and Brubaker (2010) used real organizations in their study, compared to Haigh and Dardis (2012). It's easier to control for attitude toward an organization when using a fictitious organization; however, one could argue it is hard to measure the impact of the crisis message or medium used to apologize if the participants don't have any knowledge or background—a relationship—with an organization. The end goal in strategic communications is to maintain and bolster organization-public relationships. It is important to understand how the crisis is going to impact the organization's bottom-line—usually measured through purchase intent. It is hard to measure purchase intent when using a fictitious organization because perceptions of this don't exist for participants.

Coombs (2016) addresses the use of fictitious versus real crises scenarios. He states if a real organization is used, the researcher must control for prior reputation, which is why the researcher might decide to use a fictitious one. When the experimental stimuli is based on a real organization with only the name of the organization changed, Coombs (2016) states this scenario "is equivalent to a real crisis scenario" (p. 121).

Additional research is needed to examine how paid/earned/owned messages are perceived by stakeholders. Non-crisis messages appearing on these different channels may impact stakeholders differently than the crisis messages used in this study. Additionally, this study looked at a product crisis. Additional research is needed to replicate the results for different types of crisis categories.

Future research should also continue to figure out how viewers process video messages. The sources cues in the video messages could influence how stakeholders process messages. If a CEO is awkward in front of a camera, comes across as uncaring, that impacts how the apology is interpreted. There is still more to learn on how stakeholders process video messages in terms of credibility of the source, sincerity, and believability of the apology, and if they think the video message repaired the organization's image.

Overall, this study contributes to the examination of crisis communication channel effects via experimental methods as suggested by Coombs and Holladay (2009). Additionally, the results further the utility of image restoration strategies as they are related to organization-public relationships and give practitioners a blueprint of which media and messages drive business forward while restoring the entity's image.

Note

1 Michel M. Haigh would like to thank Michael Calderon, an M.A. student in the school, for coding the open ended comments. An earlier version of this paper was presented at the International Public Relations Research Conference. This project was funded by the Arthur W. Page Center for Integrity in Public Communication at Pennsylvania State University.

References

Alsop, R. (2004). Corporate reputation: Anything but superficial – the deep but fragile nature of corporate reputation. *Journal of Business Strategy*, *25*(6), 21–29. 10.1108/02756660410699900

Arpan, L. M., & Roskos-Ewoldsen, D. R. (2005). Stealing thunder: Analysis of the effects of proactive disclosure of crisis information. *Public Relations Review*, *31*(3), 425–433. 10.1016/j.pubrev.2005.05.003

Barry, A. M. S. (1997). *Visual intelligence: Perception, image, and manipulation in visual communication*. Albany: State University of New York Press.

Benoit, W. L. (1995). *Accounts, excuses, and apologies: A theory of image restoration Strategies*. New York: State University of New York Press.

Benoit, W. L. (2015). *Accounts, excuses, and apologies: Image repair theory and research*. New York: State University of New York Press.

Broom, G., Casey, S., & Ritchey, J. (2000). Toward a concept and theory or organization-public relationships: An update. In J. A. Ledingham & S. D. Bruning (Eds.), *Public relations as relationship management: A relational approach to the study and practice of public relations* (pp. 3–22). Lawrence Erlbaum Associates: Hillsdale, NJ.

Carroll, A. B. (1999). Corporate social responsibility: Evaluation of a definitional construct. *Business and Society*, *38*(3), 268–295. 10.1177/000765039903800303

Consumer Affairs (2015). Recalls. Available at: https://www.consumeraffairs.com/recalls/2015/01/

Consumer Affairs. (2020). Recalls. Available at: https://www.consumeraffairs.com/recalls/2020/01/

Coombs, W. T. (2000). Crisis management advantages of a relational perspective. In J. A. Ledingham & S. D. Bruning (Eds.), *Public relations as relationship management: A relational approach to the study and practice of public relations* (pp. 73–93), Lawrence Erlbaum Associates, Hillsdale, NJ.

Coombs, W. T. (2006). The protective powers of crisis response strategies: Managing reputational assets during a crisis. *Journal of Promotion Management*, *12*(3/4), 241–260. 10.1300/J057v12n03_13

Coombs, W. T. (2016). Reflections on a meta-analysis: Crystalizing thinking about SCCT. *Journal of Public Relations Research*, *28*(2), 120–122. 10.1080/1062726X.2016.1167479

Coombs, W. T., & Holladay, S. J. (1996). Communication and attribution in a crisis: An experimental study in crisis communication. *Journal of Public Relations Research*, *84*(4), 279–295. 10.1207/s1532754xjprr0804_04

Coombs, W. T., & Holladay, S. J. (2002). Helping crisis managers protect reputational assets: Initial tests of the situational crisis communication theory. *Management Communication Quarterly*, *16*(2), 165–186. 10.1177/089331802237233

Coombs, W. T., & Holladay, S. J. (2008). Comparing apology to equivalent crisis response strategies: Clarifying apology's role and value in crisis communication. *Public Relations Review*, *34*(3), 252–257. 10.1016/j.pubrev.2008.04.001

Coombs, W. T., & Holladay, S. J. (2009). Further explorations of post-crisis communication: Effects of media and response strategies on perceptions and intentions. *Public Relations Review*, *35*(1), 1–6. 10.1016/j.pubrev.2008.09.011

Cos, G., Worrell, T. R., & Blosenhauser, J. D. (2016). An empirical test of image restoration strategies. In J. Blaney (Ed.), *Putting image repair to the test: Quantitative applications of image restoration theory* (pp. 85–97). Lanham, MD: Lexington Books.

Dardis, F. & Haigh, M. M. (2009). Prescribing versus describing: Testing image restoration strategies in a crisis situation. *Corporate Communications: An International Journal*, *14*(1), 101–118. 10.1108/13563280910931108
Dean, D. H. (2004). Consumer reaction to negative publicity: Effects of corporate reputation, response, and responsibility for a crisis event. *The Journal of Business Communication*, *41*(2), 192–211. 10.1177/0021943603261748
Dowling, G. (2001). *Creating corporate reputations: Identity, image, and performance*. Oxford, N.Y.: Oxford University Press.
Fombrun, C. J. (1996). *Reputation: Realizing value from the corporate image*. Boston, M.A.: Harvard Business School Press.
Food Safety News. (2020, April 22). Chipotle agrees to pay $25 million federal fine for role in some outbreaks. Available at: https://www.foodsafetynews.com/2020/04/chipotle-agrees-to-pay-25-million-federal-fine-for-role-in-some-outbreaks/
Gill, J. D., Grossbart, S., & Laczniak, R. N. (1988). Influence of involvement, commitment and familiarity on brand beliefs and attitudes of viewers exposed to alternative claim strategies. *Journal of Advertising*, *17*(2), 33–43. 10.1080/00913367.1988.10673111
Graber, D. A. (1987). Television news without pictures? *Critical Studies in Mass Communication*, *4*, 74–87. 10.1080/15295038709360115
Gribas, J., Disanza, J., Legge, N., & Hartman, K. L. (2018). Organizational image repair tactics and crisis type: Implications for crisis response strategy effectiveness. *Journal of International Crisis and Risk Communication Research*, *1*(2), 225–252. 10.30658/jicrcr.1.2.3
Haigh, M. M., & Brubaker, P. (2010). Examining how image restoration strategy impacts perceptions of corporate social responsibility, organization-public relationships, and source credibility. *Corporate Communications: An International Journal*, *15*(4), 453–468. 10.1108/13563281011085538
Haigh, M. M., & Dardis, F. (2012). The impact of apology on organization–public relationships and perceptions of corporate social responsibility. *Public Relations Journal*, *6*(1), 1–16.
Holsti, O. R. (1969). *Content analysis for the social sciences and humanities*. Reading, MA: Addison-Wesley.
Jones, G. H., Jones, B. H., & Little, P. (2000). Reputation as reservoir: Buffering against loss in times of economic crisis. *Corporate Reputation Review*, *3*(1), 21–29. 10.1057/palgrave.crr.1540096
Keyser, M. (2020, May 1). Ex-Blue Bell ceo faces 7 felony counts in cover-up of deadly listeria outbreak. Available at: https://www.khou.com/article/news/local/former-blue-bell-ceo-indicted-conspiracy-justice-department/285-5ae8633c-b879-4191-b7f5-3f5742184937
Ki, E., & Hon, L. (2007). Reliability and validity of organization – public relationship measurement and linkages among relationship indicators in a membership organization. *Journalism & Mass Communication Quarterly*, 84(3), 419–438. 10.1177/107769900708400302
Kim, S., & Sung, K. H. (2014). Revisiting the effectiveness of base crisis response strategies in comparison of reputation management crisis responses. *Journal of Public Relations Research*, *26*(1), 62–78. 10.1080/1062726X.2013.795867
Kim, Y. (2002). *Understanding crisis management*. Seoul: Chaek and Gil.
Levin, M. (2015, April 21). Timeline of the Blue Bell recall. Houston Chronicle. Available at: https://www.chron.com/business/slideshow/Timeline-of-the-Blue-Bell-recall-107965.php

Lichtenstein, D. R., Drumwright, M. E., & Braig, B. M. (2004). The effect of corporate social responsibility on customer donations to corporate-supported nonprofits. *Journal of Marketing*, *68*(4), 16–32. 10.1509/jmkg.68.4.16.42726

Liu, Y., Shankar, V., & Yun, W. (2017). Crisis management strategies and long-term effects of product recall on firm value. *Journal of Marketing*, 81, 30–48. 10.1509/jm.15.0535

Paivio, A. (1986). *Mental representations: A dual coding approach*. New York: Oxford University Press

Pfau, M., & Wan, H. (2006). Persuasion: An intrinsic function of public relations. In C. Botan & V. Hazleton (Eds.), *Public relations theory II*. (pp. 101–136). Mahwah, NJ: Lawrence Erlbaum.

Roberts, P. W., & Dowling, G. R. (2002). Corporate reputation and sustained superior financial performance. *Strategic Management Journal*, *23*(12), 1077–1093. 10.1002/smj.274

Siomkos, G. J., & Kursbard, G. (1994). The hidden crisis in product harm crisis management. *European Journal of Marketing*, *28*(2), 30–41. 10.1108/03090569410055265

Smith, A. & Garcia, A. (2016, January 15). *Chipotle to close all restaurants on Feb. 8 for food safety meeting*. CNN Money. Available at: http://money.cnn.com/2016/01/15/news/companies/chipotle-food-safety-meeting/index.html

Spence, P. R., Lachlan, K. A., & Omilion-Hodges, L. M. (2016). Examining the impact of message strategy on organizational image. In J. Blaney (Ed.), *Putting image repair to the test: Quantitative applications of image restoration theory* (pp. 29–39). Lanham, MD: Lexington Books.

Twork, J., & Blaney, J. (2013). Reputation differences between mortification- only and mortification/corrective action strategies following a transgression by a professional athlete. In J. R. Blaney, L. R. Lippert, & J. S. Smith (Eds.), *Repairing the athlete's image: Studies in sports image restoration* (pp. 395–399). Lanham, MD: Lexington Books.

Urbany, J. E., Bearden, W. O., Kaicker, A., & Smith-de Borrero (1997). Transaction utility effects when quality is uncertain. *Journal of the Academy of Marketing Science*, *25*(1), 45–55.

Wheeless, L. R., & Grotz, J. (1977). The measurement of trust and its relationship to self-disclosure. *Human Communication Research*, 3(3), 250–257. 10.1111/j.1468-2958.1977.tb00523.x

Zaichkowsky, J. L. (1985). Measuring the involvement construct. *Journal of Consumer Research*, *12*(3), 341–352. https://www.jstor.org/stable/254378

Zhou, S. (2005). Effects of arousing visuals and redundancy on cognitive assessment of television news. *Journal of Broadcasting & Electronic Media*, *49*(1), 23–42. 10.1207/s15506878jobem4901_3

3 Arab Spring Conflict Visuals

A Content Analysis of Crisis Coverage on Pan-Arab TV News

Michael D. Bruce

Arab transnational broadcasting exploded with the development of independent satellite broadcasting as the 20th century came to a close. Al Jazeera is generally viewed as the catalyst of these significant media changes in the Arab world. A 2010 survey found nearly 400 channels, several of which were 24-hour pan-Arab news channels, operating on Arabsat and Nilesat satellites (Al-Failakawi, 2010).

Satellite television viewership increased in the region at the same time. The BBC's David Lomax discovered that in the year following the fall of the Iraqi Baathist regime, more than 7 million satellite dishes were purchased (2005). This prompted an Iraqi sociologist to suggest that the Iraqis were more interested in television than food (as cited in Lomax, 2005). A field study conducted for the British Council by A.C. Nielsen (see Seib, 2007) revealed the most common media activity in the region is TV viewing (listed by 100% of respondents), followed by listening to the radio (73%), surfing the Internet (62%), and reading (55%). The survey also found that the most watched pan-Arab news channels were Al Jazeera (72%) and Al Arabiya (44%). Cottle (2011) and Pintak (2011a, 2011b) argue that in addition to social networking technologies, satellite television played an instrumental role in the recent political uprisings in the region as well.

These dramatic changes to Arab media and the simultaneous increase in risk and crisis events in the MENA region—the rise of contemporary global terrorism (Bruce & O'Hair, 2009); American-led invasions of Afghanistan and Iraq; and increased political unrest—made the Arab world a rich environment for analyzing crisis media coverage, particularly as Western government officials accused Arab media of fanning the flames of global conflict. Data for the current chapter was part of a larger project which was designed to fill voids in both pan-Arab media and visual framing research of "normal" or "routine" news coverage in transnational, pan-Arab television. One goal was to determine if Arab media coverage was as violent and sensational as critics claimed.

DOI: 10.4324/9781032619187-4

While it was expected that there would be several major international news stories within the sample frame—the World Cup, the ongoing wars in Iraq and Afghanistan, and the end of US combat operations in Iraq—there was no indication that a single crisis event—the Arab Spring—would dominate the news agenda for such a significant part of the sampling period for this project. Arab Spring started as civil demonstrations organized in Tunisia on December 18, 2010, to protest police harassment. In the following months, the popular uprisings against repressive governments spread throughout the MENA (Middle East and North Africa) region with intensity that varied from relatively peaceful demonstrations to civil war (Libya and Syria). As the uprisings spread, the Arab media was there to provide extensive coverage (Pintak, 2011b). The resulting coverage presented a unique opportunity to examine differences in visual framing of the crisis by pan-Arab TV news outlets trying to reach the same Arab audiences. Therefore, the visuals of five transnational satellite news channels that broadcast to/from the Arab world—Al Jazeera, Al Jazeera English, Al Arabiya, Alhurra, and BBC Arabic—was conducted to explore differences in the application of visual news frames in Arab Spring coverage.

Literature Review

Framing refers to organizing structures used by both media professionals and audiences to simplify complex issues (Gitlin, 1980; Gamson, Croteau, Hoynes, & Sasson, 1992; Reese, 2001). When specifically applied to the news, frames have been considered "schemes" for both presenting and comprehending the news. The term "framing" is more commonly used to describe media-located, or macro-level, frames. Frame building at this level is primarily about the decisions message producers make to give their stories meaning (Kosicki, 2003; Scheufele & Tewksbury, 2007). Frames have the potential to alter what audiences perceive as an issue, and what their reaction to the issue should be (Entman, 1993; Gitlin, 1980; Jasperson, Shah, Watts, Faber, & Fan, 1998).

A variety of methods have been developed for examining visual news frames (Matthes, 2009; Semetko & Valkenburg, 2000). Matthes and Kohring (2008) note frequency is one method for examining frames as single aspects of mediated communication grouped together in systematic patterns over multiple messages. Gitlin (1980) referred to this process as "persistent selection, emphasis, and exclusion" (p. 7).

Visual Framing

Even though images are regularly referenced as a framing device, they are often ignored in studies of television news (Grabe & Bucy, 2009; Messaris

& Abraham, 2001). Matthes' (2009) analysis confirmed this notion. He found that textual elements were generally treated as the main units of analysis. Only 5% of the studies had directly coded visuals, and only 3% used visuals as the main unit of analysis. Seventy-two percent of television content studies completely ignored the visual elements. Research has identified differences in the ways the visual and verbal aspects of mediated communication are handled by the audience (Fahmy, 2010; Fahmy & Kim, 2008; Messaris, 1992; Messaris, 1994; Messaris & Abraham, 2001). Messaris has been at the forefront of this research into the impact of images in communication. Messaris and Abraham (2001) identified three properties of visual images—analogical quality, indexicality, and lack of an explicit propositional syntax—that make visual framing distinct from verbal framing.

Messaris and Abraham (2001) argue that the analogical quality of images is what most clearly differentiates them from words. The essence of this analogical quality is the similarity of images, or analog, to the items they portray. Therefore, visuals are uniquely taken at face value without regard to prior experience or cultural references (Kepplinger, 1991). Indexicality refers to similar qualities of images that are specifically associated with photographic media (including film, television, and video). Messaris and Abraham (2001) acknowledged the writings of philosopher C.S. Peirce who referred to photographs as "signs" or "indices" of the world they represent. They argue that the indexicality of photographs presents a "true-to-life" quality that appears free from "human agency" and results in visuals being perceived as more believable than other communication sources (p. 217). They note that the use of images in the framing process could "diminish the likelihood that viewers would question what they see" (p. 217). The danger of indexicality in news images is manifested when viewers are misled by outright deceptive practices or through the subtle, often unintentional, process of image selection and editing. Messaris and Abraham (2001) recognize the Chicago MacArthur Day study (Lang & Lang, 1968) as one of the earliest studies on the systematic evaluation of the effects of the photographic selection process. The study examined how television editors shaped viewers' perceptions of the MacArthur Day event. They found shot selection in the television coverage of the event made the crowds seem larger and much more enthusiastic than they actually were. Lang and Lang determined that the discrepancy between the mediated event and the actual event was a result of selective editing. Messaris and Abraham cite the Langs' findings as a "paradigmatic illustration of the relationship between visual indexicality and framing" (2001, p. 218).

While the first two properties reference the individual image, the third distinct property—lack of an explicit propositional syntax—refers to relationships between multiple images, or "visual syntax" (Messaris & Abraham, 2001, p. 218). They note that within the communication process, verbal languages rely on specific syntactic devices for making propositions about causality, comparison, generalization, or other connections. Visual communication does not rely on an explicit syntax for making these propositions. Therefore, the various visual presentation techniques (i.e., editing, transitions, juxtaposition) can convey multiple meanings to viewers. For example, associational juxtaposition is an editing device that allows the characteristics of the subject in one image to be transferred to the subject in the next image (Reynolds & Barnett, 2002). Tuchman (1978) referred to juxtaposition as a framing technique used in news film to create relationships among various story elements. This shifts the impetus for appropriate interpretation of visual messages from the messenger to the viewer.

These three properties of the visual image create a sense of "having-been-there" (Barthes, 1978, p. 44) for the audience. Thus, scholars (Dobernig, Lobinger, & Wetzstein, 2010; Huxford, 2001; Tirohl, 2000) suggest journalists use news images to support the credibility and accuracy of their reports. Dobernig et al. (2010) state the image becomes "a piece of evidence" (p. 90). As a result, images have been found to have greater influence over opinion change than verbal or textual depictions (Kepplinger, 1991). Fahmy and Wanta (2007) go further suggesting "the way the media reports visuals become an important part of the event per se" (p. 20).

In one of the first cross-cultural content analyses involving Al Jazeera video footage, Jasperson and El-Kikhia (2003) found differences in the use of governance, military, and humanitarian frames between CNN and Al Jazeera. They also found that visuals on Al Jazeera tended to focus more on the impact of conflict, including visuals of the dead and wounded.

Aday, Livingston, and Hebert (2005) found differences in coverage of the 2003 Iraq war between US networks (ABC, CBS, NBC, and Fox News) and Al Jazeera. They concluded that Al Jazeera's coverage was generally objective unless civilian casualties were involved. They found Al Jazeera's casualty coverage to be negative and anti-American in tone. They also found unilateral reporters used more visuals of civilian and Iraqi casualties, concluding that the American networks provided a "sanitized" view of the war.

Dastgeer and Gade (2016) compared visual framing of Muslim women during the Arab Spring uprisings in Al Jazeera and CNN coverage. They found both networks framed Muslim women as active participants in the uprisings. Al Jazeera also portrayed Muslim women participating in the demonstrations significantly more than CNN. The visuals of woman as active participants in the uprisings were unexpected as it was a sharp contrast to post-9/11 coverage.

Framing analyses of international media crisis coverage often focus on examining these pre-defined frames in cross-cultural media presentations. Bruce (2014) examined the use of human interest and political frames in

Arab Spring coverage. Rather than using the typical cross-cultural approach, the study examined content from five pan-Arab networks—Alhurra, Al Jazeera, Al Jazeera English, BBC Arabic, and Al Arabiya. Results revealed no difference in the application of the human-interest frame between a taxonomy of Western and liberal networks. However, the comparison between the individual networks revealed that Alhurra invoked the political frame more often than Al Jazeera and BBC Arabic.

Visual Conflict and Violence Frames

The literature review on conflict framing outlined here suggests that media outlets frame crises differently based on the political and cultural environments in which they operate. They also reveal that predicting the framing of Arab Spring conflict by these networks can be complicated by several factors. First, in recent years, Alhurra reversed its policy and began covering breaking news. CNN, Time, and the leading pan-Arab newspaper *Al Hayat* each recognized the quality of Alhurra's Arab Spring coverage. Second, media coverage during the height of the protests was often hampered by official and unofficial disruptions. Journalists reported difficulty communicating with the outside world, were harassed, and had tapes confiscated. In Egypt, for example, the Mubarak regime knocked Al Jazeera off the government-controlled Nilesat satellite in an effort to thwart the network's coverage. Also, pro-Mubarak supporters passed out fliers (referring to Alhurra) stating, "we are going to kick you out of Egypt" (Wimbush, 2011, p. 2). Third, Fahmy (2010) postulates that differences in visual coverage will be magnified during significant international events.

Conflict was defined as "disagreements between or among parties … and needed to be obvious and clear from a casual viewing" (Groshek, 2008, p. 60). In addition to coding for the presence or absence of conflict, images were also coded for their level of violence. Klijn (2003), using a modified definition of violence from the National Television Violence Study (1996), defined violence as:

> any evidence of a credible threat of physical force or the actual use of such a force intended to physically harm or intimidate an animate being or a group of animate beings. Violence also includes certain depictions of physically or emotionally harmful consequences that occur as a result of the use of violent means against an animate being (or group of beings). (p. 132)

Fishman and Marvin (2003) note that this is a representative description of explicit violence found in most systematic studies of violent content.

Therefore, the research presented here was intended to explore how pan-Arab networks visually framed conflict and violence in their coverage of the Arab Spring crisis. It employs the same five-category coding scheme used by the author to examine conflict visuals from five Arab networks during normal daily newscasts (Bruce & Conlin, 2016) and from CNN and Al Jazeera English during the 2011 Egyptian uprisings (Haigh & Bruce, 2017). While Bruce and Haigh found differences in the level of conflict visuals between CNN and Al Jazeera coverage, both networks avoided using visuals of explicit violence (actual violent acts or the results of violence).

These questions extend this research to the broader Arab Spring uprisings on five pan-Arab networks.

> RQ1: Are there differences in the level of conflict/violence in visuals of the Arab Spring between the liberal commercial and Western networks?
>
> RQ2: Are there differences in the level of conflict/violence in visuals of the Arab Spring between each network—Al Jazeera, Al Jazeera English, Al Arabiya, BBC Arabic, and Alhurra?

Method

A content analysis was conducted on five pan-Arab satellite news channels (Al Jazeera, Alhurra, BBC Arabic, Al Jazeera English, and Al Arabiya). The two dimensions were labeled Western (Alhurra, BBC Arabic, Al Jazeera English), and liberal commercial (Al Jazeera and Al Arabiya). These five networks were chosen because they represented some of the most widely discussed examples of pan-Arab satellite news networks.

Network Taxonomy

The term "liberal commercial" was borrowed from Ayish (2002). He described the liberal commercial pattern as a new transnational pattern characterized by professional standards, presented in Western-styled "critical and pluralistic views of society" and highly volatile commercial competition (p. 142). He assigned the liberal commercial label to Al Jazeera. For the present study, Al Jazeera and Al Arabiya are labeled liberal commercial since the commercial undertones, and resulting competitiveness of these networks tends to contribute directly to other characteristics found in the liberal model. While these networks are not liberal in the truest sense of the term, they do represent "liberal" characteristics in as much as an Arab media context will allow.

Alhurra, BBC Arabic, and Al Jazeera English are considered non-commercial international broadcast networks and, therefore, represent the Western style. The term "Western" was originally chosen to classify the Western-based public diplomacy-styled Alhurra and BBC Arabic networks. AJE was included in the Western dimension because of its non-commercial status and the network's intense effort to reach an international audience.

Sample

One-hour late evening newscasts were recorded live from Alhurra, Al Jazeera, Al Arabiya, AJE, and BBC Arabic on each weekday, and many weekends, from August 1, 2010, to June 15, 2011. The goal was to create a sample that represents longitudinal "normal" or "routine" news coverage and minimizes the impact of a single major news event on the sample. There were several major international news stories during the sample frame. These events generally did not demand the kind of live 24-hour coverage that would have interrupted the normal daily news cycle. However, some news coverage during the Arab Spring was an exception. During the most intense periods of political unrest in Egypt and Libya, the international news networks interrupted their normal news cycles to provide 24-hour live, breaking news-style coverage. The bulk of this atypical coverage occurred between January 29 and February 20, 2011. Newscasts airing between these dates were excluded from the sample. This research design should result in a sample that controls for stories that overwhelmed the daily news agenda. A nonprobability sample of broadcasts was drawn for three days (Wednesday, December 29, 2010; Thursday, January 27, 2011; and Tuesday, June 14, 2011) from the entire sample frame to construct the 15-hour sample of routine news coverage. Each story from the sample (N = 438) was examined for Arab Spring content. Only stories containing Arab Spring coverage were included in the sample (n = 89). The unit of analysis from these stories was the shot (N = 1,951). The breakdown of shots by network was Al Jazeera (n = 508), Al Jazeera English (n = 213), Alhurra (n = 383), BBC Arabic (n = 386), and Al Arabiya (n = 461).

Measurement

For this study, the description of the individual shot followed the description set forth by Keith, Schwalbe, and Silcock (2009). Using their guidelines, a shot was counted "each time the shot (subject) changed by video editing or, in the case of a pan, each time the subject changed" (p. 7).

Each shot was analyzed for the presence of conflict and violence. A five-category coding scheme for conflict and violence developed by Fishman and Marvin (2003) and refined by Groshek (2008) was utilized. The categories are as follows: (1) No Conflict Frame, (2) Conflict Frame/Not Violent, (3) Conflict Frame/Dramatic Violence, (4) Conflict Frame/Latent Violence, and (5) Conflict Frame/Explicit Violence. The no conflict frame indicates the absence of conflict or violence in the image. The not violent frame contains images of conflict being handled in a peaceful manner, such as protest signs and marches. The dramatic violence frame includes images of violence that are "performed but not seriously intended," such as for sport or entertainment (Fishman & Marvin, 2003, p. 34). Images containing latent violence do not show the "immediate application of direct physical force" but suggest "that such force could be applied" (Fishman & Marvin, 2003, p. 34). Examples of latent violence include the presence of police, military personnel, and weapons. Finally, Fishman and Marvin refer to images of explicit violence as those showing either the direct application of, or consequences resulting from, violence which is "seriously intended and performed" (2003, p. 34). Explicit violence includes images of firefights, damage to buildings or property, and injuries. The harmful aftermath of violence including the image of anguished victims or eyewitnesses was also included as explicit violence. Violence caused by non-manmade agents (natural disasters, animals, weather) was excluded.

Coding and Inter-coder Reliability

Before coding could begin, the author, aided by a research assistant, determined the parameters of each news story and also the in and out (beginning and end) points for each shot. A codebook was developed as a reference for the coders to use to operationalize choices. Training consisted of two separate pre-test samples that were used to develop definitions and clarify agreement issues. After successfully completing pre-testing, with high inter-coder raw percentage agreement, the coding was conducted. For reliability purposes, it was determined that at least 10% of the sample would be double coded. The reliability scores were calculated using Krippendorff's alpha. Determination of Arab Spring content had an agreement of 0.97. The level of agreement for conflict and violence was 0.81.

Results

Research Question 1 examined differences in levels of conflict and violence in visuals used between liberal commercial networks and Western networks in coverage of the Arab Spring. To test RQ1, level of conflict and violence was cross-tabulated with network taxonomy. The frequency and percentages of conflict/violence types on Western and liberal commercial networks are shown in Table 3.1. A Chi-Square test was performed to

Table 3.1 Frequency and Percentages of Arab Spring Conflict by Network Taxonomy

Level of Conflict/Violenc	*Network Taxonomy*		*Total*
	Western	*Liberal*	
No Conflict	454 (46.2%)	425 (43.9%)	879 (45.1%)
Conflict/Not Violent	307 (31.3%)	235 (24.3%)	542 (27.8%)
Conflict/Dramatic Violence	2 (0.2%)	2 (0.2%)	4 (0.2%)
Conflict/Latent Violence	113(11.5%)	142 (14.7%)	255 (13.1%)
Conflict/Explicit Violence	106 (10.8%)	165 (17.0%)	271 (13.9%)
Total	982 (100.0%)	969 (100.0%)	1,951 (100.0%)

Table 3.2 Standardized Pearson Residuals for Arab Spring Conflict Visuals on Western and Liberal Commercial Networks

Level of Conflict/Violence	*Network Taxonomy*	
	Western	*Liberal*
No Conflict	1.05	-1.05
Conflict/Not Violent	3.46	-3.46
Conflict/Latent Violence	-2.06	2.06
Conflict/Explicit Violence	-3.98	3.98

examine the percentage differences between story type and network taxonomy. The Chi-Square was statistically significant ($\chi2 = 26.58$, df = 4, $p < 0.001$). There is a difference in level of conflict/violence in visuals used between Western networks and liberal commercial networks.

Differences were found between the use of conflict visuals on Western networks and liberal commercial networks. To determine if these differences were statistically significant, an additional procedure was conducted to decompose the chi-square by cell. The resulting standardized Pearson residuals provide a more meaningful cell-by-cell analysis regarding the differences and where they lie. Regarding the standardized Pearson residuals, Agresti (2002) states that absolute values greater than two indicate where there is a greater likelihood of difference.

Table 3.2 breaks down the standardized Pearson residuals for significant differential use of conflict and violence in Arab Spring coverage at the network taxonomy level. The "no conflict" category is the only difference not likely to be significant. Differences in the use of conflict/not violent visuals between Western and liberal networks were likely statistically significant |3.46|. Statistically significant differences for latent violent images were more likely for liberal networks |2.06| than for Western networks. Differences for use of violent images on Western and liberal |3.98| networks were also likely significant.

Research Question 2 examined differences in use of conflict visuals among each networks' Arab Spring coverage. Level of conflict/violence was cross-tabulated with all five networks. The frequency and percentages of conflict/violence types by network are shown in Table 3.3. A Chi-Square test of independence was also performed to examine the percentage differences between story type and the networks. The relationship between these variables was statistically significant ($\chi2 = 98.72$, df = 16, $p < 0.001$). Findings reveal a difference in level of conflict/violence in visuals between the networks.

Again, an additional procedure was conducted to decompose the chi-square by cell in order to determine where significant differences between networks lie. Table 3.4 illustrates the standardized Pearson residuals for significant differential use of conflict and violence in Arab Spring coverage at the network level. The table reveals BBC Arabic is more likely to air conflict-free visuals |2.93| and less likely to air visuals of latent violence |−2.47| and explicit violence |−2.69| than the other four networks. Alhurra was less likely to use latent violence visuals |−3.11| and more likely to air not violent visuals |2.88|. Al Jazeera English was less likely to present no conflict visuals |−2.53| but more likely to show visuals with latent violence |4.60|. Al Arabiya was less likely to air no conflict visuals |−2.02|. Al Jazeera was less likely to use not violent |−3.27| shots, but the only network significantly more likely to use shots of conflict/explicit violence |2.09|.

Discussion

The current study examined the visuals of five transnational satellite news channels that broadcast to/from the Arab world—Al Jazeera, Al Jazeera English, Al Arabiya, Alhurra, and BBC Arabic—to explore differences in the application of visual news frames of conflict and violence in Arab Spring coverage. Research Question 1 asked if there were differences in levels of conflict and violence in visuals used between liberal commercial networks and Western networks in coverage of the Arab Spring. The results reveal that Arab Spring visuals on all the networks were predominantly conflict free. However, when Arab Spring conflict was shown, the Western networks were more likely to use non-violent visuals while the liberal networks were more likely to present a view of the uprisings that was more explicitly violent.

Research Question 2 asked if there were differences in the level of conflict/violence in visuals of the Arab Spring between each network. Significant differences in the application of conflict/violence visuals were found.

Table 3.3 Frequency and Percentages of Arab Spring Conflict by Network

Conflict Level	*Network*					*Total*
	Al Jazeera	*Al Arabiya*	*Alhurra*	*BBC Arabic*	*AJE*	
No Conflict	246 (48.4%)	179 (38.8%)	170 (44.4%)	213 (55.2%)	71 (33.3%)	879 (45.1%)
Not Violent	102 (20.1%)	133 (28.9%)	136 (35.5%)	106 (27.5%)	65 (30.5%)	542 (27.8%)
Dramatic Violence	2 (0.4%)	0 (0.0%)	1 (0.3%)	0 (0.0%)	1 (0.5%)	4 (0.2%)
Latent Violence	70 (13.8%)	72 (15.6%)	28 (7.3%)	33 (8.5%)	52 (24.4%)	255 (13.1%)
Explicit Violence	88 (17.3%)	77 (16.7%)	48 (12.5%)	34 (8.8%)	24 (11.3%)	271 (13.9%)
Total	508 (100.0%)	461 (100.0%)	383 (100.0%)	386 (100.0%)	213 (100.0%)	1951 (100.0%)

Table 3.4 Standardized Pearson Residuals for Arab Spring Conflict Visuals by Network

Conflict Level	*Network*				
	Al Jazeera	*AJE*	*Alhurra*	*BBC Arabic*	*Al Arabiya*
No Conflict	1.16	-2.53	-0.19	2.93	-2.02
Conflict/Not Violent	-3.27	0.78	2.88	-0.14	0.41
Conflict/Latent Violence	0.46	4.60	-3.11	-2.47	1.50
Conflict/Explicit Violence	2.09	-1.01	-0.71	-2.69	1.60

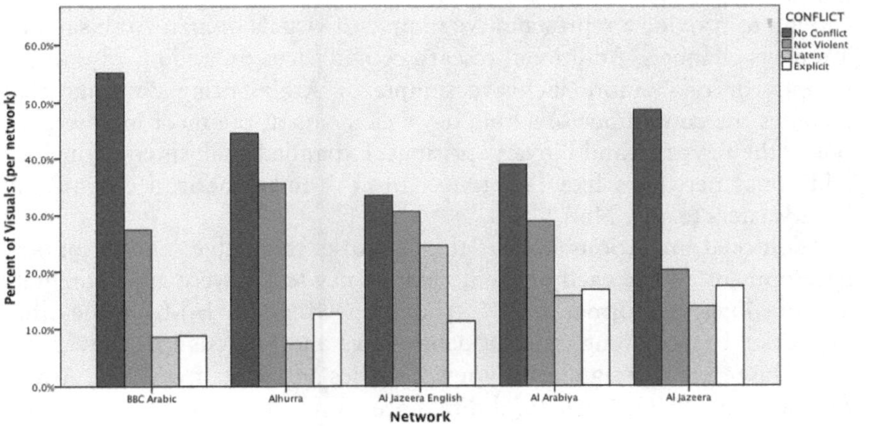

Figure 3.1 Frequency of conflict and violent imagery of Arab Spring coverage by network as represented in RQ2.

The results reveal a clear progression from the network airing the least violent visuals (BBC Arabic) to the network airing the most graphic visuals (Al Jazeera) in Arab Spring coverage. Figure 3.1 illustrates this progression of violent visuals between all five networks. Al Jazeera and Al Arabiya depicted a more violent image of the Arab Spring than Alhurra and BBC Arabic.

Stories of the Libyan uprising airing on the same day on the Alhurra and Al Jazeera networks illustrate the differences in the application of conflict/violence frames. Each story, which focused on the Libyan rebels, used the same footage from the same source. However, due to editing decisions at each network, the stories differed visually. Both networks included at least a few explicitly violent visuals (e.g., rebel forces firing artillery). However, Al Jazeera aired more conflict footage (both number and length of shots) and more shots containing explicit images, including shots of material destruction and injured civilians.

Limitations, Future Directions, and Conclusions

The most obvious limitations to this study involve the size and content of the sample. Unlike most newscast studies that use individual stories, or shots from specific time-limited selections within the newscasts as the unit of analysis, the approach of this project was to analyze every single news image from each newscast in the sample. This approach acknowledges the cumulative impact of images that are repeated multiple times in a single newscast, or over a series of newscasts. The result is an overwhelming number of shots from each newscast. In order to keep the size of the project manageable, the purposive sample consisted of only three days of programming selected from the sampling frame. These three days are not enough to provide a representative sample of visuals on pan-Arab satellite TV news channels. Additional research could focus on adding days to the sample, or on a more inclusive sample of Arab Spring coverage that includes the continuous breaking news elements of the most intense periods of the Egyptian and Libyan uprisings. Expanded analysis could include additional networks like Egyptian state TV and American commercial broadcasters (e.g., CNN).

Additional limitations involve the networks themselves and taxonomy development. While each of the networks' newscasts were approximately an hour long, the format of BBC Arabic's newscast varied from the other networks' by providing more in-depth news and analysis on a fewer stories. The result was significantly fewer stories and shots from BBC Arabic for the analysis. This structural difference alone could result in significant differences in the findings.

The inclusion of Al Jazeera English in the study also created obstacles. AJE was included because of its relationship to the sister network, Arabic Al Jazeera and its growing popularity as an international broadcaster. Placing Al Jazeera English in the taxonomy structure was difficult since Al Jazeera English clearly shares elements with both the liberal and Western networks. While AJE's financial structure more closely resembles the structure of BBC Arabic and Alhurra, the network presented a slick, high-tech newscast that emphasized more conflict (latent and explicit combined) than any of the other networks. This suggests that Al Jazeera English may share common visual approaches with its Arabic-language sister network. Future visual analysis could explore similarities and differences between Al Jazeera English and Al Jazeera.

Finally, the author recognizes the somewhat contentious nature of the terms "Western" and "liberal" among some international media scholars. Future studies could benefit from a more robust taxonomy, improved labeling, and more informed rationale for network placement.

Overall, these findings reveal the need for additional systematic analysis of visuals, and the factors shaping transnational Arab media. The results are in line with findings from previous cross-cultural comparisons of conflict visuals in pan-Arab media. The liberal networks depicted more violent images of conflict while images on the Western networks presented a more sanitized view of conflict. However, despite obvious preferences for violent images by Al Jazeera and Al Arabiya, the overwhelming majority of visuals aired on pan-Arab networks are not as graphic as critics portend.

References

Aday, S., Livingston, S., & Hebert, M. (2005). Embedding the truth: A cross-cultural analysis of objectivity and television coverage of the Iraq War. *The Harvard International Journal of Press/Politics*, *10*(1), 3–21.

Agresti, A. (2002). *Categorical data analysis* (2nd ed.). Hoboken, NJ: John Wiley & Sons, Inc.

Al-Failakawi, Y. (2010, April 15). *Media changes in the Middle East: The first decade of the 21st Century*. Paper presented at *the meeting of Broadcast Education Association*, Las Vegas, NV.

Ayish, M. (2002). Political communication on Arab world television: Evolving patterns. *Political Communication*, *19*, 137–154.

Barthes, R. (1978). *Image, music, text*. (S. Heath, Trans.). New York: Hill and Wang.

Bruce, M. D. (2014). Framing Arab Spring conflict: A visual analysis of coverage on five transnational Arab news channels. *Journal of Middle East Media*, *10*, 1–26. http://jmem.gsu.edu/files/2014/07/JMEM-2014-ENG-Bruce.pdf

Bruce, M. D., & Conlin, L. (2016). Images of conflict and explicit violence on Arab TV: A visual content analysis of five pan-Arab news networks. *Athens Journal of Mass Media and Communication*, 2(3), 151–168.

Bruce, M. D., & O'Hair, H. D. (2009). Magnifying risk and crisis: The influences of communication technology on contemporary global terrorism. In R. L. Heath & H. D. O'Hair (Eds.). *Handbook of risk & crisis communication* (pp. 629–653). New York, NY: Routledge.

Cottle, S. (2011). Media and the Arab uprisings of 2011: Research notes. *Journalism*, *12*, 647–659.

Dastgeer, S., & Gade, P. J. (2016). Visual framing of Muslim women in the Arab Spring: Prominent, active, and visible. *International Communication Gazette*, *78*(5), 432–450. doi:10.1177/1748048516640204

Dobernig, K., Lobinger, K., & Wetzstein, I. (2010). Covering conflict: Differences in visual and verbal news coverage of the Gaza crisis 2009 in four weekly news media. *Journal of Visual Literacy*, *29*, 88–105.

Entman, R. M. (1993). Framing: Toward clarification of a fractured paradigm. *Journal of Communication*, *43*(4), 51–58.

Fahmy, S. (2010). Contrasting visual frames of our times: A framing analysis of English and Arabic-language press coverage of war and terrorism. *The International Communication Gazette*, *72*, 695–717.

Fahmy, S. & Kim, D. (2008). Picturing the Iraq war: Constructing the image of war in the British and US press. *The International Communication Gazette*, *70*, 443–462.

Fahmy, S., & Wanta, W. (2007). The Perceived impact of news photographs on public opinion formation. *Visual Communication Quarterly*, *14*(1), 16–31.

Fishman, J., & Marvin, C. (2003). Portrayals of violence and group difference in newspaper photographs: Nationalism and media. *Journal of Communication*, *53*(1), 32–44.

Gamson, W. A., Croteau, D., Hoynes, W., & Sasson, T. (1992). Media images and the social construction of reality. *Annual Review of Sociology*, *18*, 373–393.
Gitlin, T. (1980). *The whole world is watching: Mass media in the making and unmaking of the new left*. Berkley, CA: University of California Press.
Grabe, M. E., & Bucy, E. P. (2009). *Image bite politics: News and the visual framing of elections*. New York: Oxford University Press.
Groshek, J. (2008). Homogenous agendas, disparate frames: CNN and CNN International coverage online. *Journal of Broadcasting & Electronic Media*, *52*, 52–68.
Haigh, M. M., & Bruce, M. D. (2017). A comparison of the visual and story frames Al Jazeera English and CNN employed during the 2011 Egyptian revolution. *The International Communication Gazette*, *79*(4), 419–433. doi:10.1177/1748048516682141
Huxford, J. (2001). Beyond the referential: Uses of visual symbolism in the press. *Journalism*, *2*(1), 45–71.
Jasperson, A. E., & El-Kikhia, M. O. (2003). CNN and al Jazeera's media coverage of America's War in Afghanistan. In K. Hafez (Ed.), *Framing Terrorism* (pp. 132–133). New York: Routledge.
Jasperson, A. E., Shah, D. V., Watts, M. D., Faber, R. J., & Fan, D. P. (1998). Framing and the public agenda: Media effects on the importance of the federal budget deficit. *Political Communication*, *15*, 205–224.
Kepplinger, H. M. (1991). The Impact of presentation techniques: Theoretical aspects empirical findings. In F. Biocca (Ed.), *Television and political advertising: psychological processes* (pp. 173–194). Hillsdale, NJ: Lawrence Erlbaum Associates, Inc.
Keith, S., Schwalbe, C. B., & Silcock, B. W. (2009). Visualizing cross-media coverage: Picturing war across platforms during the U.S.-Led Invasion of Iraq. *Atlantic Journal of Communication*, *17*, 1–18.
Klijn, M. E. (2003). Attention-getting and comprehension-raising attributes in visuals in Dutch and American, public and private television news about violence. *Journal of Broadcasting & Electronic Media*, *47*, 124–144.
Kosicki, G. M. (2003). The media priming effect: News media and considerations affecting political judgments. In J. P. Dillard & M. Pfau (Eds.), *The persuasion handbook: Developments in theory and practice* (pp. 63–81). Thousand Oaks, CA: Sage Publications.
Lang, K., & Lang, G. E. (1968). *Politics and television*. Chicago: Quadrangle Books.
Lomax, D. (2005). Iraq's television revolution [Television news story]. In *Newsnight*. London: British Broadcasting Company. Retrieved from http://news.bbc.co.uk/1/hi/programmes/newsnight/4298455.stm
Matthes, J. (2009). What's in a frame? A content analysis of media framing studies in the world's leading journals. *Journalism & Mass Communication Quarterly*, *86*(2), 349–367.
Matthes, J., & Kohring, M. (2008). The content analysis of media frames: Toward improving the reliability and validity. *Journal of Communication*, *58*, 258–279.
Messaris, P. (1992). Visual 'manipulation': Visual means of affecting response to images. *Communication*, *13*, 181–195.
Messaris, P. (1994). *Visual "literacy": Image, mind, and reality*. Boulder, CO: Westview Press.
Messaris, P., & Abraham, L. (2001). The role of images in framing news stories. In S. D. *National Television Violence Study: 1994–1995 - Scientific papers. (1996)*. California: Mediascope, Inc.

National Television Violence Study (1996) (Ed.) M. Seawell. Thousand Oaks, CA: Sage Publications.
Pintak, L. (2011a). Arab media revolution spreading change. *CNN*. Retrieved from http://edition.cnn.com/2011/OPINION/01/29/pintak.arab.media/?hpt=Sbin
Pintak, L. (2011b). The Al Jazeera revolution. *Foreign Policy*. Retrieved from http://www.foreignpolicy.com/articles/2011/02/02/the_al_jazeera_revolution
Reese, S. D. (2001). Prologue--Framing public life: A bridging model for media research. In S. D. Reese, O. H. J. Gandy, & A. E. Grant (Eds.), *Framing public life: Perspectives on media and our understanding of the social world* (pp. 7–31). Mahwah, NJ: Lawrence Erlbaum Associates.
Reynolds, A. & Barnett, B. (2002). *CNN's framing of September 11: Suggesting an appropriate response to terrorism*. Paper presented at *the meeting of the International Communication Association*. San Francisco, CA.
Scheufele, D. A., & Tewksbury, D. (2007). Framing, Agenda Setting, and Priming: The evolution of three media effects models. *Journal of Communication*, *57*, 9–20.
Seib, P. (2007). *Beyond the front lines: How the news media cover a world shaped by war*. New York: Palgrave Macmillan.
Semetko, H. A., & Valkenburg, P. M. (2000). Framing European politics: A content analysis of press and television news. *Journal of Communication*, *50*(2), 93–108.
Tirohl, B. (2000). The photo-journalist and the changing news image. *New Media & Society*, 2(3), 335–352.
Tuchman, G. (1978). *Making news: A study in the construction of reality*. New York: The Free Press.
Wimbush, S. E. (2011, April 6). *Testimony of the Broadcasting Board of Governors before the Subcommittee on Oversight and Investigations*. Committee on Foreign Affairs, US House of Representatives. Retrieved from http://foreignaffairs.house.gov/112/wim040611.pdf

4 Differentiation Versus Denial

Impact of Messaging about Player Transactions on Team Reputation, Ticket Sales, and Sports Channel Subscriptions

Joseph R. Blaney and Stephen K. Hunt

Introduction

Most fans of any professional sport are familiar with the scenario. A team with a good, but not great, season record must decide at some point during the season whether it will attempt to acquire additional talent on the available market in order to strive for postseason play *or* trade away current top performers in order to acquire players who can contribute to future championship runs. Invariably, this requires judgment calls on the part of team management: (1) can the current team's season and situation be fairly assessed as unpromising?; (2) can current productive players be retained for the next season within financial constraints?; (3) are other teams in the league willing to part with promising prospects in exchange for team talent?; and (4) do the available prospects with other teams in the league fill a need which might make the team more competitive in the future? In sum, the professional sports team has a limited amount of resources for fielding a team and must choose the best course for acquiring and divesting of player assets.

Of course, sports fans have limited resources as well. Their assignment of financial resources necessarily involves internal cost-benefit ratios. Key to these considerations is the question of whether the value being provided to them by a team merits the expenditures incurred. This study will illuminate attitudes about those expenditures and advance our understanding of the *differentiation* strategy as one option within image restoration theory (IRT), now known more appropriately as image repair theory owing to the fact that reputations ordinarily cannot be restored to perfection, merely repaired as much as possible. Using the quintessential "mid-season sell-off" of the Chicago Cubs in 2021, we'll test the impact of team statements on team reputation, fan intent to purchase tickets, and fan intent to subscribe to premium sports television.

DOI: 10.4324/9781032619187-5

This chapter will provide a short synopsis of the Chicago Cubs' 2021 mid-season player transactions and fan reaction thereto. This will include our observation that Cubs management chose to differentiate the current sets of trades from the trades which occurred in 2012 (which preceded a disastrous season). However, we offer no opinions on the wisdom of the player transactions as that subject is outside our scope of interest and expertise. We will offer a review of knowledge about image repair in sports while explaining the deficit of our understanding of the differentiation strategy. Finally, we will propose three hypotheses based on existing knowledge, explicate our method and procedures, produce results, and discuss their relevance to communication practitioners and theorists.

Image Restoration and the Athlete

Benoit's (1995) typology of image repair strategies has been the standard for understanding the nature and function of strategically defensive messages. It has been applied extensively to political, corporate, religious, and entertainment figures, but space limitations require that this section address only sports.

The image repair of athletes can be seen as early as Nelson's (1984) study of Billie Jean King following revelations of an affair with her personal assistant. She relied on the strategies of bolstering about her family life and differentiation of the indiscretion she had from a presumably unacceptable lesbian lifestyle (which was still frowned upon by many in the early 1980s). Her responses were generally well received and Nelson's assessment was that surrogates (e.g., fellow tennis players, friends, sports media) offered support that helped her repair her reputation. This case drew upon earlier examples of *apologia*, prior to the image restoration typology offered by Benoit (1995) in *Accounts, Excuses, and Apologies*.

The first application of this more detailed typology was Benoit and Hanczor's (1994) case study of the Tonya Harding controversy. Harding was credibly accused of colluding with acquaintances in a physical attack (striking her knee with a metal baton) on US Olympic Figure Skating rival Nancy Kerrigan which left the skater temporarily unable to practice prior to the 1994 Olympic Games. The study found that Harding primarily used strategies of bolstering, denial, and attacking her accuser but that her discourse on *Eye-to-Eye with Connie Chung* was not effective because her credibility leading up to the interview had been tarnished by changes in her explanations and contradictory statements from others familiar with the people involved. She also failed to challenge damning evidence. Public opinion polling supported this assessment as Harding's image never recovered and she was banned from the sport for life.

Fortunato (2008) used the typology to study the Duke University lacrosse scandal, wherein three players were accused of sexually assaulting a dancer who had been hired for a wild party where much alcohol was being consumed. This application noted that university officials used mortification, bolstering, and corrective action. Looking at the same crisis, a Len-Rios (2010) application of the case found deployment of denial of the players' assault, admissions of malfeasance (mortification) insofar as the team's reputation for drunk and disorderly parties, and ultimately the promising of replacement (a pledge to replace the coach as a form of blame-shifting and corrective action). This study found that these efforts tended to help repair the team's reputation with the local audience but did not repair a damaged national image.

Blaney et al. (2013) offered an edition with 20 image restoration studies covering a diversity of sports, genders, races, countries, and misdeeds. These studies all serve as additional examples of image repair applied to sports. Among others, Twork and Blaney (2013) called for new directions when they advocated for a turn to empirically testing image repair strategies to better assess some of the claims made in the many image repair case studies. For instance, Blaney and Benoit (2002) concluded that mortification would be more effective when combined with corrective action. However, Twork and Blaney's study found that an athlete accused of inappropriate on-field aggression who apologized *and* committed to attend anger management counseling (mortification plus corrective action) experienced no better reputation measure than the athlete who merely apologized (mortification only). Pace et al. (2010) made similar calls for the testing of claims generated by the IRT case studies.

Some scholars had been moving toward more generalizable work all along.

Jerome (2008) advanced image repair as a "rhetoric of atonement," in the case of NASCAR driver Tony Stewart's assault on a newspaper photographer after a poor race outing. In particular, she examined the situation whereby a communicator could not use denial, justification, or transcendence. This work likewise pushed the field to use quantitative approaches which test the utility of the image restoration typology. Brown et al. (2012) discovered mortification was a more appropriate strategy for LeBron James than shifting the blame or bolstering following the image crisis following his departure from the Cleveland Cavaliers for the Miami Heat. Similarly, Brown et al. (2016) discovered further support for the use of mortification over reducing offensiveness and evading responsibility strategies with the additional discovery that a white athlete (compared with Asian, Black, Hispanic, and Middle Eastern equivalents) achieved less image repair across all three of those responses. Brown et al. (2015) again pointed to both the effectiveness of mortification as an image repair choice and the unexpected higher ratings of black athletes. Most recently, Brown et al. (2018) found that the more respondents accepted NHL goalie Jordan Weal's responses to accusations of assault, the more respondents liked him and thought he could avoid repeating the transgression. Additionally, those less likely to report genuinely liking Weal were more likely to believe that repeating the misdeed was possible.

Blaney (2018) raised the specter of sports teams self-inflicting damage to reputation when they announce ticket price increases. Specifically, he noted that winning and rebuilding teams can explain the need to increase revenues without experiencing reputational damage while losing teams cannot.

The present study is one more attempt at normalizing the study of the effects of individual image repair choices quantitatively. While the rhetorical-critical approaches to image repair certainly continue (see McDormand's [2018] examination of Pete Rose, and Isaacson's [2018]) analysis of the 2017 Chicago White Sox) to provide cases for potential transferability, image repair research will only grow by testing the claims made in the ubiquitous case studies.

Consumer Intent and the Sports Fan

This chapter addresses the topic of what a perceived sell-off of the core of a professional sports team can do to team reputation and its ability to sell tickets and attract television revenue. As revenues dictate virtually all activities of an organization's expenditures, it is very important to have an acute understanding of threats to that revenue. However, like much communication research, we rely on the wisdom gained from other disciplines. Specifically, marketing findings about purchase intent must be explained.

Spears and Singh's (2004) study merged orientation toward brand and purchase intentions. Borrowing from the work of Mitchell and Olson (1981) they established reliable scales of attitude toward brand, with three characteristics: (a) attitude is held toward an object/brand, (b) attitude accompanies evaluation in terms of goodness or badness, and (c) that attitude is an internal state of mind, ultimately subject to adjustment/change and reliably self-reported by human subjects. Spears and Singh (2004) posit that from these attitudes, particular consumer behaviors will naturally follow. This is where intent to purchase becomes most central. That consumers orient their purchasing power at least partially based on attitude about the brand makes tremendous common sense and underscores the reality for most businesses that brand strength impacts revenues.

Spears and Singh (2004) conceptualize intent to purchase as personal action tendencies involving the brand. This differs from attitude to the extent that intent to purchase assumes motivation to engage in the act of commerce whereas attitude toward brand merely notes sentiment toward the brand. It is this connection between brand attitude and purchase intent that made Spears and Singh's findings so helpful as well as their offering of a reliable measure of intent to purchase. Its adaptability to live and mediated sports purchasing decisions becomes more relevant later in this study.

The Chicago Cubs 2021 Sell-Off: Rebuilding or Not?

Bastian (July 30, 2021) summarized Chicago Cubs player transactions ahead of the July 30 Major League Baseball deadline: "This will go down, without question, as one of the most important 24 hours in the long, storied history of the Chicago Cubs." This was not hyperbole. During that period the Cubs parted company with: (1) first baseman Anthony Rizzo, (2) shortstop Javier Baez, (3) third baseman Kris Bryant, and (4) closing relief pitcher Craig Kimbrel. As if these fan favorites were not enough to part with, they also traded away starting pitcher Trevor Williams, relievers Ryan Tepera and Andrew Chafin, and outfielders Joc Peterson and Jake Marisnick. While the reasoning behind these trades certainly merits an interesting discussion, it is beyond dispute that the Cubs transactions during this period constituted no less than a disassembly of the team roster as known by fans and observers.

Blaney (2018) found that the status of a team as being "winning," "losing," or "rebuilding" significantly impacted measures of organizational reputation and intent to purchase tickets after announcing ticket price increases. Specifically, teams which are perceived as losing (as opposed to winning or rebuilding) receive the least forgiveness for such damage inflicted on fans.

However, what can be learned about the impact of a planned devaluation of the team roster (i.e., trading/selling away the team core) on such measures? The summer 2021 sell-off by the Chicago Cubs provides a quintessential case ripe for study. Specifically, could the team plausibly deflect negative fallout by differentiating the current roster moves from the pain which followed the 2012 sell-off? *Differentiation* involves a communicator describing a deed as something different than a deed for which the communicator has been accused. For instance, when President George H. W. Bush was attacked for violating his pledge not to raise taxes, he differentiated them by saying that boosting income by "closing loopholes" was not a tax increase. As will be noted later, Chicago Cubs president of baseball operations differentiated his 2021 player transactions from the painful 2012 team rebuild by claiming that the new lineup had sufficient talent that it was not akin to rebuilding the team.

While image repair studies (most notably Benoit, 1995; Blaney and Benoit, 2002) have provided enough background about differentiation's effectiveness to justify predictions, quantitative tests of such have not yet taken place.

Consequently, this study offers the following hypothesis about differentiation and reputation:

> **H1:** Sports organizations who differentiate roster changes from a team rebuild will score higher on a measure of reputation than teams who simply deny a rebuild.

Likewise, as ticket sales are the lifeblood of the professional sports team, we predict the following about differentiation and intent to purchase ticket sales:

> **H3:** Sports organizations who differentiate roster changes from a team rebuild will score higher on a measure of intent to purchase tickets than teams who simply deny a rebuild.

Finally, as television viewing is another important revenue stream and contributor to market value, we predict the following about differentiation and intent to subscribe to a premium sports channel:

> **H3:** Sports organizations who differentiate roster changes from a team rebuild will score higher on a measure of intent to subscribe to a premium sports channel than teams who simply deny a rebuild.

Method

Design

Testing these hypotheses required two experimental conditions: (1) an organizational response which differentiates player transactions from a team rebuild and (2) an organizational response which simply denies that the player transactions constitute a rebuild. Taking the form of a news story which quotes Chicago Cubs president of baseball operations Jed Hoyer, these responses are detailed in Appendices A and B. Subjects were assigned to one of the two conditions in Qualtrics survey software, asked basic demographic information, and then asked to respond to the story they read with answers assessing the dependent variables of organizational reputation (of the Chicago Cubs), intent to purchase tickets (for Chicago Cubs games), and intent to subscribe to a premium sports channel (the Marquee Sports network, owned and operated by the Chicago Cubs).

Sample

Social media snowballing was deployed to solicit survey respondents who classified themselves as Cubs fans and were 18 years of age or older.

This returned 321 useable responses with 157 in the differentiation condition and 164 in the simple denial condition. Demographically, the subjects were 52.1% men and 47.6% women (one participant selected "other"); 9.8% reported income under $35,000 per year, 26.7% reported an annual income of $35,000–69,999, 18.2% reported an annual income of $70,000–99,999, 17.3% reported an annual income of $100,000–150,000, 17.6% indicated their annual income was over $150,000, and 10.4% preferred not to answer.

A strong majority (74%) indicated attendance at Cubs games while only 26% indicated rarely or never-attending games. A majority of those surveyed (57.7%) indicated that they pay for a premium service in order to receive the Chicago Cubs Marquee Sports Network. In short, this sample was largely composed of people who regularly spend money on Chicago Cubs enterprises.

Measures

Following exposure to the experimental condition, each participant answered a short survey using five-point (Likert-type, 1 to 5 with 5 as the strongest) adaptations of Coombs and Holladay's (1996) Organizational Reputational scale (five items with Cronbach's alpha = 0.81 in this study), Spears and Singh's (2004) Intent to Purchase scale (four items with Cronbach's alpha = 0.82 in this study), and Intent to Subscribe also as adapted from Spears and Singh (2004) (four items with alpha = 0.83 in this study). Item scores were reversed-recoded as necessary. Data collected from the survey were exported into SPSS in order to run tests appropriate to the hypotheses.

Results

The first hypothesis predicted that sports organizations that differentiate roster changes from a team rebuild would score higher on a measure of reputation than teams who simply deny a rebuild. An independent samples t-test provided support for this hypothesis as the differentiation strategy produced higher reputation means than the denial strategy, $t(319) = 4.51$, $p < 0.001$. Bivariate correlations and descriptive statistics for all dependent variables can be found in Tables 4.1 and 4.2.

The second hypothesis predicted that sports organizations who differentiate roster changes from a team rebuild would score higher on a measure of intent to purchase. An independent samples t-test provided support for this hypothesis as the differentiation strategy produced higher intent to purchase means than the denial strategy, $t(319) = 8.15$, $p < 0.001$.

The third hypothesis predicted that sports organizations who differentiate roster changes from a team rebuild would score higher on a measure of

Table 4.1 Bivariate Correlations for All Dependent Variables (N = 321)

	M	*SD*	*1*	*2*	*3*
1. Reputation	3.22	0.86	—		
2. Intent to Purchase	3.71	1.05	0.54**	—	
3. Intent to Subscribe	2.53	1.15	0.34**	0.41**	—

Note:
$^{**}p < 0.01$.

Table 4.2 Descriptive Statistics for Dependent Variables by Condition

	Differentiation			*Denial*		
	M	*SD*	*n*	*M*	*SD*	*n*
Reputation	3.43_a	0.74	157	3.01_a	0.92	164
Intent to Purchase	4.15_b	0.81	157	3.28_b	1.08	164
Intent to Subscribe	2.97_c	1.20	157	2.10_c	0.92	164

Note: Means with the same subscript are significantly different, $p < 0.05$.

intent to subscribe than teams who simply deny a rebuild. Again, results of an independent samples *t*-test supported this hypothesis as the differentiation strategy produced higher intent to subscribe means than the denial strategy, $t(319) = 7.31$, $p < 0.05$.

Beyond the hypotheses, we employed *t*-tests to determine if the demographic variables we measured influenced the dependent variables. Initially, looking at participants in the differentiation condition, we found no statistically significant differences based on sex for reputation, $t(152) = 3.12$, $p > 0.05$; intent to purchase, $t(152) = 1.17$, $p > 0.05$;. or intent to subscribe, $t(152) = 0.38$, $p > 0.05$. A similar pattern was repeated in the denial condition as there were no differences based on sex for reputation, $t(150) = 2.58$, $p > 0.05$ or intent to subscribe, $t(150) = 0.55$, $p > 0.05$. However, we did find differences based on sex for intent to purchase in the denial group as males reported significantly higher means than females, $t(150) = 0.28$, $p < 0.05$. Means and standard deviations for sex by condition are reported in Table 4.3.

We also found differences between the groups based on reported income.

Initially, looking at participants in the differentiation condition, we found no statistically significant differences between those reporting annual incomes of \$100,000 or over (high income) and those reporting incomes of \$100,000 or under (low income) reputation, $t(133) = -0.25$, $p > 0.05$; intent to purchase, $t(133) = -1.25$, $p > 0.05$; or intent to subscribe, $t(133) = 1.24$, $p > 0.05$. A similar pattern was repeated in the denial condition as there were no differences based on income for reputation, $t(138) = -2.49$,

Table 4.3 Descriptive Statistics for Sex by Condition

	Male			*Female*		
	M	*SD*	*n*	*M*	*SD*	*n*
Differentiation Condition						
Reputation	3.69	0.73	53	3.31	0.72	101
Intent to Purchase	4.25	0.79	53	4.09	0.82	101
Intent to Subscribe	3.00	1.22	53	2.93	1.91	101
Denial Condition						
Reputation	3.10	0.94	107	2.69	0.83	45
Intent to Purchase	3.29_a	1.16	107	3.24_a	0.98	45
Intent to Subscribe	2.14	0.94	107	2.04	0.89	45

Note: Means with the same subscript are significantly different, $p < 0.05$.

Table 4.4 Descriptive Statistics for Income by Condition

	High Income			*Low Income*		
	M	*SD*	*n*	*M*	*SD*	*n*
Differentiation Condition						
Reputation	3.44	0.77	51	3.47	0.71	84
Intent to Purchase	4.05	0.83	51	4.23	0.79	84
Intent to Subscribe	3.09	1.14	51	2.83	1.24	84
Denial Condition						
Reputation	2.78	0.89	56	3.17	0.91	84
Intent to Purchase	2.99	0.97	56	3.52	1.14	84
Intent to Subscribe	2.08_a	1.05	56	2.13_a	0.86	84

Note: Means with the same subscript are significantly different, $p < 0.05$.

$p > 0.05$ or intent to purchase, $t(138) = -2.87$, $p > 0.05$. However, we did find differences based on income for intent to subscribe in the denial group as those reporting lower incomes scored higher than those reporting higher incomes, $t(138) = -0.30$, $p < 0.05$. Means and standard deviations for income by condition are reported in Table 4.4.

Discussion

This study has provided important results for both the advancement of image repair theory and sports executives who are faced with decisions about communicating major roster changes to various team stakeholders.

Specifically, all three hypotheses were supported allowing us to claim that differentiating major roster changes from the simple denial of a roster "rebuild" will help sporting organizations improve their reputations, augment ticket sales, and increase likelihood of success for media partners.

The finding that differentiation is more effective than denial in protecting reputation not only advances image repair research, but it very likely portends relevance to the other two measures studied here: intent to purchase and intent to subscribe. To the extent that organizational reputation is closely tied to the perceived integrity of a product, the connection between reputation and revenues necessary for commercial viability must be made.

Consider also the finding that differentiation is more effective than simple denial in protecting ticket sales. Brown (2019) reported that in pre-pandemic 2019 Major League Baseball (MLB) revenues reached $10.7 billion. Thirty percent of that figure, $3.21 billion, is attributable to ticket sales. While the remaining revenues attributable to media rights and other corporate partnerships certainly merit future study, the heart of any team's financial value is the fandom whose eyes, ears, and discretionary household funds make revenue possible. In this regard, the sports organization must communicate effectively with its core audience: ticket buyers. This dynamic only increases in importance as a "post-pandemic" mindset emerges.

Likewise, the finding that differentiation is more effective than denial in protecting subscriptions to premium sports content begs to be noticed both by teams with their own proprietary carriers (such as the Chicago Cubs' Marquee Sports Network) and all those seeking compensation for broadcast/streaming rights. Statista (2022) reported that in the United States alone 57.5 million viewers watched digital live sports at least once per month in 2021. That figure is projected to reach 90.7 million viewers by 2025. As such, the organization wanting a maximum share of revenue would do well to cultivate and protect sports fan intent to subscribe.

Another significant finding was that subjects with lower incomes (under $100,000 annually) scored higher on intent to subscribe to a premium sports channel than those subjects with incomes over $100,000. One might surmise that those with higher income would have greater financial means to purchase tickets and those with lower income lesser means to do so. This may leave the team fan wanting to watch play via media as central to organizational revenues derived from broadcast rights. A more qualitative approach to sports fans via open-ended interviews and focus groups may help clarify the reasons behind the difference which upon first glance may seem counterintuitive.

The other curious finding was that of those in the denial condition men scored higher on intent to purchase tickets than women. We lack data to surmise why this may be, but it may provide heuristic value for the study of sex differences where the denial strategy is deployed.

Beyond the significant differences found, the study offers a new reliable measure for assessing an audience's intent to subscribe to premium sports offerings. This offers potential for studying media content subscriptions writ large, not just the sports media genre.

The present study is limited by the fact that many fans consume sports information via audio-visual means. As such, the text-based messaging studied here ought to be expanded to audio and video platforms.

Conclusion

The study provides a greater understanding of the effectiveness of the differentiation strategy and provides further clarification for related claims made in image restoration research. Sports teams who differentiate major roster changes from a team rebuild score higher on measures of reputation, intent to purchase tickets, and intent to subscribe to premium sports channels. On behalf of sports executives, scholars should consider the conditions under which the ability to claim differentiation is plausible with the fan base.

Appendix A: Differentiation Condition

Subjects were exposed to the following announcement:
Read the news account below then answer the questions which follow.

Cubs Deal Several Players before Trade Deadline

Chicago—The Chicago Cubs parted with key players in the week leading up to the July 30th trade deadline. First baseman Anthony Rizzo was sent to the New York Yankees for an outfield prospect and pitching prospect. Third baseman Kris Bryant was traded for two San Francisco Giants prospects. Shortstop Javier Baez and right-handed pitcher Trevor Williams were sent to the New York Mets in exchange for the highly touted outfield prospect Pete Crow-Armstrong. Finally, closer Craig Kimbrel and set-up reliever Ryan Tepera were traded to the Chicago White Sox for second baseman Nick Madrigal and pitcher Codi Heuer. These trades were on top of those sending Joc Peterson, Jake Marsinick, and Andrew Chafin to other teams as well.

Cubs president of baseball operations Jed Hoyer explained that these trades did not create a rebuild similar to the one that Cubs fan suffered through in 2012: "When we walked in, in 2012, we realized that this was going to be a really long process to get good. We didn't feel like we had the right pieces together. Now I think with the players we have I don't see any reason why this needs to be a long process."

Appendix B: Denial Condition

Subjects were exposed to the following announcement:
Read the news account below then answer the questions which follow.

Cubs Deal Several Players before Trade Deadline

Chicago—The Chicago Cubs parted with key players in the week leading up to the July 30th trade deadline. First baseman Anthony Rizzo was sent to the New York Yankees for an outfield prospect and pitching prospect. Third baseman Kris Bryant was traded for two San Francisco Giants prospects. Shortstop Javier Baez and right-handed pitcher Trevor Williams were sent to the New York Mets in exchange for the highly touted outfield prospect Pete Crow-Armstrong. Finally, closer Craig Kimbrel and set-up reliever Ryan Tepera were traded to the Chicago White Sox for second baseman Nick Madrigal and pitcher Codi Heuer. These trades were on top of those sending Joc Peterson, Jake Marsinick, and Andrew Chafin to other teams as well.

Cubs president of baseball operations Jed Hoyer explained that these trades did not create a rebuild similar to the one that Cubs fan suffered through in 2012.

References

Bastian, J. (2021, July 30). Cubs bid farewell to core on emotional day. https://www.mlb.com/news/cubs-2021-trade-deadline-moves

Benoit, W. L. (1995). *Accounts, excuses, and apologies: A theory of image restoration strategies.* State University of New York Press.

Benoit, W. L., & Hanczor, R. (1994). The Tonya Harding controversy: An analysis of image repair strategies. *Communication Quarterly*, *42*(4), 416–433. https://doi.org/10.1080/01463379409369947

Blaney, J. R. (2018). The role of team success and failure in mitigating fan dissatisfaction with ticket price increases. In Billings, A.C., Coombs, W.T., and Brown, K.A. (Eds.), *Reputational challenges in sport: Theory and application.* Routledge.

Blaney, J. R., & Benoit, W. L. (2002). *The Clinton scandals and the politics of image restoration.* Praeger.

Blaney, J. R., Lippert, L. R., & Smith, J. S. (Eds.). (2013). *Repairing the athlete's image: Studies in sports image restoration.* Lexington Books.

Brown, K.A., Billings, A, & Devlin, M. (2016). Image repair across the racial spectrum: Experimentally exploring athlete transgression responses. *Communication Research Reports*, *33*(1), 47–53. https://doi.org/10.1080/08824096.2015.1117442

Brown, K., Billings, A. C., Mastro, D., & Brown-Devlin, N. A. (2015). Changing the image repair equation: Impact of race and gender on sport-related transgressions. *Journalism & Mass Communication Quarterly*, *92*(2), 487–506. https://doi.org/10.1177/1077699015574484

Brown, K. A., Dickhaus, J., & Long, M. C. (2012). LeBron James and "The Decision": An empirical examination of image repair in sports. *Journal of Sports Media*, 7(1), 149–175. https://doi.org/10.1353/jsm.2012.0010

Brown, K. A., Zhou, Z., & Xu, Q. (2018). Love me or hate me: Predictors of perceived athlete image. In A.C. Billings, W.T. Coombs and K.A. Brown (Eds), *Reputational Challenges in Sport*. New York: Routledge, 170–184.

Brown, M. (2019, December 21). *MLB sees record $10.7 billion in revenues for 2019*. www.forbes.com

Coombs, W. T., & Holladay, S. J. (1996). Communication and attributions in a crisis: An experimental study in crisis communication. *Journal of Public Relations Research*, *8*(4), 279–295. https://doi.org/10.1207/s1532754xjprr0804_04

Fortunato, J. A. (2008). Restoring a reputation: The Duke University lacrosse scandal. *Public Relations Review*, *34*(2), 116–123. https://doi.org/10.1016/j.pubrev.2008.03.006

Isaacson, T. (2018). Is a rebuild a reputational threat? The Chicago White Sox in 1997 and 2017. In Billings, A.C., Coombs, W.T., and Brown, K.A. (Eds.), *Reputational challenges in sport: Theory and application* (pp. 185–197). Routledge.

Jerome, A. M. (2008). Toward prescription: Testing the rhetoric of atonement's applicability in the athletic arena. *Public Relations Review*, *34*(2), 124–134. https://doi.org/10.1016/j.pubrev.2008.03.007

Len-Rios, M. E. (2010). Image repair strategies, local news portrayals, and crisis stage: A case study of Duke University's lacrosse team crisis. *International Journal of Strategic Communication*, 4(4), 267–287. https://doi.org/10.1080/1553118x.2010.515534

McDormand, T.F. (2018). #14Forever: Nostalgia, Pete Rose, and the Cincinnati Reds. In Billings, A.C., Coombs, W.T., & Brown, K.A. (Eds.). *Reputational challenges in sport: Theory and application* (pp. 153–169). Routledge.

Mitchell, A. A., & Olson, J. C. (1981). Are product beliefs the only mediator of advertising effect on brand attitude? *Journal of Marketing Research*, *18*(3), 318–332. https://doi.org/10.1177/002224378101800306

Nelson, J. (1984). The defense of Billie Jean King. *Western Journal of Speech Communication*, *48*(1), 92–102. https://doi.org/10.1080/10570318409374144

Pace, K. M., Fediuk, T. A., & Botero, I. C. (2010). The acceptance of responsibility and expressions of regret in organizational apologies after a transgression. *Corporate Communications: An International Journal*, *15*(4), 410–427. https://doi.org/10.1108/13563281011085510

Spears, N. S., & Singh, S. N. (2004). Measuring attitude toward the brand and purchasing intentions. *Journal of Current Issues & Research in Advertising*, *26*(2), 53–66. https://doi.org/10.1080/10641734.2004.10505164

Statista. (2022). *Number of digital live sports viewers in the United States from 2021 to 2025*. https://www.statista.com/statistics/1127341/live-sport-viewership/

Twork, J., & Blaney, J. R. (2013). Reputation differences between mortification-only and mortification/corrective action strategies following a transgression by a professional athlete. In Blaney, J. R., Lippert, L. R., & Smith, J. S. (Eds.), *Repairing the athlete's image: Studies in sports image restoration* (pp. 395–399). Lexington Books.

5 Media Framing, Sports Activism Failure, and Crisis Communication

European Football Teams and the *One Love* Campaign at the World Cup 2022

Karoline Kokholm, Marit Lott, and Winni Johansen

Introduction

Sport has a unique ability not only to unite but to divide. Bringing politics into sports is one of those things which has a tendency to cause great divide, as sport, by many, is considered to be a haven (Cashmore et al., 2023, Kahn, 2022). A place free of daily life in all its forms, including politics. Thus, it is interesting to see that athlete activism is on the rise in spite of the potential risks and challenges following such protesting. But what happens when activism is conducted by a sports organization, and it fails? During the 2022 FIFA World Cup hosted in Qatar, we witnessed an example of this new and under-researched area of activism failures within sports activism.

This chapter is based on a case study of the *One Love* campaign initiated by the Dutch Football Association in 2020 as a way of uniting football fans and speaking out against discrimination of any kind. The campaign was joined by several European nations and football associations (Belgium, Denmark, England, France, Germany, Norway, Sweden, Switzerland, and Wales) including the Danish and the German football associations: DBU and DFB, in support of human rights during the 2022 FIFA World Cup to protest against Qatar's hosting of the World Cup and the non-observation of human rights in Qatar (Syed, 2022). The captains of the football teams were supposed to wear the *One Love* armband during the football matches at the World Cup to show their support for human rights and diversity. However, due to FIFA threatening them with sporting sanctions (presumably a yellow card for the team captain if he was wearing the armband), the engaged European football associations decided to refrain from wearing the armband (DBU, 2022). We consider not living up to their original activism promises to be activism failure. Next, when they announced their

DOI: 10.4324/9781032619187-6

decision to the public, a huge multivocal rhetorical arena (Frandsen & Johansen, 2017) opened where multiple voices started communicating around this failure: sports athletes, fans, national and international media, politicians, citizens, and NGOs, all reacted to this situation. National media formed part of these voices: not only did they have their own stances, but they also gave voice to others in their news articles. We have some insights into how news media react to protests and activism (Coombs & Cassilo, 2017, Coombs et al., 2020, Peña, 2021, Doehler, 2023). But how do news media react and frame activism failure of sports associations? What is their role? Football fans adore their sports teams, but what about the news media? How do they deal with the national football associations when the national team ends up in activism failure? Different national news media, and media in different countries, such as Denmark and Germany, reacted and framed the controversy in different ways.

Sports activism has been studied to some extent since the late 19th century. It is mostly studies on sports athletes or sports teams who in various ways have showed their socio-political stance on societal issues, such as racism (Cooper et al., 2019; Coombs & Cassilo, 2017; Leppard, 2022). Furthermore, we also find studies of media framing of sports activism, but mostly in relation to individual athletes such as LeBron James and Colin Kaepernick (Park et al., 2020, Coombs et al., 2020; Doehler, 2023). However, studies on the dilemmas occurring when the goal of conducting sports activism fails, as well as media framing of such failures are non-existent as to our knowledge at the point of writing this chapter.

Thus, the overall goal of this chapter is to investigate the reactions and framing of Danish and German national media in relation to the activism failure crisis of the Danish football association, DBU (Dansk Boldspil Union), and the German football association, DFB (Deutcher Fussball-Bund) at the onset of the crisis (November 21–23, 2022), when the two football associations decided not to wear the *One Love* armband (seen as going back on their socio-political stance on human rights and diversity) during the World Cup in Qatar in November 2022. The analysis explores the nature and variations of news media's "backlash framing" when sports organizations go back on a protest, as well as the role of national media and crisis communication in the multivocal rhetorical arena that opens during an activism failure controversy. In order to fulfill the goal this chapter aims to answer the following sub-questions:

RQ 1: How did DBU and DFB explain their positions and react to the criticism of their abandonment of the *One Love* armband—using what kind of crisis responses strategies?

RQ 2: How did the news media in Denmark and Germany frame their news reporting and positions in this activism failure controversy?

RQ 3: What were the differences and similarities of the framing of the Danish and German news media?

This chapter is divided into seven sections. After a short literature review, the theoretical framework is presented, including research and theories on sports activism, crisis communication, and media framing. Then follows a section on methodology including a short description of the involved organizations, and two sections on findings from the Danish sub-arena and the German sub-arena. Finally, the chapter ends with a discussion, conclusion, implications, and future research.

Literature review: Crises in sport, athlete activism and media coverage

Crises within sport is no new phenomenon and thus, much research has already been conducted within this field. Most of the studies dealing with crisis in sport treat athletes, teams, sports organizations, and, occasionally, even countries who have been involved in some sports-related scandals (e.g., Richards JR et al., 2017; Denham, 2019; Brown et al., 2015). Scandals covered in the literature include doping (Denham, 2019), betting (Villeneuve & Aquilina, 2016), bribery (Frederick & Pegoraro, 2018), sign-stealing (Lee & Oh, 2023), infidelity (Meng & Pan, 2013), domestic violence (Richards JR et al., 2017) and sexual abuse (Schuck, 2020; Brown et al., 2015; Meng & Pan, 2013; Hughes et al., 2017). Furthermore, research on these sports crises take on different perspectives, e.g., Villeneuve and Aquilina (2016) focus on the difference in the media coverage of football betting scandals in France and the UK. In their study they find that French newspapers are more prone to blame the system, whereas British newspapers tend to focus on individual weaknesses, especially greed. In general, and interestingly so, they also find that the actors most often presented in a negative light are teams, players, and criminals, where authorities and federations most often are represented positively. Meanwhile, Schuck (2020) investigates the use of dissociation strategies to distance from scandal, and Lee and Oh (2023) explore sports fans' behavioral response to the perceived adequacy of an organization's crisis response.

In terms of sport and crisis communication, more specifically, most studies have dealt with athletes, teams, and sports organizations' crisis response strategies (e.g., Frederick & Pegoraro, 2018; Brown et al., 2015; Meng & Pan, 2013). For instance, by employing Coombs' SCCT model, Richards JR et al. (2017) found that in spite of the American National Football League's (NFL) mismatched use of crisis response, the league's reputation did not suffer from the scandal of former football player Ray Rice as much as expected due to football's high status in America.

Athlete activism

Though an act of athlete activism in itself may not be considered a crisis or an outright scandal, the views of and increasing expectations to athletes (Meng & Pan, 2013; Rowe & Palmer, 2023; Cashmore et al., 2023) may induce a crisis when an athlete takes a socio-political stance, as doing so may be considered to be breaking down the boundaries between sport and politics (Cooper et al., 2019) causing a strong response from fans and public (Leppard, 2022).

Once the scope is narrowed down from sport and crises in general to athlete activism, the amount of research decreases. Research on athlete activism tends to focus on activism carried out by individual athletes (Cooper et al., 2019). For instance, Leppard (2022) looks into Naomi Osaka's activism and explores how she utilizes her personal and professional positionality to influence her activism and generate "points of sameness" with others. Additionally, Coombs and Cassilo (2017) studied LeBron James' role as an athlete activist and the media framing thereof finding that James' activism aligned with his brand; that he was perceived as being smart, deliberate, and purposeful in his activism and that this alignment was also visible in the media framing of his activism (Coombs & Cassilo, 2017). However, the vast majority of literature on individual athletes' activism revolves around the infamous Colin Kaepernick, former San Francisco 49ers quarterback, who knelt during the national anthem at his team's football matches in 2016 (Peña, 2021). Among others Park et al. (2020) investigated how individuals' perceived Kaepernick's protest as a result of media framing, their results indicating that the news media do indeed play a critical role in shaping perceptions of athlete activism. Meanwhile, Coombs et al. (2020) and Doehler (2023) conducted two very similar studies on Kaepernick's protest exploring the media framing of it and relating their resulting frames to the protest paradigm, a framework established by Chan and Lee (1984) to study how media reports on various protests and social norms. The main difference between the two being that Coombs et al. (2020) followed the media framing immediately after Kaepernick's protest, whereas Doehler (2023) examined the frames over a longer period of time and found that the death of George Floyd in 2020 changed the framing of Kaepernick's protest. In 2016, focus was on Kapernick's action (kneeling) rather than on the issue of racism, i.e., method rather than message, and on him as a "social deviant," while in 2020, racial injustice was discussed a bit more, and Kaepernick was applauded and framed as a social activist (Doehler, 2023). Thus, frames may change over time if a social issue becomes more apparent and urgent in society.

In comparison to the individual or a few persons athlete activism, there is a lack of research on activism performed by larger groups, teams, leagues, and sports organizations in general, although new and collective forms of activism have recently started to gain traction (e.g., Yan et al., 2018; Cooky & Antunovic, 2020; Williams, 2022). However, more importantly, studies of sports activism failure, at an individual, group, or organizational level, seem to be non-existent at this point in time, although we are witnessing more cases of activism failure at the moment.

Theoretical framework

The theoretical framework is presented in the following three sub-sections: (1) from political activism to athlete and sports activism, (2) from crisis response strategies to a multivocal rhetorical arena approach to crisis communication, and (3) from media framing to framing contests.

Defining athlete activism and activism failure

As sport and politics are closely related, it is natural that a definition of activism may take its starting point in political activism. One such definition is proposed by Shaw (2001 in Smith, 2019, p. 2378) who posited that the purpose of political activism is to communicate a need and demand for change of those in power while creating support for causes and underlining that activism is a way of demanding change and opposing those in power.

Narrowing the scope further, there are a few definitions, which relate more specifically to *athlete* activism. One such definition of athlete activism is that it is *"any amateur or professional athlete's action (collectively or individually, institutionally or informally) to promote progressive social changes"* (Presley et al., 2016 in Park et al., 2020, p. 632).

Important to note in relation to these definitions is the varying level of unconventionality, activism is thought to take on. For instance, Cooper et al. (2019) find that activism is to be of a more demonstrative and radical character, whereas Presley et al., 2016 (in Park et al., 2020) allow for activism to come across as more of a symbolic act.

Importantly, athlete activism does not exist in a vacuum but rather in the context of broader society (Cooper et al., 2019; Hartman, 2023) and, therefore, it is inherently interrelated with sport and politics (Hartman, 2023). This is also why the sporting scene provides a unique platform for an athlete to take a socio-political stance (Kaufman & Wolff, 2010), as it causes a disruption of what is otherwise thought to be good, pure, and apolitical (e.g. Kaufman, 2008; Coakley, 2015).

Taking a stand, however, is not easy because athletes today are considered celebrities and role models and thus there are high expectations to them of being good and actively engaged citizens (Kaufman & Wolff, 2010; Rowe & Palmer, 2023), which consequently makes them "agents of social change" (Park et al., 2020; Smith, 2019). However, a paradox exists here, as whenever athletes engage in apolitical acts of kindness, e.g., visiting children in hospitals, they are accepted and applauded but once they decide to take a stand and protest on the field to promote social justice, the result is, more often than not, some kind of backlash (Kaufman, 2008).

Activism failure

What is then activism failure? Following our study on the failure by European sports associations to use the *One Love* armband as a symbol of protest against the lack of human rights in Qatar during the FIFA World Cup in 2022, we define activism failure in the following way: activism failure is when an individual, group, organization, or institution for various reasons go back on their original support of a socio-political, economic, or environmental stance that may lead to social change, hence, not living up to the original promises.

Crisis communication

We consider crises to be social constructions that are interpreted and negotiated among multiple stakeholders (cf. Frandsen & Johansen, 2017, p. 48). Thus, a crisis can be defined with Coombs as "the perceived violation of salience stakeholder expectations that can create negative outcomes for stakeholder and/or the organization" (2019, p. 3).

Within crisis communication, the *Image Repair Theory* (IRT) of William Benoit (2015) and the *Situational Crisis Communication Theory* (SCCT) of Timothy Coombs (2022), have dominated the field for long. They have established inventories of the typical crisis response strategies used by an individual or an organization hit by a crisis where they have to defend themselves when accused of wrongdoing. IRT is a rhetorical and text-oriented theory that studies verbal defense when a person or organization defends itself against accusations of wrongdoing. The model relies on five main categories, and 14 strategies in total, including denial (simple denial, shifting the blame), evasion of responsibility (provocation, defeasibility, accident, good intentions), reducing offensiveness (bolstering, minimization, differentiation, transcendence, attacking the accuser, compensation), corrective action, and mortification.

SCCT forms an attempt to expand IRT and to study not only what to say but also when to say what. Thus, SCCT is a strategic context-oriented theory. It is based on relationship management and attribution theory (Coombs, 2022) claiming that the attributions of responsibility made by stakeholders have an impact on the appropriate communication strategy to choose to protect image and reputation during a crisis. The theory applies four postures, from defensive strategies to accommodative and rebuilding strategies: denial posture (attacking the accuser, denial, scapegoating), diminishing posture (excusing, justification), rebuilding posture (compensation, apology), and bolstering posture (reminding, ingratiation, victimage). Crisis history, crisis severity, and an organization's prior reputation may have an impact on the casual attributions of responsibility made by stakeholders. Hence, SCCT tries to account for intensifying factors in the context that may influence the choice of an appropriate strategy. According to Coombs and Harker (2022), sports form a unique context for crisis communication.

Another strategic, context-oriented crisis communication theory is the multivocal *Rhetorical Arena Theory* (RAT) developed by Frandsen and Johansen in 2000 (2010, 2017, 2023). RAT expands the perspectives of IRT and SCCT and tries to capture the complexity of crisis communication by taking into account the multiple voices that enter the arena and start *communicating to*, *with*, *against*, *past*, or *about* the organization hit by a crisis (Frandsen & Johansen, 2010). Some of these voices are agonists (disagreeing with one another), others are antagonists (polarized, not wanting consensus at all) (Frandsen & Johansen, 2020, 2023). Hence, RAT documents the social constructivism aspects of a crisis: an arena opens up for perceptions, negotiations, agreements as well as disagreements and framing contests. Furthermore, RAT also highlights the importance of the situational and cultural contexts, media, genres, and rhetoric for the impact of crisis response strategies (Frandsen & Johansen, 2017).

The multivocality aspect includes voices such as employees, managers, consumers, citizens, investors, media, politicians, NGOs, and third parties having their own agendas. Thus, the voices of the news media and the media logic (Fredriksson & Pallas, 2018) also play an important role during a crisis. Each news media has its own position, and interacts, e.g., by means of framing and by making room for selected voices to make themselves heard. This means that during a crisis we are typically witnessing framing contests such as corporate framing of a crisis versus news media framing.

Media framing

The basic attraction in framing, according to Olsson and Ihlen (2018), lies in "how frames provide direction for our understanding of issues" (p. 1). Frames provide direction by contextualizing information (Hallahan, 2013), and thus provide the receiver with guidelines for how a text should be interpreted. Because of this ability to contextualize a lot of power also lies in framing (Pan & Kosicki, 1993), which is evident as they provide guidelines for interpretation, which helps us make inferences about the world and thus take part in constructing our own world view (Hallahan,

1999). With this in mind, and as an important tenet of framing theory, meaning is not a given but is created (Olsson & Ihlen, 2018) in the meeting between frame and receiver (Entman, 1993).

Because of framing's breadth and usefulness in many different contexts there is, as of yet, no universally agreed-upon definition of framing or guidelines on how frames are manifested or interpreted (Fly, Bruun, & Kokholm, 2022). As such, many definitions of framing also exist, such as those of Reese (2001 in Olsson & Ihlen, 2018) and Hallahan (2013), but in spite of the many available definitions many scholars (e.g., Scheufele, 1999; Hallahan, 1999; Boykoff & Carrington, 2020; Coombs et al., 2020; Cornelissen, 2020; Fly et al., 2022) still revert to Robert Entman (1993) when defining framing.

According to Entman (1993), framing involves two essential features: selection and salience. Selection being to highlight certain pieces of information, and thus leaving out others, thereby directing the receiver's attention to what the communicator finds important, and salience meaning to promote a certain piece of information, thus making it more easily perceptible to the audience and, thereby, increasing the chances that the receiver will identify the intended meaning and remember it (Entman, 1993). In other words, selection is used to increase the salience of the information. Based on this, Entman (1993) put forward the following definition of framing:

> To frame is to select some aspects of a perceived reality and make them more salient in a communicating text, in such a way as to promote a particular problem definition, causal interpretation, moral evaluation, and/or treatment recommendation for the item described.
>
> (p. 52)

An important notion within framing is that in spite of the abilities of framing to create meaning, there is no guarantee that a frame may influence its audience as may have been the intention, as salience is the result of interaction between frame and receiver (Entman, 1993).

Framing contests

Depending on who the sender of the frame is, the framing of a situation may vary and cause framing contests between communicators (Olsson & Ihlen, 2018). For instance, an organization in crisis will frame the crisis according to the organization's view of it, i.e., applying a *corporate* frame, whereas the media, who may apply a *news* frame portraying the crisis differently (Cornelissen, 2020). However, framing contests may also be identified, for instance, in news media articles presenting two or more clearly conflicting or opposite frames at once. This is seen, for instance, in Doehler's study of media framing of Kaepernick's protest where a conflict or clash occurs between a frame claiming that he paid disregard to the patriotic nature of the United States, against another frame claiming his right to freedom of speech (Doehler, 2023).

Importantly, because of the presence and impact of the media and the fact that a frame provides a context for which to create meaning, the media cannot be considered a neutral communicator (Olsson & Ihlen, 2018). This, as frames put forward by the media are impacted by journalists' personal ideologies and pressures from external stakeholders, as well as the inherent pressure to conform to the expectations of owners, executives, and the media's ideologies (Entman, 2007), what is also known as the media logic (Cornelissen, 2020).

Thus, the power of framing is once again highlighted by the way that the media has the ability to influence and even change the individual's and public's opinion through frames (Hughes & Shank, 2005; Olsson & Ihlen, 2018).

News media framing

As established by Olsson and Ihlen (2018), frames "shape the way an issue is reported" and, therefore, significantly influences the audience's perception of the issues. Because framing may be considered a "fractured paradigm" (Entman, 1993), the types of frames used also vary. Hallahan (1999) puts forward seven types of framing within public relations: framing of situations, attributes, choices, actions, issues, responsibility, and news. Other scholars, such as Semetko and Valkenburg (2000), find there to be five overall frames used by the news media, namely, that of a conflict, human interest, economic, morality, and responsibility frame, confirmed again in a study by An and Gower (2009). The purpose of the conflict frame is to emphasize the conflicts between groups, individuals, and other institutions in order to capture the interest of the audience. Further, the conflict frame is used to dramatize and simplify complex conflicts to make them more suitable for news coverage. The human interest frame presents an issue, event, or problem from an emotional angle, thus providing it with a "human face," which is a way of personalizing or emotionalizing the news to gain the attention of the audience. The frame of economic consequences is used to hone the economic consequences of a certain issue, event, or problem and the impact it will have on an individual, group, organization, or country. The morality frame places the news in a moral context, however, as the news media are expected to be objective, the morality frame is often referenced indirectly by journalists through quotations and inferences. Lastly, the responsibility frame is used to attribute responsibility, for a problem or issue, either for causing or solving it, to the government, a group, or individual.

Finally, some of the frames found in the study of Kaepernick's activism by Doehler (2023), who used the protest paradigm for his study, also seem to be relevant to the study of framing of the *One Love* controversy between DBU, DFB and FIFA, e.g., "the action, not the issue-frame," i.e., the action of protesting versus the issue based on which the protest is carried out.

Methodology

Applying a social constructivist approach to crisis, we perceive a crisis to be something that is created through social interactions and ways of speaking about it (Holm, 2018). Thus, it is a matter of perception. Aligned with this, we apply a qualitative research design based on an embedded case study (Yin, 2018): the abandonment of the armbands during the World Cup in Qatar in 2022, containing two sub-units: DBU and DFB. It is an unusual case, the fact that the activist protest of wearing the *One Love* armbands was never accomplished by the Danish and German football associations, DBU and DFB, makes it an unusual case (Yin, 2018), as athlete activists normally follow through on their protests. For that reason, the case also led to a very critical media coverage and media framing of the event, among others in Denmark and Germany. Hence, it is ideal for the study of the reactions and criticism of activism failure as they appear in texts.

Key actors: DBU, DFB, and FIFA

The Danish national football association, DBU, Dansk Boldspil-Union, was founded in 1889 (DBU, 2023a). DBU is responsible not only for the management and coordination of rules and tournaments, but also football's role in Denmark in a broader perspective (DBU, 2023b). Thus, it is DBU's responsibility to attend to football at both the amateur and professional level, which also makes the organization the employer of the Danish professional football players (DBU, 2023c). Furthermore, Denmark, i.e. DBU, is one of the founding fathers of FIFA, which was established in Paris in 1904 (DBU, 2023b; Levy, 2023).

The German national football association DFB, Deutscher Fußball-Bund e.V. is the German counterpart to DBU. It was founded in 1900 (DFB, 2020), and joined FIFA in 1904 (tz, 2022). It consists of professional as well as amateur football teams and it employs association staff, referees, coaches, teachers, and professional football players (DFB, 2023).

The Federation Internationale de Football Associations, FIFA, is the international administrative authority and thus ultimate governing body of football worldwide (US Soccer, 2023). FIFA was founded in 1904 with the purpose of promoting a mutual association of football through which to foster relationships between football associations and to control and organize the game. Today FIFA's mission is "to truly globalise, popularise and democratise football for the benefit of the entire world" (FIFA, 2020).

Data collection

Two sets of data were collected for this study: (1) online texts and press conference statements from DBU and DFB and (2) news media articles from five Danish and four German national media. To obtain the data relevant for this study, a purposive sampling strategy, i.e., sampling according to purpose and research questions (Bryman, 2016) was employed. Accordingly, as the research questions for this study aim to understand the case of the abandonment of the *One Love* armband primarily from the perspective of the news media at the onset of the crisis, data in the form of news articles from select news media during the first three days of the crisis have been collected. Furthermore, a heterogeneous sampling strategy (Daymon & Holloway, 2011) was employed to be able to investigate the presumed different framings of the news media along with criterion sampling, used to select the news media.

Statements and texts from DBU and DFB

As a result of the sampling criteria, two texts and a collection of statements from each of the press conferences being held in the wake of the announcement of the withdrawal of the armbands (November 21–23, 2022) have been selected for analysis. The articles are authored by DBU and DFB and were obtained through DBU's and DFB's own websites in the section in which they publish news related to the 2022 World Cup. As for the press conferences, as neither video material nor a transcript of the entire press conference was obtainable, the statements, i.e., quotes from the press conferences, have been gathered from video clips of the press conference and from different news articles about the press conference.

Danish and German news media

In order to gain insight into the media framing by the Danish and German news media, a sample was created to represent a cross section of the news media landscape. The inclusion criteria encompassed that the media selected must be national in terms of reach, as the nationwide news media are the sources through which the majority consume their news (Danmarks Statistik, 2023; AWA, 2023), and that the news media must have significant weekly readership figures, as this indicates a high reach, and presumably impact on, consumers. For investigating the onset of the crisis, another inclusion criterion is that the articles must have been published between November 21 and 23, 2023, as the discontinuation of the armband use was announced on November 21, DFB held a press conference on November 22, and DBU did similar on November 23.

Based on these criteria the following news media were selected for Denmark: *Politiken*, *Jyllands-Posten*, *Berlingske*, and *Ekstra Bladet*, as these are the four independent Danish news media with the highest readership figures (Kantar Gallup, 2022). Furthermore, the media vary in terms of genre, *Politiken*, *Berlingske*, and *Jyllands-Posten* are daily papers, whereas *Ekstra Bladet* is a tabloid (Maressa, 2015), and orientation, *Politiken* is considered to be slightly left-wing; *Berlingske* slightly right-wing; *Jyllands-Posten* right-wing; whereas, being a tabloid, *Ekstra Bladet* focuses primarily on sensation and entertainment (Lånekassen, 2023). Additionally, as a large part of news consumers in Denmark also rely heavily on public service media (DR, 2022), it was decided to include the Danish public service media with the highest readership figures, namely *TV2* (Lindhardt, 2023). This, in order to ensure that the sample of data sources reflected the news consumption of the Danish public as accurately as possible.

For the German perspective, the following news media were selected: *BILD*, *Süddeutsche Zeitung (SZ)*, *Frankfurter Allgemeine Zeitung (FAZ)*, and *Der Spiegel online*. *BILD* is a tabloid and has the highest readership figures in Germany, followed by the nationwide daily newspapers *SZ* and *FAZ* (AWA, 2023). In order to also cover mainly online media recipients, the news website *Der Spiegel online*, which is editorially independent of the print version, is included as one of the most popular online news websites in Germany (Statista, 2023). Additionally, the media also vary in orientation as *SZ* and *Der Spiegel online* are slightly left-wing, *FAZ* is slightly right-wing and *BILD* is rather right-wing and publishes mainly sensational content (Freilich, 2023). See Table 5.1 for an overview.

In order to access the Danish news media articles, *Infomedia*, a Danish online news article database, was used. Searching for "One Love" in the given time period and in the given media resulted in 151 articles, which were then sifted through according to the sampling criteria. Accordingly, a total of 11 articles were selected for analysis.

For the German news media articles research were collected by going through the archives of each media. Accordingly, filter functions were used to search for the explicit time period and the term "One Love." This research resulted in 15–20 articles for each media. After reading them and applying the defined sampling criteria, nine articles were selected for the analysis.

Table 5.1 Overview of newspaper articles and characteristics

Danish news media	*Genre*	*Orientation*	*No of selected articles*
Politiken	Daily newspaper	Slightly left-wing	3
Jyllandsposten	Daily newspaper	Right-wing	1
Berlingske	Daily newspaper	Slightly right-wing	2
Ekstra Bladet	Tabloid	Sensation and entertainment	2
TV2	Public service media		3
In total			= 11
German news media			
BILD	Tabloid	Right-wing, sensational	3
Süddeutsche Zeitung (SZ)	Daily newspaper	Slightly left-wing, liberal	2
Frankfurter Allgemeine Zeitung (FAZ)	Daily newspaper	Slightly right-wing, conservative, liberal	2
Der Spiegel (online)	Online news website	Slightly left-wing, liberal	2
In total			= 9

Data analysis of crisis communication and media framing

The crisis communication strategies applied by DBU and DFB were analyzed using the inventories of crisis response strategies of Benoit (2015) and Coombs (2022) presented in section 3.2. As for analyzing the media framing in the 20 articles, we conducted a framing analysis as put forward by Pan and Kosicki (1993). According to them, each text is made up of "signifying elements" or "framing devices," which collectively make up a frame through which the intended interpretation of an article is promoted. Thus, to uncover the frames of the articles, each article was read and analyzed according to these signifying elements, which are made up of lexical choices and structural dimensions, i.e., the syntactical, script, thematic, and rhetorical structure. Hence, after an analysis of the signifying elements, the subthemes were uncovered (see Appendix 2 and 4) and, in spite of many overlaps between subthemes and frames, it was then possible to derive the main themes and thus identify the overall frame of each article (see Appendix 1 and 3). Finally, the frames were clustered, and conflicting frames and framing contests were identified.

In order to refer to the articles and distinguish between different articles from the same news media, each article has been given an abbreviation, e.g., article number three from *Politiken* is P-3 and article number two from FAZ is FAZ-2.

Findings part I: DBU crisis response and the Danish news media framing

In this section, we will present the findings from the case study of the Danish Football Association, DBU, and the framing of the *One Love* campaign controversy in Danish news media. Before presenting the media frames used by the five Danish news media selected for this study, we briefly describe the reactions, positions, and crisis response strategies used by DBU to explain themselves to the public.

DBUs abandons the use of the One Love *armband*

On November 21, 2022, the UEFA working group, of which DBU is a member, issued a statement announcing the abandonment of the use of the *One Love* armband. The statement appeared in DBU's online newsroom and contains several crisis communication strategies such as shifting the blame, attacking the accuser and victimage, and thus serves to depict FIFA as the aggressor and the *One Love* campaign nations as the victims.

Following the announcement and the initial reactions of the news media and the public, DBU hosted a press conference on November 23 and posted an article in its online newsroom, using the same crisis response strategies as previously to maintain their victim position. No apology is given by DBU, but they are defending their position by shifting the blame, excusing and trying to deflect the responsibility from the players, as stated by DBU chairman Jesper Møller during the press conference: "One thing is what I have to be subjected to, both in the media, politically and so on, but they have to leave our players alone, that's just how it is."

Danish news media framing

In the wake of the announcement of the discontinuation of the use of the armbands on November 21, 2022, a lot of actors and voices reacted to the news, including the media. In order to gain insight into the Danish news media's portrayal of the situation, 11 news articles have been analyzed. In this section, we will present some of the most important findings (news media frames) found in the four newspapers *Politiken* (P), *JyllandsPosten* (JP), *Berlingske* (BE), the more sensational *Ekstra Bladet* (EB), and in news articles from one of the Danish public service broadcasting media, *TV2*. We identified seven overall frames, each of them covering a series of subthemes (see Appendix 2) for an overview of the use of frames and subthemes within each of the five sets of news articles.

The seven frames are presented in the following order: cowardice frame, fear frame responsibility frame, uncertainty frame, dominance frame, divergence frame, and contrast frame. They seemingly relate to the moral values of DBU, the sanctions of FIFA and consequences for DBU, and the moral values of FIFA, as well as comparisons with other teams.

Cowardice frame

The cowardice frame is one of the important frames found in the Danish news media. Coward, gutless, and spineless are all words used in the news media texts and refer to DBU giving up, not having the courage to stand up for their activistic stance for human rights in Qatar, for reasons such as being spineless, not having the guts, being scared, but also, not wanting to risk the consequences of protesting; being conflict-averse, not standing up to their bully.

This frame was found, for instance, in both EB articles describing DBU as gutless not daring to follow through on their promises and take a stand against FIFA and Qatar: "Frightened by FIFA they do not dare to dress captain Simon Kjær the 'One-Love' armband which signals resistance against homophobia and racism" (EB-2), and "Could risk a yellow card" (EB-1).

In the TV2 articles, the cowardice frame also comes clearly forward, describing how DBU does not want to risk the consequences of protesting: "... the protest would have too big a sporting impact" (TV2-2). And in *Berlingske* focus is upon DBU being conflict-averse, lacking the will to stand up for their cause: "When it counted, the will to take a stand was little" and complying with the will of FIFA: "But again FIFA said no and again DBU complied" (BE-2).

Fear frame

The fear frame refers to giving up wearing the armband due to fear of sanctions from FIFA and being scared. In this case fear is seen as the determining factor in DBU's decision to abandon the use of the armbands. *Politiken* (P-3) has an overall theme where DBU is portrayed as getting cold feet and the overall frame of fear is used to depict DBU as being scared: "[...] the Danish national football team will not be wearing the captain's armband against discrimination at the World Cup in Qatar anyways for fear of sporting sanctions" and "For fear of sporting sanctions the national football team will not be wearing the rainbow-colored captain's armband, which shows the wearer's dissociation with discrimination" (P-3).

Responsibility frame

The responsibility frame refers to the need of someone to take responsibility for what is going on by standing up against FIFA. In this case, the responsibility is considered to rest upon DBU and its chairman, Jesper Møller, in particular, as he is the elected representative of DBU in FIFA and, therefore, has the ability to influence FIFA's actions. The responsibility frame is evident in the article *Denmark can no longer wait to criticise FIFA and the arrow points at one man* (P-2) from *Politiken*. Here the main theme is Jesper Møller as needing to take action and stand up to FIFA as FIFA is described as "an elephant running wild in the display window and destroying what, with another host nation, could have been a beautiful presentation of the global team sport's qualities" and thus as someone who needs to be dealt with. Furthermore, Jesper Møller is being accused of hiding and is urged to step forward to "manage the binding mandate he has received by the Danish national sport's large support base," thus implying that he now needs to take responsibility by taking action.

Uncertainty frame

Another frame, which recurs across different articles and news media, is the uncertainty frame. This frame refers to the uncertainty as unpredictability and not knowing what is to come. Here the uncertainty is created by FIFA through the way it is acting in an unusual and unpredictable way, especially in regard to its stance on human rights, which makes it increasingly hard for DBU and the other *One Love* nations to know what they may expect from FIFA going forward. In *Politiken* (P-1), this becomes evident in the overall theme of FIFA as playing by their own rules by opposing the sporting norms, which in itself is unusual and unexpected. "But ahead of Denmark's first match at the World Cup in Qatar FIFA's handling of the anti-discrimination campaign with that exact name [i.e. the *One Love* campaign] is creating a mix of politics and the game on the field, which has not been seen in modern finals history." By following FIFA's own agenda, "Denmark and the six other nations are also surprised, to say the least, that they could wear the *One Love* captain's armbands back in September under the auspices of UEFA for the matches in Nations League and that FIFA, back then, did not react. The world federation has known about the wish to wear the *One Love* captain's armband for months" (P-1). In *Jyllands-Posten* (JP-1), the uncertainty frame becomes clear in the way that DBU and the rest of the *One Love* campaign nations are unwilling to risk carrying out their protesting not knowing what consequences to expect because FIFA seems to be changing its direction. As Stanis Elsborg, senior analyst at Play the Game, explains: "It is completely unheard to be threatened with sporting sanctions for wearing an armband, which symbolizes something that falls in line with FIFA's own policies" (JP).

Dominance frame

The dominance frame refers to an actor using power and bullying others. This frame is evident in *TV2s* article, *Denmark abandons much-debated armband* (TV2-3) and shows FIFA as being in charge and having the last say, thus posing as a dominating character. This is evident in the way that FIFA is described as having its own agenda and as being superior: "They have known about our stance for a long time. We stand for inclusion just like FIFA says they stand for inclusion. I cannot see that our messages conflict with the messages that FIFA wishes to communicate" and "FIFA dictating captain's armbands." The overall theme thus becomes clear that FIFA is considered a dictator who has the power to rule according to its preferences and does so at the expense of some of its members.

Divergence frame

The divergence frame refers to the existence of paradoxes, discrepancies, and divergences from the norm. In this case how the 2022 World Cup differs from the norm of how a football world cup is conducted, and how FIFA, Qatar, and the football associations that are parts of the *One Love* campaign are acting in contrast to the norm. The divergence frame can be found in *Berlingske* (BE-1), an article whose main theme is the World Cup as being full of contrasts, thus underlining the divergence and paradoxes at play. This becomes clear from the way that it is described in the article how Qatar and FIFA allow certain forms of protests but not others, "You are allowed to kneel against racism. But an armband supporting homosexuality is forbidden" (BE-1), and how FIFA is being self-contradictory: "In spite of previous assurances of the opposite spectators and football players with »rainbow-support« of homosexuals' rights are facing problems." This implies that the two actors are being self-contradictory in terms of at least FIFA's usual stance toward human rights. Additionally, the *One Love* nations are being portrayed as weak-willed: "The threat that it will trigger a warning to the team captain before the match begins has caused the national football associations to give in," while the Iranians are portrayed as strong-willed and willing to stand up for themselves: "A 17-year-old woman from Iran, by contrast, tells she doesn't care what people tell her she can and cannot do" (BE-1).

Contrast frame: DBU versus Iranian players

The last frame identified is found in *TV2* and is about contrasting DBU (the Danish team) and Iranian players. *TV2* uses a frame of contrast to highlight how Denmark and DBU could do better in the article entitled "Iranian players applauded for protest, while Denmark backs down on armbands" (TV2-3). The article gives way to the main theme being Iran as the ideal that Denmark should be following, highlighting Iran's courage and willingness to take risks, e.g., "The Iranian players risk harsh punishments to show their support in public to the protesters in the home country." In contrast, Denmark and the *One Love* nations are portrayed as weak and yielding to FIFA by collectively backtracking on the use of the armbands. The contrast between Iran and Denmark is further underlined when the two are directly compared: "For the Iranian players, there is likely a lot more at stake by publicly challenging the Iranian regime than a yellow card," implying that Denmark should have kept fighting.

As it appears from the analysis, the Danish news media were framing the controversy in different ways giving voice to different perceptions and perspectives and revealing various themes and subthemes (see App. 1 and 2).

Findings part II: DFB crisis response and the German news media framing

In this section we will present the findings from the case study of the German football association, DFB, and the framing of the *One Love* campaign controversy in German news media. First, we briefly describe the immediate reactions, positions, and crisis response strategies used by DFB to explain their abandonment decision to the public. Next, we present the media frames used by the selected four German news media.

Crisis communication of DFB

As DFB belongs to the UEFA working group, they are also part of the joint statement on November 21, when the abandonment of the *One Love* armbands was announced. DFB published the statement on their website in the "News"-section (DFB, 2022a), followed by another article the next day tackling the issue of the armband. In this article entitled "Hansi Flick: 'The national team stands for diversity,'" the national coach uses different crisis communication strategies in an attempt to defend the national team's stand on diversity (DFB, 2022b). He is *denying* DFB's responsibility in this scenario blaming FIFA for banning the armbands and not allowing DFB *"to stand up for human rights anymore"* (DFB, 2022b). Besides he is pointing out the *good intentions* of the *One Love* campaign and the national team wanting to wear it. Additionally, *excuses* (explanations) and *transcendence*, by pointing out the intention to remove pressure from the player' shoulders, are applied illustrating how DFB is taking a very defensive stance and displaying themselves as victims.

After the first reactions by the fans and the media to the abandonment of the *One Love* armband, DFB president Neuendorf and DFB manager Bierhoff held a press conference on November 22. In the analysis of press conference, several crisis communication strategies were identified: *shifting the blame*, *attacking the accuser*, *transcendence*, *victimage*, *minimization*, *bolstering*, *defeasibility*, and *corrective action* (SZ, 2022a–2022d). Neuendorf is trying to justify how DFB became victims of the misbehavior of FIFA (Leicher, 2022). In contrast to the other *One Love* nations, the German team attempted to take a stance in the controversy between DFB and FIFA, by taking a photo where the players cover their mouth as a sign of being silenced by FIFA, using an *attacking the accuser* response strategy. Thus, they applied a very defensive crisis communication strategy.

In spite of DFB's very defensive stance, however, three weeks after the press conference, Neuendorf ended up apologizing by admitting that he made a mistake in how he handled the situation: "I would have acted sooner today. I should have sought a direct line to Infantino to get clarity. That's what I've learned" (Sportschau, 2022).

German news media framing

Nine articles from four different German news media were analyzed in order to gain knowledge about how the German media was reacting to the abandonment of the *One Love* armband. The included news media are *BILD* (BI), *Frankfurter Allgemeine Zeitung* (FAZ), *Süddeutsche Zeitung* (SZ), and *Der Spiegel (online)* (SPo). We identified eight overall frames in our analysis, each of them covering a series of subthemes (see App. 4).

The eight frames are presented in the following order: cowardice frame, hypocrite frame, naivety frame, pathetic frame, weakness frame, non-credibility frame, cowardice-dominance frame, and embarrassment frame. Overall, the frames mainly relate to four topics: the character and moral values of DFB, judgment of DFB's actions, the responsibility of DBU versus FIFA, as well as consequential feelings of the public toward the act of DFB.

Cowardice frame

Similar to the Danish news media, the cowardice framing is the most important frame found in the German analysis. The frame is connected to FIFA throughout, by highlighting that DFB are cowards who do not dare stand up against FIFA. The term "cowardice" is used several times throughout the media articles, e.g., in the headline of BILD (BI-1): *Comment on the armband scandal at the World Cup "You are nothing but COWARDS!"*

Besides that, the cowardice frame was identified in SPo-2, where DFB is portrayed as backtrackers: "an association that ducks away when things get serious." In FAZ-2, it is also stressed that the photo of the national team holding their hands in front of their mouths supports this impression of gutlessness, thereby missing its original goal.

Hypocrite frame

The hypocrite frame refers to an organization not "walking the talk," and mainly relates to DFBs general position on diversity. According to the article SZ-1, the justification for not wearing the armband is hypocritical, because the reason given by DFB, that the sanctions were unpredictable, is simply not believable. It is claimed that the real reason for coming up with the armband in the first place was advertisement deals rather than diversity. Furthermore, BI-1 claims that the armband was just a "hypocrite rainbow action," and that it turns out to be all "empty words" (BI-1).

Naivety frame

The naivety frame refers to being naïve or credulous. It also relates to DFB's relationship with FIFA and who is to blame for the crisis situation. The article FAZ-1 points out that FIFA is the real bad guy in banning the *One Love* armband. It emphasizes that DFB should have known better and should have been more proactive in ensuring FIFA's approval earlier. In the end, this means the failure of the campaign and the crisis could have been avoided by DFB by tackling the issue differently, but out of naivety they missed their chance. As FAZ-1 puts it: "It may also have been a bit naive of the associations to push ahead with their agenda to the end without the appropriate safeguards, so they share responsibility for the situation despite all their good intentions."

Pathetic frame

The pathetic frame refers to something being deplorable and pitiful. It is about the judgment of DFBs behavior, acting in a disappointing way, and being incapable of standing up for its protest. This is found in SPo-1 where the whole conflict regarding the *One Love* armband and especially the way it ended is described as "regrettable and a little pathetic. In fact, it is unbelievable." Besides, it appears also in SZ-2, which is complaining about Germany's "collective weepiness." However, it refers not only to DFB itself, but also to all of Germany and, therefore, kind of alludes to the failed role of the country's representation by DFB (SZ-2).

Weakness frame

The weakness frame refers to a lack of strength and, therefore, not having the ability to take a stance, which is again related to the missed expectations of DFB standing up to FIFA. This frame is used in FAZ-2 where it is already stressed through the headline *Germany without courage and strengths*. The article is not only about DFB being gutless and, therefore, cowards, but mainly about their weakness referring to a lack of ability (FAZ-2). DFB and the national team itself is perceived as being overwhelmed by the ban from FIFA with the only reaction was the "alibi photo" of putting their hands in front of their mouths, which does not make it anything better (FAZ-2).

Non-credibility frame

The non-credibility frame refers to not being credible or trustworthy. It describes how the DFB's behavior makes their intentions unbelievable and, hence, how they have lost their credibility for future actions similar to this one. In SZ-2, the situation is pictured as follows: "DFB and the players have now severely damaged their credibility with regard to discrimination and non-violence." Furthermore, the national players are also perceived to have damaged their position as a role model for fighting against racism in the stadium (SZ-2).

Cowardice-dominance frame

Dominance refers to one party being more powerful than another. BI-3 deals with a discussion between the ZDF World Cup expert Christoph Kramer and moderator Jochen Breyer. Here it is contrasted how, on the one hand, DFB acted cowardly as "Germany is also buckling before FIFA, forgoing the 'One Love' armband at the World Cup in Qatar as a sign AGAINST discrimination and FOR diversity," but on the other hand, FIFA is the more powerful party and, therefore, bears more responsibility as well as being the real loser of the debate: "It's just that FIFA gets to decide. You are powerless." This way of displaying it indicates a *framing contest* between the portrayal of FIFA as the dominant bad guy and DFB as the weak coward.

Embarrassment frame

The final frame, the embarrassment frame refers to the feeling of being uneasy or ashamed, and it relates to the German public being ashamed of DFBs behavior. This is found in BI-2 where the head of sports, Brügelmann, is totally condemning DFB for not wearing the armband, and also for how the decision went down. He emphasizes that DFB is reacting completely wrong regarding the *One Love* armband and that the whole team makes a really poor showing, by stating: "It's the day we're ashamed of DFB & national team, even though the first German match hasn't even taken place yet." This frame distinguishes itself from the other frames, as it is about what DFB's action means and does to the fans and public—it embarrasses—whereas the former frames mostly connect to the character and/or values of DFB.

As it appears from the analysis, the German news media were also framing the controversy in many different ways using specific frames and subthemes (see App. 3 and 4) when presenting the controversy and the ones to blame.

Discussion

As the analyses of key frames in sections 5 and 6 have shown, there are a lot of exciting findings from each of the two countries and an important variation of the news media framing. In this section, we will concentrate on the most exciting and interesting findings, including the media frames as such but also compare for similarities and differences of media reactions and frames in the two countries of Denmark and Germany. However, we will start with a very short reflection on the crisis response strategies of the two football associations that contributed to the news media framing.

How did the two football associations handle the issue of the One Love *armband?*

The overall *One Love* campaign including the team captains wearing the *One Love* armband during the World Cup in Qatar in 2022 was a way to protest against discrimination and non-observation of human rights in Qatar. However, as it appears from the analysis, the event that triggered the crisis was the joint statement made by DBU and DFB as well as other European football associations (part of the UEFA working group), that they were *not* going to wear the *One Love* armband as planned during the games due to the threat of pressure and sporting sanctions from FIFA, the governing body of football worldwide.

Both DBU and DFB explained that they were the victims of FIFA's decision to (potentially) sanctioning the captains (getting a yellow card in the games) if they went through with wearing the *One Love* armband. For that reason, they applied a denial and evading responsibility strategy claiming that FIFA was the one to blame, attacking FIFA for denying them a voice, and stressing their good intentions as they with this symbol had wanted to fight for human rights. They clearly considered themselves to be in a victim crisis, and they kept this viewpoint also when they were hit by the strong reactions and criticism of the news media in the rhetorical arena of the crisis.

However, the views of the voices in the rhetorical arena on the nature of the crisis and responsibility of the associations are clearly conflicting. According to our findings, news media mostly seem to think that it is a preventable crisis caused by the football associations themselves taking a wrong decision of not going through with the protest, although some news media also admit that FIFA plays the role of "a bully." In case of a preventable crisis, a more accommodative crisis response strategy could have been expected in order to reduce the criticism (Coombs, 2022; Coombs & Harker, 2022).

Danish and German news media framing: What was it all about?

Both the Danish and the German news media used various frames to present the situation of the abandonment of the *One Love* armband. When looking at all of the frames and subthemes used in the Danish news media (see Table 5.2), four main topics can be identified: character, values, and behavior of DBU (cowards afraid of FIFA); role, decision, and power of FIFA (unsure of what FIFA would do); FIFA values (paradoxical behavior of FIFA); DBU compared to other football teams going through with their protest (e.g., Iranian players).

The first main topic is about the attribution of character traits to DBU, especially being cowards, and this was also the most dominant frame found in the analysis. Additionally, the media attributed a fear frame which includes being fearful before FIFA and the potential sanctions if they go through with the protest. This also leads to the second main topic, which is about the perception of FIFA's sanctions. This topic is characterized by

Table 5.2 Frames used by Danish and German news media in the One Love controversy

Danish News Media	*German News Media*
Cowardice	Cowardice
FearResponsibility	Hypocrite
Uncertainty	Naive
Dominance	Pathetic
Divergence	Weakness
Contrast	Non-credibility
	Cowardice-dominance
	Embarrassment

the uncertainty frame of being unsure what actually is going to happen (just expecting a fine, not a yellow card for the captains) and the dominance frame of FIFA being the powerful authority and DBU having to subordinate. The third one is about FIFA having paradoxical values, appearing in the divergence frame. On the one hand claiming in their statutes that FIFA is fighting for human rights and diversity, but on the other hand banning the armband, which shows that they do not want to live up to these rights. The fourth main topic relates to the comparison with other teams, including the contrast frame, where the behavior of DBU is contrasted with the positive example of the Iranian players, or the English captain, Harry Kane (see App. 2).

When looking at the German news media, four themes can also be identified: character traits of DFB; behavior of DFB; responsibility of DFB versus FIFA; and reactions and feelings of the general public (embarrassment frame). As already mentioned, the German news media also attributed frames to the character and values of DFB including cowardice, weakness, and pathetic frames, with the cowardice frame being the dominant one as well. Additionally, the German news media focused more on the judgment of DFB's behavior, the action itself, using the hypocrite and the non-credibility frame. These frames are both interpreting the withdrawal of the armband as an expression of hypocrisy not wanting to fight for human rights in the first place or just when such a fight does not include any risks or pains. Such a behavior causes a lack of credibility that may result in not trusting them if they engage in actions like this in the future. The third main topic is about the question of responsibility between DFB and FIFA, which comes forward in the naivety and the cowardice versus dominance frame. The naivety frame is mainly about FIFA being the main responsible, but because DFB knows how FIFA is acting, they could have anticipated the situation, thus DFB is also responsible for the handling the situation. The last main topic is about the feelings of the general public caused by this protest failure. The embarrassment frame is used to tell how people in Germany are feeling hurt, ashamed, and embarrassed by the action of DFB.

Danish versus German news media framing: Similarities and differences

The identified frames, depicted in Table 5.2, give important clues not only about the diversity of frames but also about the country-specific perspectives of the media. A comparison of these perspectives shows similarities but also differences in how the *One Love* armband controversy is displayed.

The most obvious *similarity* is clearly the cowardice frame, which is the most dominant frame in both of the countries' news media. DBU and

DFB are both presented as gutless and spineless in how they backtrack on their promise of taking a stance for human rights and diversity. A reason for this being so dominant could be, that in general, both media and the public have a very high opinion and admiration for their country's football team. The national football teams in both countries are seen as national symbols representing the whole country to the world. This is emphasized in the media when they replace the association's name with the country name, as, for example, in the FAZ article "Germany without courage and strength" (FAZ, 2022), using Germany as a metaphor for DFB. In this case, it makes sense that the media is disappointed by the action of the national football association and teams linking Germany to protest failure.

Another *similarity* can be found in the evaluation of FIFA being the main party responsible for the abandonment of the *One Love* armband. However, this surprisingly did not result in a more negative judgment of FIFA compared to the national football associations, but rather the other way around. The media went a lot harder on DBU and DFB than on FIFA, indicating in this way that they somehow expected the misbehavior of FIFA because of previous morally questionable actions (Esposito, 2016), whereas they had not expected well-reputed associations not to stick to their positive action of protesting against discrimination. Having a fine reputation creates obligations! However, we also found a *difference* between Germany and Denmark in relation to this topic. The German news media clearly communicates that they find DFB to be responsible in the scandal as well, as DFB should have known better and not acted in such a naïve way. This judgment does not come across the same way in the Danish news media. This may lead to different possible conclusions of what should have been done to avoid a crisis like the one that happened. According to the analysis of the Danish articles, the best option for DBU would have likely been to go through with the protest without asking FIFA for permission beforehand, whereas the German media suggests that they should have ensured approval by FIFA a lot earlier.

Another interesting *difference* relates to the overall impressions created by the way of reporting the topics. In this respect, the presentation of the controversy is slightly different in the Danish versus the German news media. The tone in the German news media articles is throughout very negative, having nothing good to say about DFB. This especially comes forward when they are talking about the mouth-shut photo, interpreting it as another display of weakness rather than acknowledging the national team's attempt to take a stance beyond the armband. Opposed to this, the Danish news media coverage is surprisingly more nuanced in their use of frames, and not as negative as one might expect, when also taking into account the highly negative illustration of the general situation of Qatar hosting the World Cup including severe violations of human rights. When looking at the different news media of the two countries, it becomes clear that the news media themselves also communicate differently, having different communication styles, as in Germany and Denmark the tabloid is negative throughout, and the other ones are a little or in the case of the Danish media a lot more nuanced.

Finally, and interestingly, specific frames were found in the Danish media that did not occur at all in the German media and vice versa. The contrast frame of the Danish media, contrasting the behavior of DBU to that of the Iranian players or the UK captain Kane, is completely missing in the German news media, whereas the embarrassment frame tackling the feelings of the public and Germany of being ashamed and embarrassed, was only identified in the German media. These differences may be a matter of news media wanting to position themselves differently from other news media, but it may also be a matter of differences within national contexts of football and/or protest actions.

What is the role of the media? How can the framing variations be explained?

The most surprising finding from the analysis was the differences in framing across the news articles. Though some differences in the degree of negativity toward DBU and DFB were assumed, it was not expected that the media's framing would fall into three distinct categories: blaming DBU and DFB, blaming FIFA, or focusing on the paradox of the situation in general. The media coverage of Qatar and the lead up to the World Cup was generally negative and, therefore, it was expected that the abandonment of the *One Love* armband would be similarly negative, when the promise of protest was broken. Such a decision could be perceived as giving in to the demands of FIFA and Qatar. The differences in framing by the individual media may be explained in different ways.

Firstly, the differences may be due to *media's responsibilities and positioning*, i.e., the responsibility to present news from different angles (Fredriksson & Pallas, 2018) and to comply with the media logic of a given media (Cornelissen, 2020). Of the media investigated both the Danish news media *Politiken*, *Jyllands-Posten*, *Berlingske*, and *TV2*, and the German news media *Süddeutche Zeitung* and *Frankfurter Allgemeiner Zeitung* presented the controversy from different angles, which is consistent with these media being independent daily papers and one being a public service media. For instances, *Berlingske* employs both a contrast frame to the overall situation as well as a cowardice frame to present DBU as being conflict-averse and not willing to stand up to FIFA. In comparison,

Ekstra Bladet only applies a cowardice frame and does so with more emphasis than the other media, which corresponds to *Ekstra Bladet* being a tabloid. In contrast, the German tabloid *BILD* also strongly emphasizes the cowardice frame but also applies, as the only one, an embarrassment frame taking the perspective of the German population feeling ashamed. Hence, the media's positioning may explain the surprising differences in framing among the news media.

Another reason for the media to not just be criticizing DBU and DFB but also, surprisingly, FIFA could be *the loyalty of the media*. Though DBU and DFB are largely criticized and considered weak-willed by the media, FIFA is also, unexpectedly, framed as a bully and behaving in a scandalous way which could indicate a loyalty toward DBU and DFB and their framing of the FIFA controversy. What may speak against this, however, is how severely DBU and DFB are being criticized by some of the media, and the very negative tone especially of the German media even if the media in general are also critical of FIFA.

Lastly, some of the nuances in attributing responsibility to DBU and DFB could be the result of DBU and DFB's *framing of the situation* having an impact on the media. In other words, DBU and DFB's promotion of a victim frame and simultaneous emphasis on how absurd and abnormal the situation is could potentially have a mitigating effect on the framing by some of the media and, as such, have caused some of the nuances present in the framing of the football associations as scared or weak as opposed to being a coward. It may also explain why some of the media also focus on criticizing FIFA as opposed to DBU and DFB.

The focus on DBU and DFB as cowards and FIFA as dominating and a bully in the news media also indicates the presence of a *framing contest* in terms of the attribution of responsibility. As the media generally has great reach and impact on the public (Park et al., 2020; Pan & Kosicki, 1993), the framing contest is important to note. Although this contest opens for nuances of perceptions among stakeholders and the general public, the cowardice frame still remains predominant, as FIFA described as a bully also means that the two organizations are not daring to stand up to a powerful opponent and authority. This emphasis on the cowardice angle will have an impact on the outcome of the protest failure, and on the outrage of people in general (cf. Stie & Mørk, 2022; Kristensen, 2022).

Overall news media framing versus news media framing of an activism failure crisis

If we compare our findings to the five overall frames identified by Semetko and Valkenburg (2000) used by news media when they frame critical issues, situations, and crises, our findings show that three of these frames are also found in this study:

- *A morality frame*: DBU/DFB being framed as cowards, having no guts, being scared, weak, hypocritical, and non-credible are all about morality. DBU and DFB lack the morals to stand up for human rights and diversity, and to live up to their promises, messages, and values.
- *A conflict frame*: between DBU/DFB and FIFA, as they are not agreeing on how to deal with the lack of human rights and diversity in Qatar. FIFA is referring to the rule of not mixing sports and politics against DBU/DFB wanting to support diversity in public, during the games.
- *A responsibility frame*: about who is to blame and being responsible for the matter. Is it DBU/DFB or FIFA? Is DBU/DFB a victim of FIFA's sanctions, did they cause this matter themselves and do they simply not want to take the responsibility for this backlash and activism failure? Or is FIFA the bad guy, using its power of sanctioning to oppress the will of associations?

To find these three types of frames during the *One Love* armband controversy is perhaps not that surprising when we look at the crisis type: activism failure. Not living up to the promises in relation to the protesting action for human rights and diversity in Qatar, violates expectations of stakeholders in relation to values and norms. Hence, as human rights and diversity are also about ethics, morals, and norms, it would be expected for the news media to debate this theme. Second, one of the important news criteria, often seen in the media, is to take or at least include the perspective of both sides in a conflict. Thus, the activation of a conflict frame would be expected too. Finally, as it is about a crisis, people want explanations not only on why such a situation occurred, but also on who or what is to blame, as well as on how to prevent this from happening again. Thus, a responsibility frame is also important when reporting on crises. This is confirmed by Villeneuve and Aquilina (2016) who state that "The question of attributing fault and root causes is relatively central in the development of a narrative. This could, in the long run, determine the actions that are deemed appropriate or not, to tackle the situation" (p. 198).

Finally, the study also confirms the use of the *action, not the issue frame* by news media found in Doehler's study (2023) of Kaepernick's activism. In our study of activism failure, focus is mainly on the action, abandoning the wearing of the armband, rather than on the issue itself of human rights and diversity in Qatar. This is surprising, as we could expect a certain focus on what the failure of the protest would mean to the activism cause itself, and on the possibility of influencing the debate on human rights and diversity in Qatar. On the other hand, we may claim that getting so much media coverage on the activism failure, indirectly also gave a lot of attention to the cause, and in this way, the football associations got their message out to the public anyway.

Conclusion, implications, and future research

The overall goal of this chapter was to investigate the reactions and framing of Danish and German national media in relation to the *One Love* armband activism failure crisis of DBU and DFB at the onset of the crisis, November 21–23, 2022, and to discuss the nature and variations of news media's "backlash framing" of the event. As it appears from the above, a lot of interesting findings have given us first insights into a crisis of this nature: activism failure. We did identify similarities to news media framing during crisis and to sports activism crisis in general, such as the appearance of morality frames, conflict frames, and responsibility frames. However, the findings also show how going back on a socio-political stance creates huge and negative reactions although or perhaps especially because an organization originally had taken a stance approved by the public for showing socio-political responsibility on human rights, even if you are part of sports, where separating sports and politics for long has been the norm. Showing the need for changes also in sports were applauded, but the organizations did not dare to walk the talk.

For theory, our study has added valuable first insights into a new crisis type of activism failure, and to the risk of not living up to social responsibilities when going back on a socio-political stance. Furthermore, the study attributes new perspectives to rhetorical arena theory as it sheds light on the specific framing of news media that are very influential voices in the rhetorical arena of such a backlash crisis.

For practitioners these findings imply that they have to not only be aware of the strong negative reactions when trying to do good turns bad, but they also have to anticipate the reactions, feelings, and disappointments of their fans and people in general. It is not possible to go back, once you have taken a socio-political stance perceived to be ethically correct.

However, our study only followed the reactions and framing of the news media at the onset of the crisis. It would be relevant to follow the media over a longer period, as well as to look into reactions of other kind of voices, such as activist groups, politicians, and fans. Did this controversy in fact really damage the reputation of DBU, DFB, or FIFA for that matter? Furthermore, it would be interesting to conduct other studies of activism failure, because we are definitely going to see more protest failures in the years to come, with the complicated crisis landscape of the world today.

Appendix 1: Danish news media framing of DBU and FIFA

Article	Frame	Example
Politiken, 21.11-22 *The matter of the rainbow-coloured armband has created a mixture of politics and the game on the field, which has not been seen in modern World Cup history*(P-1)	**Uncertainty frame** ➔ FIFA as playing by their own rules	—"But ahead of Denmark's first match at the World Cup in Qatar FIFA's handling of the anti-discrimination campaign with that exact name [i.e., the *One Love* campaign] is creating a mix of politics and the game on the field, which has not been seen in modern finals history." —"Denmark and the six other nations are also surprised, to say the least, that they could wear the One Love captain's armbands back in September under the auspices of UEFA for the matches in Nations League and that FIFA, back then, did not react. The world federation has known about the wish to wear the One Love captain's armband for months."
Politiken, 21/11-22 *Denmark can no longer wait to criticise FIFA and the arrow points at one man* (P-2)	**Responsibility frame** ➔ Jesper Møller as needing to take action	—"Even after the World Cup has started the international football association (FIFA) with Gianni Infantino in the lead is tumbling around like an elephant running wild in the display window and destroying what, with another hostnation, could have been a beautiful presentation of the global team sport's qualities." —"DBU's chairman, Jesper Møller, has hidden in a hole for so long that it is embarrassing. Now he must resurface and manage the binding mandate he has received by the Danish national sport's large support base."

(*Continued*)

(Continued)

Article	Frame	Example
Politiken, 21/11-22 *Denmark will not be playing with the One Love captain's armband at the World Cup anyways* (P-3)	**Fear frame** ➔ DBU as getting cold feet	—"For fear of sporting sanctions, the national football team will not be wearing the rainbow-coloured captain's armband, which is carried to show the wearer's dissociation with discrimination."
JyllandsPosten, 21/11-22 *Is a little piece of fabric a big limitation of the freedom of speech?* (JP-1)	**Uncertainty frame** ➔ FIFA as a joker	— "»It is completely unheard of to be threatened with sporting sanctions for wearing an armband, which symbolises something that falls in line with FIFA's own policies« he says."
Berlingske, 22/11-22 *Diary from Qatar: Was that a rainbow I just saw?*(BE-1)	**Divergence frame** ➔ The World Cup as being full of contrasts	—"You are allowed to kneel against racism. But an armband supporting homosexuality is forbidden [...]" —"In spite of previous assurances of the opposite spectators and football players with »rainbow-support« of homosexuals' rights are facing problems." —"The threat that it will trigger a warning to the team captain before the match begins has caused the national football associations to give in."
Berlingske, 22/11-22 *Berlingske believes: DBU and the players have lost in credibility* (BE-2)	**Cowardice frame** ➔ DBU as being conflict-averse	—"When it counted, the will to take a stand was little." —"But again FIFA said no and again DBU complied." —"Before the World Cup in Qatar both players and DBU had heralded activist markings but these were cancelled after opposition from the international football association (FIFA)."

(*Continued*)

(Continued)

Article	Frame	Example
Ekstra Bladet, 21/11-22 *Massive turnaround: Denmark ditches 'One Love'-armband* (EB-1)	**Cowardice frame** ➔ DBU as being scared	—"Could risk a yellow card."
Ekstra Bladet, 22/11-22 *Cowards* (EB-2)	**Cowardice frame** ➔ DBU as spineless	—"Frightened by FIFA they do not dare to dress captain Simon Kjær the 'One Love'-armband, which signals resistance against homophobia and racism."
TV2, 21/11-22 *Denmark abandons much debated armband* (TV2-1)	**Dominance frame** ➔ FIFA as the dictator	—"With that being said we are extremely disappointed in FIFA in this case. They have known about our stance for a long time. We stand for inclusion just like FIFA says they stand for inclusion. I cannot see that our messages conflict with the messages that FIFA wishes to communicate." —"FIFA dictating captain's armbands."
TV2, 21/11-22 *Criticism hails on DBU: -Beyond embarrassing* (TV2-2)	**Cowardice frame** ➔ DBU as not standing up to their bully	—"CEO of DBU, Jakob Jensen, says to TV2 that the protest would have too great a sporting impact."
TV2, 22/11-22 *Iranian players applauded for protest, while Denmark backs down on armbands* (TV2-3)	**Contrast frame** ➔ Iran as the ideal Denmark should be following	—"The Iranian players risk harsh punishments to show their support in public to the protesters in the home country." —"But instead the English captain, Harry Kane, ran onto the field wearing a FIFA-approved armband with the words 'no discrimination'." —"For the Iranian players, there is likely a lot more at stake by publicly challenging the Iranian regime than a yellow card."

Appendix 2: Compilation of subthemes in Danish news media

SUBTHEMES	
Number	**Name**
News media: *Politiken*	
P-1	
1	FIFA as opposing sporting norms
2	Other actors as intending to oppose FIFA
3	FIFA as resisting change
4	Other actors as respecting FIFA
5	FIFA as having their own agenda
6	DBU as needing to take action
7	Denmark as challenging FIFA
P-2	
1	FIFA as the culprit
2	Some participants as being unfairly held accountable
3	Jesper Møller as neglecting his responsibility
P-3	
1	The change of heart as being the result of fear
News media: *Jyllands-Posten*	
JP-1	
1	Discontentment with FIFA
2	Unwillingness to risk protesting
3	FIFA as losing grip
News media: *Berlingske*	
BE-1	
1	FIFA & Qatar as self-contradictory
2	The *One Love* nations as being weak-willed
3	Iranians as strong-willed
4	Protesting as having serious consequences for Iranians
5	Qatar opposing protests
6	FIFA & Qatar as opposing rainbow support
7	Kneeling as an approved

(*Continued*)

(Continued)

SUBTHEMES	
Number	**Name**
BE-2	
1	DBU and the national team as lacking will
2	The players as being blamefree
3	DBU as compliant
4	FIFA as being a bully
5	Change as being a necessity
6	DBU as feeling criticised
News media: *Ekstra Bladet*	
EB-1	
1	DBU as changing their position
2	DBU's change of position as being a joint decision
3	The decision being a result of feeling threatened
EB-2	
1	Wrong-doing taking place
1a	DBU as being gutless
1b	FIFA as bribable
1c	The players as being weak
1d	DBU as hypocrites
2	Qatar as dictating the progress of events
3	Iran as being a role model
News media: *TV2*	
TV2-1	
1	DBU as dissatisfied and uncomprehending
2	Risk of punishment causing the abandonment of the armband
3	FIFA as having their own agenda
4	FIFA as superior
TV2-2	
1	FIFA as the aggressor
2	DBU & the national team as giving up

(*Continued*)

(Continued)

SUBTHEMES	
Number	Name
3	FIFA as having double standards
4	FIFA as directed by Qatar
5	DBU & the national team as yielding
6	DBU as not wanting to risk the consequences of protesting
7	DBU & the national team as being spineless
TV2-3	
1	Iranian players as being willing to take risks
2	Iranian players as being courageous
3	Denmark and other nations as being yielding
4	Iran as the hero, the other nations as cowards

Appendix 3: German news media framing of DFB and FIFA

Article	Frame	Example
BILD, 21/11.2022 *Comment on the armband scandal at the World Cup "You are nothing but COWARDS!"* (BI-1)	**Cowardice Frame** → DFB as cowards buckling out of fear	"You are nothing but COWARDS!"
BILD, 21/11.2022 *Comment from Head of Sport Matthias Brügelmann—We're ashamed of you!* (BI-2)	**Embarrassment Frame** → DFB as causing embarrassment and shame	"It's the day we're ashamed of the DFB & national team, even though the first German match hasn't even taken place yet."
BILD, 22/11.2022 *Dispute over "One Love" bandage—ZDF expert talks himself into a rage!* (BI-3)	**Cowardice vs. Dominance Frame** → DFB as coward vs. FIFA as the powerful	"Germany is also buckling before FIFA, forgoing the 'One Love' armband at the World Cup in Qatar as a sign AGAINST discrimination and FOR diversity." Versus: "It's just that FIFA gets to decide. You are powerless."

(*Continued*)

(Continued)

Article	Frame	Example
SZ, 23/11.2022 *Germany is world champion... in justification* (SZ-1)	**Hypocrite Frame** ➔ DFB as hypocrite with their justification	"An intelligent person can morally justify anything. [...] Until in the end you can hardly feel the boundary between 'well' and 'well justified'. And then not only expect absolution, but preferably also recognition."
SZ, 23/11.2022 *The martyr poses of the national team players are causing damage* (SZ-2)	**Non-Credibility Frame** ➔ DFB as losing credibility	"DFB and the players have now severely damaged their credibility with regard to discrimination and non-violence."
FAZ, 22/11.2022 *A total damage. The FIFA threat turns the Europeans' protest into a weakness attack (FAZ-1)*	**Naivety Frame** ➔ DFB as being too naïve and therefore also sharing responsibility	"It may also have been a bit naive of the associations to push ahead with their agenda to the end without the appropriate safe-guards, so they share responsibility for the situation despite all their good intentions."
FAZ, 23/11.2022 *Germany without courage and strengths (FAZ-2)*	**Weakness Frame** ➔ DFB as weak and helpless	"Germany without courage and strengths."
Der Spiegel (online), 21/11.2022 "One Love" captain's armband at the World Cup—Infantino and the seven dwarves (Spo-1)	**Pathetic Frame** ➔ DFB as being pathetic in handling the conflict	"This end to the conflict is regrettable and a little pathetic. In fact, it is unbelievable."
Der Spiegel (online), 23/11.2022 Ban on the one-love captain's armband—The president's failing (Spo-2)	**Cowardice Frame** ➔ DFB as backtracker	"An association that ducks away when things get serious."

Appendix 4: Compilation of subthemes in German news media

SUBTHEMES	
Number	Name
BI-1	
1	DFB as sending an empty message
2	*One Love* nations as buckling out of fear
3	DFB as cowards
4	DFB as engaging in hypocrite actions for diversity
5	US as a good example
BI-2	
1	DFB as embarrassing
2	DFB as having lost its credibility
3	DFB as too cowardly to wear the bandage
4	FIFA as behaving scandalous
5	DFB as missing the right reaction
6	DFB as making a poor showing
BI-3	
1	DFB as cowards
2	FIFA as the powerful
3	FIFA as the loser of the debate
SZ-1	
1	Germany as world champions in justifying
2	DFB as cowards and being stupid with their insecure back and forth
3	DFB as hypocrite with their justification
4	DFB as a good example for misbehavior
SZ-2	
1	DFB as presenting weak reasons for following FIFA
2	DFB as sending an empty message
3	Germany as collectively whining
4	DFB as harmfully rejecting responsibility
5	DFB as losing credibility
6	DFB as damaging their existence as a role model

(*Continued*)

(Continued)

SUBTHEMES	
Number	**Name**
FAZ-1	
1	Europeans as cowards before FIFA's threat
2	DFB as being too naïve and therefore also sharing responsibility
3	FIFA as being the main responsible
FAZ-2	
1	DFB as weak and helpless
2	DFB as coward
3	DFB as coward (with the photo)
4	Germany as responsible for their own situation
5	Germany as overwhelmed and disappointing with the Alibi-photo
SPo-1	
1	DFB as being too convenient to take a stance
2	Nations as being laughable followers of FIFA's rules
3	DFB as being pathetic
SPo-2	
1	DFB as backtracker
2	DFB as coward
3	DFB as naïve regarding FIFA's position

References

An, S.-K., & Gower, K. K. (2009). How do the news media frame crises? A content analysis of crisis news coverage. *Public Relations Review*, *35*, 107–112.

AWA (2023). Printtitel mit der größten Reichweite in Deutschland im Jahr 2023. Retrieved November 8, 2023 https://de.statista.com/statistik/daten/studie/261537/umfrage/reichweite-von-zeitschriften-in-deutschland/

Benoit, W. (2015). *Accounts, Excuses and Apologies: Image repair theory and research*. New York: State University of New York Press, 1st ed., 1995.

Boykoff, J., & Carrington, B. (2020). Sporting dissent: Colin Kaepernick, NFL activism, and media framing contests. *International Review for the Sociology of Sport*, *55*(7), 829–849.

Brown, N. A., Brown, K. A., & Billings, A. C. (2015). "May No Act of Ours Bring Shame": Fan-Enacted Crisis Communication Surrounding the Penn State Sex Abuse Scandal. *Communication & Sport*, *3*(3), 288–311.

Bryman, A. (2016). *Social Research Methods* (5th ed.). Oxford, UK: Oxford University Press.

Cashmore, E., Dixon, K., & Cleland, J. (2023). The new politics of sport. *Sport in Society*, 1–10.

Chan, J. M., & Lee, C-C. (1984). The journalistic paradigm on civil protests: A case study of Hong Kong. In A. Arno & W. Dissanayake (Eds.). *The News Media in National and International Conflict* (pp. 183–202). Boulder: Westview.

Coakley, J. (2015). Assessing the sociology of sport: On cultural sensibilities and the great sport myth. *International Review for the Sociology of Sport*, *50*(4-5), 402–406.

Cooky, C., & Antunovic, D. (2020). "This Isn't Just About US": Articulations of Feminism in Media Narratives of Athlete Activism. *Communication & Sport*, *8*(4-5), 692–711.

Coombs, D. S., & Cassilo, D. (2017). Athletes and/or Activists: LeBron James and Black Lives Matter. *Journal of Sport and Social Issues*, *41*(5), 425–444.

Coombs, D. S., Lambert, C. A., Cassilo, D., & Humphries, Z. (2020). Flag on the Play: Colin Kaepernick and the Protest Paradigm. *Howard Journal of Communications*, *31*(4), 317–336.

Coombs, W.T. (2022). *Ongoing crisis communication. Planning, Managing, and Responding*. LA: SAGE. 1st ed. 1999.

Coombs, W. T., & Harker, J. L. (2022). Crisis Communication and Reputation Management in Sports. In T. W. Coombs, & J. L. Harker, *Strategic Sport Communication: Traditional and Transmedia Strategies for a Global Sports Market* (pp. 150–164). New York: Routledge.

Cooper, J. N., Macaulay, C., & Rodriguez, S. H. (2019). Race and resistance: A typology of African American sport activism. *International Review for the Sociology of Sport*, *54*(2), 151–181. https://doi.org/10.1177/1012690217718170

Cornelissen, J. (2020). *Corporate Communication. A Guide to Theory & Practice* (5th ed.). London, United Kingdom: SAGE.

Danmarks Statistik. (2023). *Forbrug af nyhedsmedier (kvartal) efter alder og køn, medie og tid*. https://www.statistikbanken.dk/KVUNYH03

Daymon, C., & Holloway, I. (2011). *Qualitative Research Methods in Public Relations and Marketing Communications* (2nd ed.). Abingdon, Oxon, UK: Routledge.

DBU (2022, November 21). DBU dropper One Love-anførerbind [DBU abandons captain's One Love armband], *DBU*. https://www.dbu.dk/nyheder/2022/november/dbu-dropper-one-love-anfoererbind

DBU. (2023a). *1961-1980*. Retrieved May 29, 2023: https://www.dbu.dk/om-dbu/dbu-s-historie/1961-1980/

DBU. (2023b). *1889-1920*. Retrieved May 29, 2023: https://www.dbu.dk/om-dbu/dbu-s-historie/1889-1920/

DBU. (2023c). *Ansatte*. Retrieved May 29, 2023: https://www.dbu.dk/om-dbu/ansatte/

Denham, B. E. (2019). Coverage of the Russian Doping Scandal in the New York Times: Intramedia and Intermedia Attribute Agenda-Setting Effects. *Communication & Sport*, 7(3), 337–360. https://doi.org/10.1177/2167479518765188

DFB (2020, January 28). *Vor 120 Jahren: Der DFB wird gegründet*. DFB. https://www.dfb.de/news/detail/vor-120-jahren-der-dfb-wird-gegruendet-212342/

DFB (2022a, November 22). *Hansi Flick: "The national team stands for diversity"* DFB. https://www.dfb.de/news/detail/hansi-flick-the-national-team-stands-for-diversity-246529/

DFB (2022b, November 23). *Voice silenced - Germany players make a statement.* DFB. https://www.dfb.de/news/detail/voice-silenced-germany-players-make-a-statement-246565/

DFB (2023). *DFB-Mitgliederstatistik 2022/2023.* Retrieved December 13, 2023, from https://www.dfb.de/verbandsstruktur/mitglieder/aktuelle-statistik/

Doehler, S. (2023). Taking the star-spangled knee: the media framing of Colin Kaepernick. *Sport in Society*, *26*(1), 45–66. https://doi.org/10.1080/17430437.2021.1970138

DR (2022). *Medieudviklingen 2022.* DR.

Entman, R. M. (1993). Framing: Toward Clarification of a Fractured Paradigm. *Journal of Communication*, *43*(4), 51–58.

Entman, R. M. (2007). Framing Bias: Media in the Distribution on Power. *Journal of Communication*, *57*(1), 163–173. https://doi.org/10.1111/j.1460-2466.2006.00336.x

Esposito, C. (2016). A red card for FIFA: Corruption and scandal in the world's foremost sports association. *Rich. J. Global L. & Bus.*, *16*, 45.

FIFA (2020). Football in 2020 vision. *FIFA*. Retrieved May 29, 2023, from FIFA: https://publications.fifa.com/en/annual-report-2020/the-global-game/the-vision-2020-2023/

FAZ (2022, November 23). *Germany without courage and strengths.* Retrieved from https://www.faz.net/aktuell/sport/fussball-wm/deutsches-team/fussball-wm-deutschland-ohne-mut-und-kraft-beim-auftakt-gegen-japan-18482625.html

Fly, E., Bruun, J. L., & Kokholm, K. (2022). *The news media's framing of ECCO in an unprecedented situation.* Unpublished exam project, MSc in Strategic Communication Aarhus: Aarhus School of Business and Social Sciences, Aarhus University

Frandsen, F., & Johansen, W. (2010). Crisis communication, complexity and the cartoon affair: a case study. In W.T. Coombs & S.J. Holladay (Eds.). *The Handbook of Crisis Communication* (pp. 425–448). Malden, MA: Wiley Blackwell.

Frandsen, F., & Johansen, W. (2017). *Organizational Crisis Communication.* London: SAGE.

Frandsen, F. & Johansen, W. (2020). Arenas and voices in organizational crisis communication. In F. Frandsen & W. Johansen (Eds.). *Crisis communication. Handbooks of Communication Science* (pp. 195–211). Berlin: Walter de Gruyter

Frandsen, F. & Johansen, W. (2023). Rhetorical Arena Teory: Revisited and Expanded. In W. Timothy Coombs & S. J. Holladay (Eds.). *The Handbook of Crisis Communication* (2nd ed., pp. 169–182). Hoboken: Wiley Blackwell

Frederick, E., & Pegoraro, A. (2018). Scandal in College Basketball: A Case Study of Image Repair via Facebook. *International Journal of Sport Communication*, *11*, 414–429. https://doi.org/10.1123/ijsc.2018-0076

Fredriksson, M., & Pallas, J. (2018). Media Relations. In R. L. Heath, & W. Johansen (Eds.). *The International Encyclopedia of Strategic Communication* (pp. 916–927). Hoboken: John Wiley & Sons.

Freilich (2023, June 14). Deutsche Zeitungen und Zeitschriften: Ihre politische Ausrichtung. Retrieved November 8, 2023. https://www.freilich-magazin.com/kultur/deutsche-zeitungen-und-zeitschriften-ihre-politische-ausrichtung

Goos, H. (2002, November 21). "One Love"-Kapitänsbinde bei der WM—Infantino und die sieben Zwerge, ["One Love" captain's armband at the World Cup - Infantino and the seven dwarves.] *Der Spiegel online.* https://www.spiegel.de/sport/fussball/wm-2022-streit-um-one-love-binde-gianni-infantino-und-die-sieben-zwerge-kommentar-a-60b8e111-5d9a-4b46-9c6a-c899b47d03bc (SPo-1).

Hallahan, K. (1999). Seven Models of Framing: implications for Public Relations. *Journal of Public Relations Research*, *11*(3), 205–242. https://doi.org/10.1207/s1532754xjprr1103_02

Hallahan, K. (2013). Framing Theory. In R. L. Heath (Ed.). *Encyclopedia of Public Relations* (pp. 340–343). Thousand Oaks: SAGE Publications, Inc.

Hartman, D. (2023). Sport, Social Movements, and Athlete Activism. In L. A. Wenner (Ed.). *The Oxford Handbook of Sport and Society* (pp. 571–594). New York: Oxford University Press.

Holm, A. B. (2018). Social Constructivism. In A. B. Holm (Ed.). *Philosophy of Science* (2nd ed., pp. 141–162). Samfundslitteratur.

Hughes, R. L., Giles, M. S., Haywood, J., & Snipes, J. T. (2017). Media perceptions and constructions of race and sports: reflections on the duke lacrosse scandal. *Journal for the Study of Sports and Athletes in Education*, *11*(3), 161–174. https://doi.org/10.1080/19357397.2017.1343176

Hughes, S., & Shank, M. (2005). Defining Scandal in Sports: Media and Corporate Sponsor Perspectives. *Sport Marketing Quarterly*, *14*(4), 207–216.

Jensen, C. T. (2022). *Fodbold i Danmark, ca. 1880-* [Football in Denmark, approx. 1880-] Retrieved May 29th, 2023, from *Danmarkshistorien*: https://danmarkshistorien.dk/vis/materiale/fodbold-i-danmark-ca-188

Kahn, D. (2022, December 18). Not just a game: Why sports and politics cannot be separated. *The Business Standard*, Retrieved March 3, 2023: https://www.tbsnews.net/features/panorama/not-just-game-why-sports-and-politics-cannot-be-separated-553706

Kantar Gallup. (2022). *Index Danmark/Gallup Helår 2022*. KANTAR Gallup.

Kaufman, P. (2008). Boos, Bans, and Other Backlash: The Consequences of Being an Activist Athlete. *Humanity & Society*, *32*, 215–237. https://doi.org/10.1177/016059760803200302

Kaufman, P., & Wolff, E. A. (2010). Playing and Protesting: Sport as a Vehicle for Social Change. *Journal of Sport and Social Issues*, *34*(2), 154–175. https://doi.org/10.1177/0193723509360218

Kristensen, T. M. (2022, November 22). Danmark havde vundet—hvis man da bare havde turdet vælge det rigtige anførerbind. *Jyllands-Posten*. https://jyllands-posten.dk/debat/kommentar/ECE14614184/danmark-havde-vundet-hvis-man-da-bare-havde-turdet-vaelge-det-rigtige-anfoererbind/

Lee, S., & Oh, T. (2023). The role of trust in sports organization crisis communication: the case of the Houston Astros' sign-stealing scandal. *International Journal of Sports*, *24*(1), 90–107. https://doi.org/10.1108/IJSMS-12-2021-0231

Leicher, D. (2022, November 22). Angst vor einer Strafe, die sie nicht kennen! Der Rausred-Auftritt der DFB-Bosse. *BILD*. https://m.bild.de/sport/fussball/nationalmannschaft/wm-2022-der-auftritt-der-dfb-bosse-angst-vor-einer-strafe-die-sie-nicht-kennen-82012798.bildMobile.html?t_ref=https%3A%2F%2Fwww.bild.de%2Fsport%2Ffussball%2Fnationalmannschaft%2Fwm-2022-der-auftritt-der-dfb-bosse-angst-vor-einer-strafe-die-sie-nicht-kennen-82012798.bild.html

Leppard, T. R. (2022). Athlete activism and the role of personal and professional positionality: The case of Naomi Osaka. *International Review for the Sociology of Sport*, *57*(8), 1214–1233. https://doi.org/10.1177/10126902211073907

Levy, M. (2023, December 5). *FIFA*. *Britannica*. https://www.britannica.com/topic/Federation-Internationale-de-Football-Association

Lindhardt, K. (2023, January 30). TV 2 topper listen over udgivere med flest digitale brugere. *Media Watch*. https://mediawatch.dk/Medienyt/Web/article14888029.ece

Lånekassen. (2023). *Danske aviser*. Retrieved May 9, 2023, from *Lånekassen*: https://www.laanekassen.dk/abonnement/avis/
Maressa, J. E. (2015, October 29). Det danske mediebillede. *Jyllands-Posten*. https://jyllands-posten.dk/skole/detfrieord/ECE8166808/det-danske-mediebillede1/
Meng, J., & Pan, P.-L. (2013). Revisiting Image-Restoration Strategies: An Integrated Case Study of Three Athlete Sex Scandals in Sports News. *International Journal of Sport Communication*, 6, 87–100. https://doi.org/10.1123/ijsc.6.1.87
Olsson, E.-K., & Ihlen, Ø. (2018). Framing. In R. L. Heath, & W. Johansen (Eds.) *The International Encyclopedia of Strategic Communication*. Hoboken: John Wiley & Sons. https://onlinelibrary.wiley.com/doi/10.1002/9781119010722.iesc0076
Pan, Z., & Kosicki, G. M. (1993). Framing Analysis: An approach to News Discourse. *Political Communication*, *10*, 55–75. https://doi.org/10.1080/10584609.1993.9962963
Park, B., Park, S., & Billings, A. C. (2020). Separating Perceptions of Kaepernick From Perceptions of His Protest: An Analysis of Athlete Activism, Endorsed Brand, and Media Effects. *Communication & Sport*, *8*(4-5), 629–650. https://doi.org/10.1177/2167479519894691
Peña, V. (2021). From Protest to Movement: A Longitudinal Content Analysis of ESPN's Colin Kaepernick Coverage. *The International Journal of Sport and Society*, *12*(1), 191–204. https://doi.org/10.1080/16184742.2023.2287471
Presley R. G., Shreffler M. B., Hancock M. G. & Schmidt S. H. (2016). *Issues & ethics in sport: A practical guide for sport managers*. Dubuque, IA: Kendall Hunt.
Reese, S. D., Gandy Jr, O. H., & Grant, A. E. (Eds.). (2001). *Framing public life: Perspectives on media and our understanding of the social world*. Routledge.
Richards, J.R., Wilson, C., Boyle, K., & Mower, J. (2017). A knockout to the NFL's reputation?: A case study of the NFL's crisis communications strategies in response to the Ray Rice scandal. *Public Relations Review*, *43*, 615–623. https://doi.org/10.1016/j.pubrev.2017.02.015 Get rights and content
Rowe, D., & Palmer, C. (2023). Sport, Scandal, and Social Morality. In L. A. Wenner, *The Oxford Handbook of Sport and Society* (pp. 550–570). New York: Oxford University Press.
Scheufele, D. A. (1999). Framing as a Theory of Media Effects. *Journal of Communication*, *49*(1), 103–122. https://doi.org/10.1111/j.1460-2466.1999.tb02784.x
Schuck, R. I. (2020). What We Aren't When We Are Penn State: Dissociation Strategies in the Penn State Sexual Abuse Scandal. *Journal of Global Sport Management*, *5*(2), 184–201. https://doi.org/10.1080/24704067.2019.1576145
Semetko, H. A., & Valkenburg, P. M. (2000). Framing European Politics: A Content Analysis of Press and Television News. *Journal of Communication*, 93–109. https://doi.org/10.1111/j.1460-2466.2000.tb02843.x
Shaw, R. (2001). *The activist's handbook*. University of California Press.
Smith, L. R. (2019). Stand Up, Show Respect: Athlete Activism, Nationalistic Attitudes, and Emotional Response. *International Journal of Communication*, *13*, 2376–2397.
Sportschau (2022, December 13). DFB-Präsident gesteht Fehler bei "One Love"-Binde ein [DFB president admits mistake around the One Love armband]. *Sportschau*. https://www.sportschau.de/fussball/fifa-wm-2022/dfb-praesident-neuendorf-gesteht-fehler-ein-100.html

Statista (2023). *Reichweite der Top-10-Nachrichtenseiten in Deutschland im März 2023*. Retrieved November 8, 2023, from https://de.statista.com/statistik/daten/studie/165258/umfrage/reichweite-der-meistbesuchten-nachrichtenwebsites/

Stie, H.-H. B., & Mørk, M. B. (2022, November 21). Kritikken hagler ned over DBU: - Pinligt ud over alle grænser [Criticism hails on DBU: -Beyond embarrassing.] *TV2*. https://sport.tv2.dk/fodbold/2022-11-21-kritikken-hagler-ned-over-dbu-pinligt-ud-over-alle-graenser (TV2-2).

Syed, A. (2022, November 21). The 'One Love' LGBTQ Rights Armband Is Causing a Stir at the Qatar World Cup. *Time*. https://time.com/6235503/one-love-armband-qatar-world-cup

SZ (2022a, November 22). "One-Love"-Eklat: Bierhoff beklagt "Drucksituation". *SZ*. https://www.sueddeutsche.de/sport/fussball-one-love-eklat-bierhoff-beklagt-drucksituation-dpa.urn-newsml-dpa-com-20090101-221122-99-612479

SZ (2022b, November 23). "*One-Love: Bierhoff wirbt um Verständnis für WM-Spieler*". *SZ*. https://www.sueddeutsche.de/sport/fussball-one-love-bierhoff-wirbt-um-verstaendnis-fuer-wm-spieler-dpa.urn-newsml-dpa-com-20090101-221123-99-630067

SZ (2022c, November 21). DFB kritisiert "One Love"-Verbot der Fifa. *SZ*. https://www.sueddeutsche.de/sport/fussball-wm-kapitaene-binde-one-love-fifa-1.5699875

SZ (2022d, November 23). Hand vor den Mund: DFB-Auswahl mit Zeichen gegen FIFA. *SZ*. https://www.sueddeutsche.de/sport/fussball-hand-vor-den-mund-dfb-auswahl-mit-zeichen-gegen-fifa-dpa.urn-newsml-dpa-com-20090101-221123-99-632884

Tz (2022, November 4). DFB: Gründung, Geschichte, Erfolge, Mitglieder—alle Infos zum Deutschen Fußball-Bund. *Tz*. https://www.tz.de/sport/fussball/dfb-geschichte-erfolge-mitglieder-praesident-infos-90033822.html#id-Comments

US Soccer (2023). *FIFA*. Retrieved May 29, 2023, from US Soccer: https://www.ussoccer.com/history/organizational-structure/fifa

Villeneuve, J.-P., & Aquilina, D. (2016). Who's fault is it? An analysis of the press coverage of football betting scandals in France and the United Kingdom. *Sport in Society*, *19*(2), 187–200. https://doi.org/10.1080/17430437.2015.1067772

Williams, A. L. (2022). The Heritage Strikes Back: Athlete Activism, Black Lives Matter, and the Iconic Fifth Wave of Activism in the (W)NBA Bubble. *Cultural Studies, Critical Methodologies*, 22(3), 266–275. https://doi.org/10.1177/15327086211049718

Yan, G., Pegoraro, A., & Watanabe, N. M. (2018). Student-Athletes' Organization of Activism at the University of Missouri: Resource Mobilization on Twitter. *Journal of Sport Management*, *32*, 24–37. https://doi.org/10.1123/jsm.2017-0031

Yin, R. K. (2018). *Case Study Research and Applications: Design and Methods*. Los Angeles: SAGE Publications, Inc.

6 Lessons Learned from the Early Days of the COVID-19 Pandemic

Communicating about Public Health Risks on Social Media

Elina R. Tachkova and Grace Ellen Brannon

The COVID-19 pandemic of 2020 has been an unprecedented health crisis. As of January 2024, since the start of the pandemic globally there have been more than 700 million confirmed cases and over 7 million deaths (WHO, 2024). This public health crisis developed quickly and unexpectedly, shutting down the world in a matter of weeks. The virus posed such a serious threat because of the way it secretly attacks the body; in the early stages of an infection, the body is unable to detect it (Yanes-Lane et al., 2020). It takes between 7 and 14 days until the virus reaches its peak and most people feel fine until they suddenly feel very sick. Unfortunately, by the time someone is diagnosed with COVID-19, they have most likely already spread the virus to others. The fact that the virus kept mutating into highly contagious variants additionally complicated the response to the pandemic (O'Dowd, 2021).

Because of its fast spread, COVID-19 created many challenges for public sector risk communicators. Successful risk communication efforts must be accurate and timely. Moreover, the goal of any risk communication message is to convince people that the threat is real and that they must act to reduce the likelihood of exposure to the risk (Mitchell & Beanlands, 2020). Effective risk communication should be persuasive enough for people to engage in the desired behavior and respond to the threat (ter Huurne & Gutteling, 2009).

COVID-19 put public health organizations to the test. The public risk communication sector is often overlooked. There is scarce research on how these organizations communicate to the public (Coombs, 2020). The United States is the country with most deaths. As of January 2024, approximately 1 million people have lost their lives due to COVID-19 (CDC, 2024) This chapter aims to investigate the communicative response to COVID-19 of various public sector organizations in the United States. Specifically, the purpose of our analysis is to understand how risk communication about health crises could be improved in the future.

DOI: 10.4324/9781032619187-7

The chapter starts with a literature review explaining the intersectionality of public health crises and presenting the research question. The next section explains the methodology adopted to approach the research question, namely content analysis. We then present the findings in a quantitative and qualitative manner. Finally, the chapter concludes with a discussion of the results and their theoretical and practical implications.

Public health crises: The intersection between health, risk, and crisis communication

Public health crises represent a unique intersection between the fields of health, risk, and crisis communication. This section will provide definitions of the three separate fields and will discuss their connectedness in the context of public health crises.

Health communication

Health communication encompasses communication related to health in a variety of contexts, including within families, between patients and their healthcare teams, through organizations' communications with the masses, and others. Topics can cover health and well-being, disease prevention, quality of life, and health promotion (Rimal & Lapinski, 2009). While previous pandemics show how important it is for health organizations to share quality and accurate information to the public (Edelman et al., 2020; Paek et al., 2008), COVID-19 is particularly unique given the wide variety of media sources people can use, such as social media and television, to get information about the virus. Health communication research is pertinent for studies involving risk communication (Abraham, 2011), especially given the inherent public health challenges from viruses like COVID-19 like misinformation and disinformation.

Misinformation is defined as information which is incorrect or false, while disinformation is conceptualized as information which is *deliberately* deceptive (Karlova & Fisher, 2013). At the early stages of the COVID-19 pandemic, very little information was known about the virus, for instance, where it originated from and how it transmits. This contributed to the spread of misinformation as we will demonstrate in our analysis. However, later stages of the pandemic were characterized by a strong presence of disinformation. For instance, there were false and dangerous statements that drinking bleach can cure coronavirus infections, conspiracy theories that the pandemic was caused by worlds' elites for reducing population growth and even claims that 5G installations would be spreading the virus (European Commission, 2024).

Risk communication emphasizes the social understanding of risk (Palenchar, 2005). The goal of risk communication is to reduce the likelihood of exposure to a risk for those prone to the threat, or risk bearers. Moreover, risk communication is an interactive process, which seeks to increase awareness of a risk and improve the response to that risk. Lastly, successful risk communication is rooted in understanding how people perceive risks (Heath et al., 2018). A risk communication effort will be successful if the information is personally relevant and people are provided with clear steps to control the risk (ter Huurne & Gutteling, 2009).

Extended parallel process model

The extended parallel process model (EPPM) is one of the predominant frameworks utilized in risk communication (Barnett et al., 2014; Witte, 1992). The model helps understand how people make sense of risks and threats and what factors influence their decision-making. The next section will briefly discuss the key points of the EPPM.

The model acknowledges that people process messages in different ways and, therefore, understanding risks and information about risks is subjective. The idea is that risk messages are fear appeals, which prompt people to adopt a desired behavior. In the EPPM, there are two main outcomes related to a risk message: fear control and danger control. When people decide to engage in fear control, they revert to managing their fear with the help of different psychological responses such as denial, avoidance, or message distortion. However, when people choose to engage in danger control, they adopt the desired behavior, and comply with the recommended actions. Therefore, the desired outcome of a risk message is to elicit danger control rather than fear control. In the context of COVID-19, danger control behaviors could be wearing a face mask properly, washing hands regularly, and practicing social distancing.

But what exactly determines people's responses? The EPPM proposes two sets of factors, namely threat appraisal and efficacy appraisal. Each of these are comprised of a set of sub-factors. The first step is for people to evaluate the threat (in other words, threat appraisal). In this stage a person will assess if he/she is vulnerable to the risk (susceptible) and if the threat is serious enough to require any action (severity). If people see a threat as irrelevant and not serious, they will dismiss the risk message. However, if the threat is perceived as relevant, people will engage in a second appraisal, namely whether the proposed response is effective in managing the threat or not (in other words, efficacy appraisal). Efficacy assessments of the desired response to a risk include plan and self-efficacy. Plan efficacy focuses on evaluating the effectiveness of the proposed course of action. In other words, will this help to eliminate the risk or not? Self-efficacy is whether people believe they have the skills and resources to execute the recommended plan. The idea of efficacy appraisal is that if people do not think a certain plan is effective or that they can implement it, they will not bother to follow it. We argue that analyzing risk communication messages through the lens of the EPPM will provide a better understanding of how people have made sense of risk communication messages and what factors guide their decision-making when choosing to engage in either danger or fear control.

Crisis communication

Public health crises such as the COVID-19 pandemic also create the need for effective crisis management. Crisis management is comprised of a set of factors designed to combat crises and reduce the damage of the crisis (Coombs, 2019). Crisis communication is the heart of crisis management and represents what should be said and done to manage the crisis. Any crisis communication effort should start with what is termed the ethical-base response (Coombs, 2019). An ethical-base response contains instructing and adjusting information (Sturges, 1994a). Instructing information tells people how to physically protect themselves from the threat. For instance, instructing information in the case of COVID-19 would be washing hands and wearing a face mask. Adjusting information aims to reduce people's psychological distress. Adjusting information explains what type of corrective action was taken to reduce the damage of the crisis and what is being done to make sure it will not repeat again. An example of corrective action related to COVID-19 would be identifying positive cases, isolating them, and tracing contact persons to be placed under quarantine. Instructing and adjusting information help people deal with a crisis by providing guidance and reducing stress and anxiety during a crisis.

Summary

The COVID-19 pandemic created unique challenges and demands for public sector organizations. This novel coronavirus proved to be exceptionally difficult to manage. This was partly not only due to its sudden development and rapid spread but also due to the uncertainty associated with it. Lack of trust in public leadership, particularly in polarized atmospheres (Paulik et al., 2020; Ranjit, Shin, First, & Houston, 2021), is another challenge. Moreover, the lack of truthful and credible information is a fundamental challenge to crisis communicators, especially related to misinformation and disinformation (Ratzan et al., 2020). Van der Meer and Jin (2020) conducted an experimental study to identify information strategies which can increase awareness and trigger people to act during infectious disease outbreaks. They found that government agencies and news media are more successful in improving people's beliefs than, for example, their social peers. This means that public health organizations are the go-to sources and have significant credibility and trustworthiness in the eye of the public. Local public health organizations are often overlooked as crisis communicators (Coombs, 2020), which in turn negatively affects the quality and efficacy of their risk communication efforts, particularly for communities that avoided urgent actions (Paulik et al., 2020).

This chapter expands on our understanding of risk communication in the public sector. The EPPM is a useful framework for applying to risk messages because it helps explain how people make sense of risk messages and proposes ways to enhance their perceived susceptibility to the risk. In the context of our study, we were interested in examining what kind of information has been given to the public in the early stages of the COVID-19 pandemic in hopes to better understand why people did not see the threat as serious. Specifically, we examined what types of frames have been utilized by local public health organizations across the United States when communicating the risk of COVID-19.

Studying unique and challenging crisis cases like this one is a way of learning about crisis management and risk communication while simultaneously providing information for designing health interventions. Specifically, there is a need to understand how uncertainty is communicated to the public to be able to study how risk is in turn understood (Brown, 2020). Although COVID-19 is unique because of the plethora of misinformation and disinformation which surrounded the pandemic. Additionally, the threat of pandemics remains. We are likely to experience more pandemics in the future and such outbreaks will require similar risk and crisis communication skills (Coombs, 2020). Therefore, health organizations on every level will have to be ready for such challenging situations.

Method

The study employed inductive content analysis (van Gorp, 2009) to determine what frames have been used by public health authorities in the United States to communicate about the threat of COVID-19. For the purposes of this research, we were interested in what types of frames, both generic and issues-specific, have been utilized to communicate about the health risks of the virus. The study employed a combination of quantitative and qualitative content analysis. The quantitative analysis allows us to study the frequency of the generic frames used in the public health messages and the qualitative analysis provides a deeper and more meaningful understanding of the COVID-19 issues-specific frames.

Table 6.1 Counties selected for inclusion in the study

State	*County*	*Population*
California	Los Angeles County	10,081,570
	San Diego County	3,316,073
	Orange County	3,168,044
Texas	Harris County	4,646,630
	Dallas County	2,606,868
	Tarrant County	2,049,770
New York	Kings County	2,589,974
	Queens County	2,287,388
	New York County	1,631,993

Source: United States Census Bureau (2019).

We chose to focus on the three biggest states in the United States, namely New York, Texas, and California. Specifically, we selected the three largest counties in each state to have a representative sample across the country (Table 6.1).

The time frame for selection of the different messages was the first two weeks of March 2020. The pandemic developed rather quickly in the United States, the beginning of March 2020 was critical for the containment of COVID-19. The second part of March 2020 was characterized by nation-wide lockdowns and mandatory stay-at-home orders across the country. The selected time frame was, therefore, most appropriate because it captured the individual risk communication efforts of local public health authorities in the most accurate and timely manner.

The sample consisted of press releases and tweets issued by local public health departments in the nine counties. Twitter is becoming a more common and preferred channel for communication in public health and emergency management because it enables the public to receive credible and timely information (Dalrymple et al., 2016).

The unit of analysis was a paragraph or a single tweet. Following Van Gorp's (2009) definition of frames and frame packages, using a single paragraph as a unit of analysis allows to "unpack" the framing and reasoning devices employed.

The coding procedure began with an initial exploratory analysis where both authors coded a sample of press releases in order to measure intercoder reliability (Cohen's $\kappa = .89$). Intercoder reliability helps establish the objectivity and validity of the analysis. Poor intercoder reliability suggests unclear coding categories and problems with the coding methods of the individual coders (Lavrakas, 2008).

Moreover, the inductive approach, adopted for this study, involved analyzing the various press releases and tweets with an open view to attempt

Table 6.2 List of generic frames

Frame	*Description*
Information about new cases	Number of new cases reported in the county
Instructing information	Information about what actions the public should take to limit the spread of the coronavirus
Adjusting information	Information about what specific action the local authorities are taking to protect the public
Credible sources for additional information	Information about credible and trustworthy sources the public could use to keep informed

to identify the different types of frames used. To be able to have a more comprehensive overview of the data, we searched for both generic and issue-specific frames. A limitation to this approach is that it can detect many possible ways in which an issue can be framed as in the first stage of the coding process. In other words, as the coders are reading through the texts for the first time, they are working with very loose preconceptions of possible frames (Semetko & Valkenburg, 2000). To avoid such drawbacks, we started by conceptualizing the possible generic frames which are most relevant and likely to appear in risk communication messages concerning pandemics. Table 6.2 represents the generic frames we identified based on the initial exploratory analysis.

The *Information about new cases* frame refers to providing detailed information about the new cases which have been recorded in each county. At the very early stages of the pandemic, when it was still possible to identify and track every new case, the authorities provided a summary to the public stating the number of cases and where they have been tracked from.

Instructing and *adjusting* information are terms borrowed from crisis communication (Sturges, 1994b). Instructing information tells people what actions to take to physically protect themselves from a crisis. In the context of the COVID-19 pandemic, instructing information consists of instructions about how to wash your hands, wearing a face mask, and keeping social distance. Adjusting information aims to help people cope psychologically with the effects of a crisis and consists of corrective actions. An example of adjusting information provided by public health authorities would be the actions taken to limit the spread of the novel coronavirus such as tracing contact persons, limiting public gatherings, and imposing stay-at-home orders.

Finally, a *Credible sources* frame was also identified and represented references to credible state and federal authorities which the public was encouraged to use as sources of information. The idea was that people should only rely on trustworthy sources of information regarding the pandemic and thus most of the messages concluded with a reference to such credible institutions where further information could be sought. Once the generic frames were identified and conceptualized, we worked through the texts with these in mind.

The next step in the analysis was to organize the raw data through an open coding (Matthes, 2009). During this open coding process, the coders reviewed the materials, making notes and headings in the text as they read through the articles. A limitation of such type of coding is that it requires repeated reading of the material and is thus labor intensive and time-consuming (Semetko & Valkenburg, 2000). The final step in the analysis included grouping the data and reducing the number of frames by combining them into broader categories and defining exactly what type of information these broader frames include. This approach allowed us to (1) explore the frequency of the generic frames and (2) identify issue-specific frames particularly unique for the COVID-19 pandemic.

Findings

Quantitative

Most of the content came from New York (n = 47, 36.7%), followed by Texas (n = 41, 32.0%), and California (n = 40, 31.3%). LA County, California, had the highest county-level number of publications (n = 19, 14.8%). Both Texas and California released information at the county level, with New York releasing press releases at the state level and tweets at county or department of health level. Most information was disseminated via press release (n = 72, 56.3%) compared with Twitter (n = 56, 43.8%). Much of that content was specific to COVID-19 (n = 103, 80.5%). Less than half of the posts (n = 53, 41.4%) referred readers to credible sources. Most of the posts focused on adjusting information (n = 75, 58.6%), followed by information about new cases (n = 61, 47.7%), and instructing information (n = 58, 45.3%).

Much of the examples of adjusting information focused on contact tracing including, "Public Health has identified persons who may have had close personal contact with these individuals" (LA County, March 4) and "DCHHS [Dallas County Health and Human Services] has completed contract tracing and has directly notified anyone who was in close contact with the individual while they were in Texas" (Dallas County, March 11). Other press releases and tweets discussed updating a county-level COVID-19 dashboard daily and providing notice of a new call center resource for residents in unincorporated Harris County without a healthcare provider and who need access to coronavirus-related care.

Many of the press releases and tweets also provided information about the new cases. However, due to oft-cited privacy concerns, the descriptions of the individuals who had contracted COVID-19 were minimal. Two separate Tarrant County (March 10 and 11) press releases described, "The case had travelled to a conference..." rather than describing the diagnosis using person-first language. In most cases, however, when a new case was identified, the gender and age range of the individual was also reported.

Instructing information described the types of actions the general public could and should be taking during the pandemic. These included: staying home when sick, washing hands with soap and water for at least 20 seconds often, avoiding touching eyes, nose, and mouth with unwashed hands, limiting close contact, cleaning and disinfecting high-touch surfaces regularly, and other hygiene-related recommendations. Early on, face masks were not regularly recommended (often due to PPE shortages), with one LA County (March 9) press release stating, "Face masks are most effective when used appropriately by healthcare workers and those directly caring for people who are sick and by people who are sick."

Several of the press releases referred readers to the websites of local county Department of Public Health, with the CDC and WHO's websites being other commonly referenced credible sources of other COVID-19 material. Less often referenced credible sources included Health and Human Services Agency, My Health My Resources (Tarrant County), and the social media pages for the local county public health departments. In New York, the governor's website was also described as a credible source. Tweets often included infographics as well.

Qualitative

Community involvement and buy-in was central to many of the press releases, particularly in Texas. One quote from a March 14, 2020, Dallas County, Texas, press release said, "The rate at which they [COVID-19 cases] rise will depend on the extent to which we all act responsibly to prevent community spread." Religious groups were directly addressed in one March 15, 2020, Dallas County, Texas, press release: "Times of uncertainty make us want to come together. Worshipping at home or in small groups is a break in habit for many," said Dallas County Judge Clay Jenkins. "I thank all who normally would attend a larger service, especially our faith leaders for your sacrifice and focus on fighting community spread."

'Flattening the curve' was mentioned often. On March 13, a Los Angeles County, California, press release stated, "We are all in this together and we must all do our part to slow the spread," said Barbara Ferrer, PhD, MPH, MEd, Los Angeles County Public Health Director. The next day, on March 14, "flattening the curve" was the primary focus of the Twitter feed. March 16, 2020, San Diego County, California's press release echoed LA County's tweet.

Because of the novelty of COVID-19, much information shared in the early days was later found to be erroneous. A March 8, 2020, Harris County, Texas, press release instructed the community to NOT wear a mask unless recommended by a healthcare professional. Similarly, a March 2, 2020, New York press release from the governor stated, "We have the best health-care system in the world...," which was reiterated on March 6, "In New York we have the most sophisticated healthcare system on the globe..." In San Diego County, California, a March 9 press release implied that the homeless population were spreading the virus.

Extending empathy was minimal but existed. A March 11, 2020, Los Angeles County, California, press release stated, "Public Health extends our deepest condolences to the patient's loved ones in the wake of this tragedy," said Barbara Ferrer, PhD, MPH, MEd, Los Angeles County Public Health Director.

Minimizing the potential threat was another common theme. A March 10, 2020, Harris County, Texas, press release, "Coronavirus does not discriminate between those who have access to health care and those that do not," said Harris County Judge Lina Hidalgo. While HCPH (Harris County Public Health) understands residents may be concerned, evidence so far suggests that most people who have become infected with COVID-19 only experience mild to moderate symptoms and fully recover.

Lessons learned

This chapter aimed to investigate what information has been communicated to the public by local public health organizations in the early stages of the COVID-19 pandemic. The sample consisted of tweets and press releases which were analyzed through the lens of the EPPM. The United States is among the countries which has been most severely affected by the pandemic (CDC, 2024). This is partly due to the fact that the public did not perceive the threat from the virus to be serious and severe enough. Therefore, the purpose of this study was to assess how the public health authorities communicated about the threat to the general public. The EPPM is a useful model to assess these messages because it helps in understanding how people make sense of risk.

Instructing and adjusting information

The results of the content analysis reveal that public health authorities in the United States communicated about the risk of COVID-19 primarily by providing adjusting and instructing information to the public. Crises can generate many different emotions including anger, sympathy, and anxiety. Anxiety makes people worry about how the crisis will affect them and the people around them (Jin, 2009). Anxiety is a powerful emotion because it produces stress which in turn has a negative effect on a person's cognitive abilities. In other words, when people experience anxiety, their comprehension is reduced and they are slow to respond to the crisis and risk messages (Rai et al., 2011). Adjusting information reduces anxiety because it provides specific information about what measures have been taken to limit the damage of the crisis or the virus in this case. Adjusting information helps people cope psychologically with the threat of risk (Sturges, 1994a). It is useful in risk and crisis messages because it reduces uncertainty and thus anxiety. Information about the virus and new cases could also be classified as adjusting information because it gives a sense of reassurance that the authorities are in control of the situation and can be trusted with the way they are handling it.

Most of the information distributed from public health organizations also included instructing information. These messages included specific guidance for how to properly wash hands, advice to wear face masks as well as practicing social distancing. Instructing information helps people cope physically with the risk (Sturges, 1994a). Moreover, it provides information about specific actions that people can take to protect themselves. Instructing information plays a central role for the effectiveness of a risk communication effort because it can be directly linked to the notion of *efficacy* in the EPPM.

Perceived threat and efficacy

Efficacy is central idea in the EPPM because it tells us when people are going to adopt the behavior change and act in a resilient manner (Witte et al., 2001). If people believe that adopting the new behavior is effective from protecting them from the risk, they are likely to adopt it. This is also known as engaging in danger control. The higher the perceived efficacy of the desired behavior, the more likely it is that constituents will contribute to resolving the public health crisis. The idea of efficacy helps explain the presence of instructing information is the risk communication messages that we analyzed. Furthermore, the #Flattenthecurve messages are another example of efforts to enhance efficacy. The idea behind the hashtag was that everyone can take simple steps to reduce the spread of COVID-19, and therefore it reinforced efficacy. The purpose of a risk communication effort is also to convince the public that the desired behavior will reduce the threat. Gaining compliance, however, is heavily dependent on how severe people perceive the threat to be.

Risk communication centers around the evaluation of risk (Sandman, 2006). Therefore, risk messages focus on convincing people that the threat and the risk is real and thus gaining their compliance to engage in danger control. In a public health crisis such as the COVID-19 pandemic, communicators should encourage the public to be more concerned about a risk they might be underestimating (Coombs, 2020). If the public is underestimating a risk, the threat assessment part of the EPPM will be negatively affected. In other words, if people perceive the risk of COVID-19 to be low, they will underestimate it and will not see the threat as a risk for them. Our results indicate that public health organizations across the United States did very little to enhance the perceive severity of the risk early in the pandemic. In fact, we found messages that actually downplayed the seriousness of the virus:

> *HCPH* [Harris County Public Health] *does not recommend that healthy individuals wear a facemask to protect themselves from respiratory illnesses, including COVID-19. Residents should only wear a mask if recommended by a healthcare professional.*
>
> (Harris County, March 3, 2020)

> *While HCPH understands residents may be concerned, evidence so far suggests that most people who have become infected with COVID-19 only experience mild to moderate symptoms and fully recover.*
>
> (Harris County, March 10, 2020)

Additionally, only 5% of the messages in our sample emphasized gaining compliance or enhancing efficacy. Instructing and adjusting information alone are not sufficient to encourage action, as the purpose of these messages is quite different. Specifically, we argue that the threat assessment part of the EPPM was compromised which in turn led to the public's reluctance to engage in danger control and protect themselves from the virus by adopting the recommended behavior. In other words, the public (1) did not perceive to be susceptible to the threat and (2) did not think that the threat was serious enough. The risk communication messages which public health authorities used in the early stages of the pandemic did not communicate effectively how serious the virus is and, therefore, people did not feel compelled to protect themselves.

In summary, the findings suggest that the authorities effectively communicated instructing and adjusting information regarding the virus in the early stages of the pandemic. Instructing information included specific actions to alleviate the risk and adjusting information consisted of communicating about the steps taken by the authorities to limit the spread of the virus. This type of information helped enhance the perceived efficacy of the response. However, what was lacking was emphasis on the threat in terms of likelihood and severity. One way to explain these inconsistencies is the uncertainty and lack of information about the virus. As the pandemic developed, new information emerged, and at times it was contradicting earlier information. Consider the previous example regarding wearing face masks from Harris County. At first people were told that healthy individuals do not need to wear a mask. This is an example of misinformation, which was later disproved. Nevertheless, such contradictions affected the credibility of public health authorities in the United States and resulted in people not perceive the risk to be severe enough.

Conclusion

The aim of this study was to examine the types of information local public health organizations across the United States communicated to constituents about the risk of COVID-19 in order to bridge the gap in current understanding of risk communication in the public sector as well as provide an account as why the country had such a bad response to the pandemic. This study's findings, interpreted through the lens of EPPM, show a glimpse of how local public sector organizations in New York, California, and Texas communicated to constituents about the COVID-19 threat. Findings provide context for future studies. Understanding more about how risk communication about health crises can be improved is vital for individual-level health outcomes as well as societal-level health outcomes.

The findings have several important implications. From a practical standpoint, there is very little research on how public health organizations communicate about risk on social media such as Twitter. Although the media is a key player in the social construction of risk (Dan & Raupp, 2018), the public sector should not be overlooked. The COVID-19 pandemic is a black swan crisis. A black swan crisis is unique and unlikely to happen again (Coombs, 2020). This public health crisis is unique and has some very specific communicative demands and challenges. However, it is unrealistic to assume that the world will never again face another infectious disease-related pandemic. The focus of our analysis is not to generalize idiosyncratic insights that are highly specific and contextual. Rather we are interested in understanding how communication could have been improved by studying what messages and frames have been employed by the authorities in the early stages of the pandemic. Instructing and adjusting information are valuable message strategies, they are necessary for an effective risk communication. However, perceptions of threat and ultimately gaining compliance to adopt the desired behavior is the key to minimizing risk damages and building resilience (Wang & Mao, 2021; Wong & Jensen, 2020). The public sector needs to recognize the importance of this to be able to communicate more effectively (Hansson et al., 2021).

From a theoretical perspective, the finings enhance our understanding of how the EPPM could be used to create risk messages. The model helps explain what factors affect decision-making processes. The EPPM has value for guiding public health crisis communication (Barnett et al., 2014). The notions of threat and efficacy are essential for the effectiveness of a risk message. Moreover, the model is valuable because it can be used to identify issues that could potentially obstruct the public from adopting the desired response. The model should be considered when planning public health crisis communication efforts.

The present study should be considered within the context of its limitations, yet these allow for recommendations for future research. While the publication numbers were fairly symmetrical across the three states, the average of 40 press releases or tweets per state is not necessarily indicative of each state's COVID-19 response during the first weeks of the pandemic. Future research should expand the social media type (for example, to Facebook or Instagram) as the audiences differ between social media types (Shane-Simpson et al., 2018). Further, this study is limited by the US context. Other countries had already begun facing the COVID-19 pandemic head-on by the time the virus was identified in the United States, and as such, their responses during this time frame would likely differ. Finally, this study should be repeated with a timeline expansion, including more of 2019 so that comparisons can more accurately be made. Future research should also examine how visual media (for example, infographics) were used during the COVID-19 pandemic, as well as their effectiveness.

References

Abraham, T. (2011). Lessons from the pandemic: the need for new tools for risk and outbreak communication. *Emerging Health Threats Journal*, *4*(1). https://doi.org/10.3402/ehtj.v4i0.7160

Barnett, D. J., Thompson, C. B., Semon, N. L., Errett, N. A., Harrison, K. L., Anderson, M. K., Ferrell, J. L., Freiheit, J. M., Hudson, R., McKee, M., Mejia-Echeverry, A., Spitzer, J., Balicer, R. D., Links, J. M., & Storey, J. D. (2014). EPPM and willingness to respond: The role of risk and efficacy communication in strengthening public health emergency response systems. *Health Communication*, *29*(6), 598–609. https://doi.org/10.1080/10410236.2013.785474

Brown, P. (2020). Studying COVID-19 in light of critical approaches to risk and uncertainty: Research pathways, conceptual tools, and some magic from Mary Douglas. *Health, Risk & Society*, 22(1), 1–14. https://doi.org/10.1080/13698575.2020.1745508

Centers for Disease Control and Prevention. (2024). COVID data tracker. *Retrieved from* https://covid.cdc.gov/covid-data-tracker/#datatracker-home

Coombs, W. T. (2020). Public sector crises: Realizations from Covid-19 for crisis communication. *Partecipazione e Conflitto*, *13*(2), 990–1001. https://doi.org/10.1285/I20356609V13I2P990

Coombs, W.T. (2019). *Ongoing crisis communication: Planning, managing, and responding* (5th). Sage.
Dalrymple, K. E., Young, R., & Tully, M. (2016). "Facts, not fear": Negotiating uncertainty on social media during the 2014 Ebola crisis. *Science Communication*, *38*, 442–467. https://doi.org/10.1177/1075547016655546
Dan, V., & Raupp, J. (2018). A systematic review of frames in news reporting of health risks: Characteristics, construct consistency vs. name diversity, and the relationship of frames to framing functions. *Health, Risk & Society*, *20*(5-6), 203–226. https://doi.org/10.1080/13698575.2018.1522422
Edelman, E. J., Aoun-Barakat, L., Villanueva, M., & Friedland, G. (2020). Confronting another pandemic: Lessons from HIV can inform our COVID-19 response. *AIDS Behavior*, *24*, 1977–1979. https://doi.org/10.1007/s10461-020-02908-z
European Commission. (2024). Tackling coronavirus disinformation. Retrieved from https://commission.europa.eu/strategy-and-policy/coronavirus-response/fighting-disinformation/tackling-coronavirus-disinformation_en
Hansson, S., Orru, K., Torpan, S., Bäck, A., Kazemekaityte, A., Meyer, S. F., Ludvigsen, J., Savadori, L., Galvagni, A., & Pigrée, A. (2021). COVID-19 information disorder: six types of harmful information during the pandemic in Europe. *Journal of Risk Research*, *24*(3-4), 380–393. https://doi.org/10.1080/13669877.2020.1871058
Heath, R. L., Lee, J., Palenchar, M. J., & Lemon, L. L. (2018). Risk communication emergency response preparedness: Contextual assessment of the protective action decision model. *Risk Analysis*, *38*(2), 333–344. https://doi.org/10.1111/risa.12845
Jin, Y. (2009). The effects of public's cognitive appraisal of emotions in crises on crisis coping and strategy assessment. *Public Relations Review*, *35(*3), 310–313. https://doi.org/10.1016/j.pubrev.2009.02.003
Karlova, N. A., & Fisher, K. E. (2013). A Social Diffusion Model of Misinformation and Disinformation for Understanding Human Information Behaviour. *Information Research*, *18*(1).
Lavrakas, P. J. (2008). *Encyclopedia of survey research methods*. Sage publications. https://doi.org/10.4135/9781412963947
Matthes, J. (2009). What's in a frame? A content analysis of media framing studies in the world's leading communication journals, 1990-2005. *Journalism & Mass Communication Quarterly*, *86*(2), 349–367. https://doi.org/10.1177/107769900908600206
Mitchell, S. S. D., & Beanlands, J. (2020). Rethinking Risk Communication: Lessons from a Pandemic. *Topia (University of Toronto Press)*, *41*, 88–95. https://doi.org/10.3138/topia-011
O'Dowd, A. (2021). Covid-19: Cases of delta variant rise by 79%, but rate of growth slows. *BMJ*, *373*:n1496. https://doi.org/10.1136/bmj.n1596
Paek, H.-J., Hilyard, K., Freimuth, V. S., Barge, J. K., & Mindlin, M. (2008). Public support for government actions during a flu pandemic: Lessons learned from a statewide survey. *Health Promotion Practice*, *9*(4_suppl), 60S–72S. https://doi.org/10.1177/1524839908322114
Palenchar, M. J. (2005). Risk communication. In R. L. Heath (Ed.), *Encyclopedia of public relations* (Vol. 2, pp. 752–755). Sage.
Paulik, L. B., Keenan, R. E., & Durda, J. L. (2020). The case for effective risk communication: Lessons from a global pandemic. *Integrated Environmental Assessment and Management*. https://doi.org/10.1002/ieam.4312

Rai, M. K., Loschky, L. C., Harris, R. J., Peck, N. R., & Cook, L. G. (2011). Effects of stress and working memory capacity on foreign language readers' inferential processing during comprehension. *Language Learning*, *61*(1), 187–218. https://doi.org/10.1111/j.1467-9922.2010.00592.x

Ranjit, Y. S., Shin, H., First, J. M., & Houston, J. B. (2021). COVID-19 protective model: the role of threat perceptions and informational cues in influencing behavior. *Journal of Risk Research*, *24*(3-4), 449–465. https://doi.org/10.1080/13669877.2021.1887328

Ratzan, S. C., Sommarivac, S., & Rauh, L. (2020). Enhancing global health communication during a crisis: Lessons from the COVID-19 pandemic. *CUNY SPH Graduate School of Public Health & Health Policy Publications and Research*. Retrieved from https://academicworks.cuny.edu/sph_pubs/265/

Rimal, R. N., & Lapinski, M. K. (2009). Why health communication is important in public health. *Bulletin of the World Health Organization*, *87*, 247–247a. https://doi.org/10.2471/BLT.08.056713

Sandman, P. M. (2006). Crisis communication best practices: Some quibbles and additions. *Journal of Applied Communication Research*, *34*(3), 257–262. https://doi.org/10.1080/00909880600771619

Semetko, H. A., & Valkenburg, P. M. (2000). Framing European politics: A content analysis of press and television news. *Journal of Communication*, *50*(2), 93–109. https://doi.org/10.1111/j.1460-2466.2000.tb02843.x

Shane-Simpson, C., Manago, A., Gaggi, N., & Gillespie-Lynch, K. (2018). Why do college students prefer Facebook, Twitter, or Instagram? Site affordances, tensions between privacy and self-expression, and implications for social capital. *Computers in Human Behavior*, 86, 276–288. https://doi.org/10.1016/j.chb.2018.04.041

Sturges, D. L. (1994a). Communicating through crisis: A strategy for organizational survival. *Management Communication Quarterly*, 7(3), 297–316. https://doi.org/10.1177/0893318994007003004

Sturges, D. L. (1994b). Communicating through crisis: A strategy for organizational survival. *Management Communication Quarterly*, 7(3): 297–316. https://doi.org/10.1177/0893318994007003004

Ter Huurne, E. F., & Gutteling, J. M. (2009). How to trust? The importance of self-efficacy and social trust in public responses to industrial risks. *Journal of Risk Research*, *12*(6), 809–824. https://doi.org/10.1080/13669870902726091

United States Census Bureau. (2019). Retrieved from https://www.census.gov/quickfacts/fact/table/US/PST045219

van der Meer, T. G., & Jin, Y. (2020). Seeking formula for misinformation treatment in public health crises: The effects of corrective information type and source. *Health Communication*, *35*(5), 560–575. https://doi.org/10.1080/10410236.2019.1573295

van Gorp, B. (2009). Strategies to Take Subjectivity Out of Framing Analysis. In *Doing News Framing Analysis: Empirical and Theoretical Perspective* (pp. 84–109). Routledge.

Wang, D. & Mao, Z. (2021). From risks to catastrophes: How Chinese Newspapers framed the Coronavirus Disease 2019 (COVID-19) in its early stage. *Health, Risk & Society*, *23(*3), 93–110, https://doi.org/10.1080/13698575.2021.1901859

Witte, K. (1992). Putting the fear back into fear appeals: The extended parallel process model. *Communications Monographs*, *59*(4), 329–349. https://doi.org/10.1080/03637759209376276

Witte, K., Meyer, G., & Martell, D. (2001). *Effective health communication messages: A step-by-step guide*. Sage.

Wong, C. M. L., & Jensen, O. (2020). The paradox of trust: perceived risk and public compliance during the COVID-19 pandemic in Singapore. *Journal of Risk Research*, *23*(7-8), 1021–1030. https://doi.org/10.1080/13669877.2020.1756386

World Health Organization. (2024). WHO Coronavirus (COVID-19) dashboard. Retrieved from: https://covid19.who.int

Yanes-Lane, M., Winters, N., Fregonese, F., Bastos, M., Perlman-Arrow, S., Campbell, J. R., et al. (2020). Proportion of asymptomatic infection among COVID-19 positive persons and their transmission potential: A systematic review and meta-analysis. *PLoS One*, *15*(11): e0241536. https://doi.org/10.1371/journal.pone.0241536

7 The Effectiveness of Converging Alert Messages from Multiple Weather Communicators

*Saymin Lee, Jiyoun Kim, Anita Atwell Seate, and Brooke F. Liu**

When high-impact weather is on the horizon, such as hurricanes and tornadoes, experts must coordinate their messages to help community members prepare for potential devastating consequences of these storms. This coordination is crucial for managing these crises, as it facilitates the timely development and dissemination of critical information from experts such as government officials and media partners (e.g., Herovic et al., 2014; Sellnow et al., 2019). With the advent of social media, the landscape of crisis actors has further diversified to include active members of the public, introducing new dynamics to multiactor coordination in crisis communication (e.g., Coombs & Holladay, 2014; Johansen et al., 2016). The field of weather crisis communication, in particular, has been transforming to accommodate this diversification of crisis communicators (Atwell Seate et al., 2022; Spence et al., 2021). In addition to core weather communicators, including government agencies and broadcast media, active individuals such as weather enthusiasts have started taking on the role of weather communicators, particularly on social media (Atwell Seate et al., 2022; Liu et al., 2020a, 2020b). While these varied actors send out messages to alert communities to threats and/or instruct on appropriate safety measures in the face of high-impact weather, the field calls for efforts to maintain consistency in multiple weather messages across various actors for effective weather crisis communication (Williams & Eosco, 2021). Some weather communicators, meanwhile, are concerned that message consistency might undermine public understanding regarding the inherent uncertainty of weather forecasting (Williams & Eosco, 2021).

Yet, little quantitative work has examined how effectively multiple actors can coordinate their crisis messages, especially when considering

* We thank the National Oceanic and Atmospheric Administration (NOAA) for funding this research through the VORTEX-SE Program (Grant No. NA20OAR4590454). The views and conclusions contained in this paper are those of the authors and should not be interpreted as necessarily representing the official policies, either expressed or implied, of NOAA.

DOI: 10.4324/9781032619187-8

message convergence. Crisis communication scholarship, through the lens of rhetorical arena theory (Frandsen & Johansen, 2010), has identified the interplay among multiple actors in crisis communication (e.g., Rodin et al., 2019; Zhang & Chen, 2022; Zhao & Oh, 2021). However, a micro approach to explicate the process of that multiactor communication is lacking, particularly in public crisis contexts like high-impact weather. The message convergence framework, in the meantime, has explored the process of multiactor communication, with the focus on the convergence of multiple voices at a message level (Anthony et al., 2013, 2017). The message convergence literature confirms that crisis messages from multiple actors become more believable when they converge; they become less believable when they diverge (Anthony et al., 2013; Mayer et al., 2023; Sellnow et al., 2019). These studies provide strong evidence that the literature needs to consider communicative ecosystems to understand crisis response processes; however, these findings are primarily from qualitative studies, and further empirical evidence guiding how multiple crisis actors can optimize the level or type of message convergence, especially to effectively promote public safety, remains scarce.

To address this gap, this study seeks to uncover the effectiveness of converging messages from multiple actors in weather communication. Specifically in the context of high-impact weather, we examined how weather alert messages from multiple actors that varied in their convergences on the threat and the recommended preparatory actions influenced individuals' perceptions of message credibility and their preparatory action-taking intentions. Our findings extend existing understanding of multivocal crisis communication by providing additional empirical evidence on how crisis messages from multiple actors can work effectively depending on the ways they converge. Accordingly, these findings have practical implications for risk and crisis communicators charged with public safety.

In the following section, we review the rhetorical arena theory—the multivocal approach to crisis communication—as our theoretical base to understand the emergence of multiple actors in public crisis communication and their interactions. We then review the message convergence framework for our micro-level analysis on the process of multiactor communication.

Literature review

Rhetorical arena theory: A multivocal approach to public crisis communication

Rhetorical arena theory (RAT; Frandsen & Johansen, 2010) is premised on the idea that crises involve a variety of social actors creating a multivocality of crises. The notion of multivocality allows us to explore the communicative ecosystems that various actors engage in, when understanding crisis communication. The theory posits that, as a crisis arises, not only the organization responsible for managing the crisis but also other organizations and publics begin communicating about the crisis, opening the rhetorical arena. This multivocal approach shifts the focus of crisis communication research from a single organization managing a crisis to multiple actors' communicative interactions in the arena, which also align with the relational realities between organizations and publics (e.g., Atwell Seate et al., 2022; Heath, 2006). Based on RAT, the initial line of research has identified multiple voices and their interaction patterns in the crisis arena, primarily in the context of corporate crises (e.g., Frandsen & Johansen, 2010, 2018; Johansen et al., 2016).

Although initially proposed for organizational crises, RAT has been extended to other crisis contexts involving multivocality—particularly, public crises such as natural disasters (e.g., Ndlela, 2019) or public health emergencies (e.g., Pulos, 2020; Rodin et al., 2019; Zhang & Chen, 2022). Public crisis communication, aiming primarily to achieve public safety, inherently involves a myriad of actors, including governmental agencies, NGOs, and citizens, all connected to the crisis context (Frandsen & Johansen, 2020b, 2022). Thus, the multivocal approach is integral to understanding public crisis communication, including weather crisis communication.

While taking a different theoretical tack to RAT, communication scholarship has explored multivocality in the weather communication context as well, confirming the communicative dynamics among multiple actors. Work by Atwell Seate and colleagues (Atwell Seate et al., 2022; Liu & Atwell Seate, 2021) has shown that US National Weather Service (NWS) achieves its mission through a relational constellation of emergency managers, broadcast media, and active individuals sharing its life-saving messages. Work by Liu et al. (2020a) showed that active individuals are crucial on social media as they help translate weather science for their social networks and act as important information conduits of weather risk and crisis information. In times of high-impact weather, these individuals function much like "social media-rologist" and, therefore, should be regarded as critical actors collaborating on weather crisis communication (Atwell Seate et al., 2022; Liu et al., 2020a). Given this multivocality, researchers have begun addressing the importance of communicative coordination among these various actors for effective weather crisis communication (Atwell Seate et al., 2022; Liu et al., 2020b). Specifically, the weather communication scholarship has called for the guidance on effective multivocal communication, in which multiple actors send their warnings collectively in the face of a high-impact weather event (e.g., Weyrich et al., 2019; Williams & Eosco, 2021).

However, existing RAT literature lacks micro models to specify the process of effective multivocal communication, particularly for public crisis contexts, despite the qualitative insights on the importance of communicative coordination among multiple actors. The framework of RAT actually comprises two perspectives: a macro perspective to overview multiple actors and their interactions in the arena and a micro perspective to investigate each individual communication process (Frandsen & Johansen, 2010, 2020a, 2022). Existing literature has mainly overviewed multiple actors and their interactions in given public crisis arenas at the macro level, primarily through case studies (e.g., Iannacone, 2021; Maier et al., 2022; Ndlela, 2019). The micro-level analyses in the literature are limited to revealing what was communicated and by whom (e.g., Rodin et al., 2019; Zhang & Chen, 2022). Little research has paid attention to how multivocal communication can be processed.

In the meantime, the message convergence framework may serve as a micro model to explore the coordination of multiactor crisis communication, especially where multiple messages from various actors come together. In the following section, we review the message convergence framework as an additional basis for deciphering multivocal communication at a micro level.

Micro-level process with multivocality: Message convergence framework

As various actors communicate in an arena, multiple arguments arise. These arguments may be converging, "lead[ing] to a single conclusion" (Perelman & Olbrechts-Tyteca, 1969, p. 471). The message convergence framework (MCF) theorizes the process and effects of such convergence, especially within the context of public crises (Anthony et al., 2013; Perelman & Olbrechts-Tyteca, 1969). The framework posits that when crisis or risk arguments from multiple actors converge on certain points, the arguments become more persuasive. Given this core proposition, MCF has been employed to study the process of multivocal communication across crisis or risks contexts, especially at the micro level, such as how individuals seek and consume multiple messages that may be converging (Anthony et al., 2013; Anthony & Sellnow, 2016; Soares et al., 2023; Ye & Ki, 2018; Zhao et al., 2022).

Message convergence occurs when multiple messages from different actors have overlapping points within them, namely converging points. Converging points can be understood as some elements that consistently appear across multiple messages (Herovic et al., 2014; Perelman & Olbrechts-Tyteca, 1969). In public crisis messages, these converging points can be on the information about a crisis event, including its probability and impacts, and/or the recommendation of preventive or protective actions (Herovic et al., 2014; Mileti & Sorensen, 1990; Sellnow et al., 2019). When publics recognize the converging points of messages, where different actors stand on the same, they may accept or follow what is advocated by those points (Anthony et al., 2013). Accordingly, it has been recommended that multiple actors in public crisis communication collaborate proactively to construct converging points, such as the information on threats and appropriate safety measures, to manage crisis situations effectively (Herovic et al., 2014; Sellnow et al., 2019; Zhao & Oh, 2021).

However, existing literature lacks empirical evidence to guide which point(s) multiple messages from different actors could converge on to achieve the most communicative effects in a given public crisis context. Weather communication, in particular, covers a range of elements (e.g., location and date of an event, level of threat, and recommended preparatory actions) in its emergency messages (Mileti & Sorensen, 1990; Williams & Eosco, 2021). With these as potential converging points, the field strives to be consistent in weather messages across various communicators, but lacks empirical evidence to guide effective convergence (Williams & Eosco, 2021). This study draws attention to potential points of convergence in weather messages and explores varying convergence types where multiple weather communicators converge on a certain point only or on other points as well.

Meanwhile, the MCF scholarship has contemplated how message convergence could lead to desirable communication outcomes (e.g., Anthony et al., 2013; Anthony & Sellnow, 2016; Sellnow et al., 2019). The following section reviews these qualitative insights, specifically in terms of the links between message convergence and (1) message credibility and (2) behavioral intentions.

Message credibility

When multiple messages converge on certain points, MCF theorizes that the audience goes through a process evaluating the veracity of these converging points (Anthony et al., 2013; Perelman & Olbrechts-Tyteca, 1969). In line with broader communication scholarship, this process can be referred to as message credibility, defined as "an individual's judgment of the veracity of the content of communication" (Appelman & Sundar, 2016, p. 63). MCF research has confirmed that, generally, if multiple actors are communicating the same arguments, the audience tends to consider those arguments as credible, particularly if those actors are seen as credible (e.g., Anthony et al., 2013; Anthony & Sellnow, 2016; Sellnow et al., 2019). However, the literature also notes that excessive or seemingly contrived convergence can cause distrust (Anthony et al., 2013).

Following these qualitative insights on the credibility of converging messages, a recent experimental study has made one of the first attempts to test the relationship between message convergence and message credibility (Soares et al., 2023). This study demonstrated that a condition where multiple messages converge leads to higher credibility of the given messages, compared to low or no message convergence. Specifically, the researchers found that, when separate news stories about a public health threat echoed each other over time, they yielded a higher level of message credibility than less converging stories in a shorter period or a single story (Soares et al., 2023).

Despite quantitative evidence that a higher level of convergence tends to increase message credibility, however, the field still lacks an understanding of the credibility of converging messages in relation to their types of convergence—i.e., how the different ways that multiple actors converge on certain point(s) lead to message credibility. As previously noted, this study draws attention to elements of weather messages as converging points of multiple messages, such as the information on the threat and recommended preparatory actions. Having the convergence on the threat or the convergence on the threat and recommended preparatory actions as the types of convergence, we propose our first research question as follows.

> RQ1: How, if at all, does message credibility vary by convergence type?

Preparatory action-taking

Exploring the communicative effects of message convergence, particularly in public crisis contexts, the MCF literature highlights the impacts of message convergence on promoting advocated actions, such as recommended safety measures (e.g., Anthony et al., 2013; Sellnow et al., 2019). Qualitative findings have confirmed that people tend to take actions as advocated in converging messages from multiple actors once they recognize the message convergence (e.g., Anthony et al., 2013; Anthony & Sellnow, 2016). For example, Anthony et al. (2013) noted the responses from their focus group participants that, in the public health crisis context, they tend to take the actions as advocated multiple times across multiple sources.

While not explicit, these qualitative studies have implied that the driving factors in the relationships between message convergence and behavioral decisions can be message credibility. For example, when reporting their qualitative findings, scholars described one's course of decision making followed by message convergence that people trust and/or feel confident when there are points of convergence and it prompts the intention to adhere recommended measures in those convergent messages (Anthony et al., 2013; Anthony & Sellnow, 2016). While there is no empirical evidence of the mediating role of message credibility in the MCF literature yet, other lines of communication scholarship provide strong evidence for the intervening role of message credibility in the relationship between communication strategies and behavioral intentions (e.g., Huang et al., 2022; Kim et al., 2023 in environmental communication context). Therefore, we also expect that the heightened credibility of converging messages from different weather communicators will lead to encouraging the audience to take recommended preparatory actions as in the weather messages. However, there is scarce evidence to gauge how the mediating role would vary depending on convergence type. Therefore, we propose the following research question, instead of a hypothesis.

> RQ2-1: How, if at all, does message credibility mediate the relationship between convergence type and intentions to take preparatory actions?

Information sharing

Along with taking recommended preparatory actions, another desired behavioral outcome of weather communication is having publics share given weather information to others (e.g., Ploran et al., 2018; Sutton et al., 2019). As the audiences share the weather message from core weather communicators with their friends and family, it helps government organizations achieve their mission of public safety by getting life-saving information to more members of the at-risk public (Atwell Seate et al., 2022; Liu et al., 2020b; Sutton et al., 2019). Also, as people tend to listen to their neighbors in taking protective actions such as evacuation under a severe weather event (Ploran et al., 2018), the action of sharing the weather information with others could help to ensure the safety of the community. However, the MCF literature has yet to explicitly explore how message convergence would influence the spread of convergent information. In the line with exploring individual's action taking under varying message convergences, we also propose the following research question.

> RQ2-2: How, if at all, does message credibility mediate the relationship between convergence type and the intention to share the weather information with others?

Social media engagement

As previously mentioned, scholarship examining the multivocality of crises, such as that found in the RAT literature, has focused on social media as communicative spaces where a variety of social actors, including organizations and publics, can engage in communication (Coombs & Holladay, 2014; Johansen et al., 2016; Rodin et al., 2019; Zhang & Chen, 2022). While the MCF literature is also premised on multivocality and explores how publics process converging messages from multiple actors, only recently has research started to draw attention to message convergence on social media (e.g., Zhao & Oh, 2021). However, the literature still lacks an understanding of public engagement on social media, such as interactions with message sources, as the process or outcome of message convergence.

Meanwhile, broader communication scholarship has confirmed that message credibility can lead to social media engagement with the message source, such as liking and sharing the message (e.g., Lee, 2022; Men & Tsai, 2013; Nedelcu & Balaban, 2021). To further explore social media engagement with converging messages from multiple actors, we propose our final research question as follows.

> RQ3: How, if at all, does message credibility mediate the relationship between convergence type and an individual's social media engagement with each message?

Methods

We conducted a between-subjects experiment to explore the varying effects of convergence type on message credibility. We also explored the mediating role of message credibility in the relationships between convergence type and communication outcomes—specifically, taking preparatory actions, sharing the information with others, and social media engagement.

Stimuli development

Based on the literature review and in collaboration with our NWS forecaster partners, we developed experimental stimuli presenting convergences of multiple weather messages in a high-impact weather alert context. First, the chosen hypothetical context was a severe storm alert in the Southeastern U.S.—specifically, a watch indicating a slight risk for severe storms at night. The actors sending out severe storm alert messages were threefold: 1) the NWS, 2) a broadcast meteorologist, and 3) a social media-rologist. Specifically, given the hypothetical alert area, the three actors were the NWS Birmingham (a local weather authority), James Spann (an actual broadcast meteorologist based in Birmingham), and a fictitious individual serving as a social media-rologist. Twitter was the chosen social media platform, displaying all messages from multiple actors simultaneously on a single page.

Next, we identified three alert elements as the points of message convergence: (1) threat information, (2) the recommendation of communicative preparatory actions, and (3) the recommendation of sheltering preparatory actions. While the specific wording in addressing each point could vary (Williams & Eosco, 2021), all three actors included these points of convergence in their alert messages. We then set the convergence type by varying the converging point(s) included in the messages. For the first convergence type (convergence type 1), all three actors addressed only the threat information in their messages. For the second convergence type (convergence type 2), the messages from the three actors included both the threat information and the recommendation of communicative preparatory actions. For the third convergence type (convergence type 3), the messages from the three actors addressed all points—the threat information, the recommendation of communicative preparatory actions, and the recommendation of sheltering preparatory actions. In total, there were three convergence types (i.e., the convergence on the threat, the convergence on the threat and communicative preparatory action, and the convergence on the threat, communicative preparatory action, and sheltering preparatory action), and each convergence displayed three messages (i.e., a tweet from the NWS, one from a broadcast meteorologist, and one from a social media-rologist). The order of the messages was counterbalanced to prevent order effects.

Considering the weather communication ecology where weather messages often include graphical elements such as maps or infographic (Olson et al., 2019; Sutton et al., 2019), each actor's message in this experiment was accompanied by an image of alert information. While the images varied slightly between actors, we ensured that the color usage in each image aligned across actors, to maintain consistency (Williams & Eosco, 2021). See Appendix A for the final experimental stimuli.

Participants and procedure

After IRB approval, we conducted an online experiment from November 2022 to February 2023, which was administered via the survey firm Qualtrics. We recruited participants who resided in one of the following states: Arkansas, Mississippi, Tennessee, Alabama, and Missouri, for two reasons. First, the NWS seeks to enhance weather communication, especially in the Southeastern U.S. given regional vulnerabilities to high-impact weather (National Severe Storms Laboratory, n.d.). Second, these states align with the social media reach of the two weather communicators in our study (i.e., NWS Birmingham, James Spann). Additionally, we limited our participants to individuals who had an active Twitter account and were 18 years or older. To ensure sample diversity, we set quotas for age, sex, and race. We incorporated a brief screening survey to check participants' eligibility and fill the quotas.

Once participants passed the screening and consented to participate in the study, they were randomly assigned to one of the three convergence conditions, where the tweet messages of severe storm alerts were presented. After reading the messages, participants were asked to answer survey items on their thoughts and responses to those messages. Participants were compensated by Qualtrics after the study.

Responses from 985 participants who passed the attention check and completed the study were collected. We excluded responses from participants who took over 2 hours to complete the study or who did not answer more than half of the items, resulting in a loss of 32 respondents. A total of

953 participants' responses were used in the analysis. The average study completion time was approximately 24 minutes (M = 23.66, SD = 13.63). The average participant age was 38 years (*Range* = 18–87, M = 38.26, SD = 13.97). In our sample, 59.71% reported as female (n = 569), 40.19% as male (n = 383), and .1% as intersex (n = 1). Additionally, 78.07% reported as White (n =744) and 18.68% as African American/Black (n = 178), followed by Hispanic/Latinx (n = 51, 5.35%), American Indian/Native (n = 27, 2.83%), Asian/Pacific Islander (n = 12, 1.26%), and other (n = 9, .94%), selecting all that apply.

Measures

To measure each variable, we adapted the measurement items from prior research. All items were measured on a 9-point scale ranging from 1 (Strongly disagree) to 9 (Strongly agree).

Message credibility. We measured the perceived credibility of each actor's weather message with three items, adapted from Appelman and Sundar (2016) and Weyrich et al. (2019): "(The message from [the actor] is) Credible," "Believable," and "Accurate" (NWS: M = 6.64, SD = 2.21, α = .96; Broadcast meteorologist: M = 6.61, SD = 2.15, α = .95; Social media-rologist: M = 6.22, SD = 2.09, α = .94).

Preparatory actions. We specified preparatory actions into two components: communicative preparatory action and sheltering preparatory action. First, to measure the intention to take communicative preparatory actions, we developed the following three items: "(If I saw the messages on my Twitter feed, I would) Ensure I have multiple ways to receive messages about the severe weather," "Ensure that I leave my cell phone turned on to receive messages about the severe weather," and "Ensure that my weather radio is turned on and ready to receive messages about the severe weather" (M = 6.67, SD = 1.83, α = .74). Next, the intention to take sheltering preparatory actions were measured with four items, adapted from Morss et al. (2016), as follows: "(If I saw the messages on my Twitter feed, I would) Change my schedule to ensure that I am in a safe place during the severe weather event," "Leave my residence to stay in a location where sturdy shelter is readily available," "Put lawn furniture, trash bins, etc. in a secure location," and "Park my vehicle in a garage" (M = 6.06, SD = 1.8, α = .73).

Sharing information. We measured the intention to share the given information with others with six items, adapted from Liu et al. (2016). The items include, for example, "(If I saw the messages on my Twitter feed, I would) Call people I know (family, friends and coworkers, etc.) via telephone to talk about the severe weather," or "Tell others to follow the local National Weather Service office's instructions about the severe weather." (M = 5.43, SD = 1.92, α = .84).

Social media engagement. Individuals' social media engagement with each actor's message was measured with four items, also adapted from Liu et al. (2016). The items were: "I would retweet [the actor]'s message," "I would use the like button in response to [the actor]'s message," "I would reply with a positive comment to [the actor]'s message," and "I would reply with a question to [the actor]'s message" (NWS: M = 5.02, SD = 2.28, α = .86; Broadcast meteorologist: M = 4.98, SD = 2.29, α = .87; Social media-rologist: M = 4.76, SD = 2.28, α = .87).

See Appendix B for all measurement items and descriptive statistics.

Results

Convergence types and message credibility (RQ1)

A one-way analysis of variance (ANOVA) was conducted to compare the message credibility of each actor (i.e., the NWS, a broadcast meteorologist, a social media-rologist) across three convergence types (i.e., the convergence on the threat, the convergence on the threat and communicative preparatory action, and the convergence on the threat, communicative preparatory action, and sheltering preparatory action). Additionally, we performed Tukey's test for pairwise comparisons among the three convergence types to investigate any statistical differences between them.

Our data showed statistically significant differences in the message credibility of each actor among the three convergence types. Firstly, the credibility of the NWS message varied across the convergence types (F [2, 947] = 3.49, η^2= .01, p = .03). Similarly, the credibility of the broadcast meteorologist's message also varied across the convergence types (F[2, 948] = 4.44, η^2 = .01, p = .01), as did the credibility of the social media-orologist's message (F [2, 949] = 3.78, η^2 = .01, p = .02).

Pairwise comparisons revealed that messages were perceived as more credible under the condition of converging on the threat and communicative preparatory action, when compared to the condition of converging on the threat, communicative preparatory action, and sheltering preparatory action. The credibility of the NWS message under the convergence on the threat and communicative preparatory action (M = 6.86, SD = 2.00) was higher than under the convergence on the threat, communicative preparatory action, and sheltering preparatory action (M = 6.40, SD = 2.44); the difference was statistically significant at $p < .05$. Furthermore, the credibility of the broadcast meteorologist's message under the convergence on the threat and communicative preparatory action (M = 6.87, SD = 2.01) was higher than under the convergence on the threat, communicative preparatory action, and sheltering preparatory action (M = 6.32, SD = 2.36), with a statistically significant difference at $p < .01$. The credibility of the social media-rologist's message under the convergence on the threat and communicative preparatory action ($M = 6.39$, $SD = 2.09$) was higher than under the convergence on the threat, communicative preparatory action, and sheltering preparatory action ($M = 5.95$, $SD = 2.21$), with a statistically significant difference at $p < .05$. Other pairwise comparisons (i.e., comparisons to the condition of converging only on the threat) did not show statistical significance. See Table 7.1 for the mean message credibility of each actor under each convergence type.

The mediating role of message credibility (RQ2)

To answer RQ2 on the mediating role of message credibility, we ran the PROCESS macro for R (Model 4; Hayes, 2022) and investigated the indirect effects of message credibility on the relationships between convergence type and preparatory actions. Indirect effects were estimated using bias-corrected 95% bootstrap confidence intervals with 5,000 bootstrap samples. Given that we found the statistical difference in message credibility only between the convergence on the threat and communicative preparatory action and the convergence on the threat, communicative preparatory action, and sheltering preparatory action when answering RQ1, these two convergence types were the focus for RQ2. Hereinafter, convergence type refers to these two types (i.e., the convergence on the threat and communicative preparatory action versus the convergence on the threat, communicative preparatory action, and sheltering preparatory action).

Preparatory actions (RQ2-1)

The two preparatory actions were examined in this study: communicative preparatory action and sheltering preparatory action. Results showed statistically significant indirect effects of message credibility on the

Table 7.1 Message credibility across three convergence types

Convergence type		*Message Credibility*					
		NWS		*Broadcast Meteorologist*		*Social media-rologist*	
	n	*M*	*SD*	*M*	*SD*	*M*	*SD*
Convergence on the threat	333	6.64	2.14	6.60	2.04	6.29	1.95
Convergence on the threat & communicative action	315	6.86	2.00	6.87	2.01	6.39	2.09
Convergence on the threat, communicative action, & sheltering action	305	6.40	2.44	6.35	2.36	5.95	2.21

relationships between convergence type and publics' intentions to take communicative preparatory actions (Table 7.2). Specifically, the indirect effect of message convergence on communicative preparatory action via the credibility of the NWS message was statistically significant, as the confidence interval did not include zero (B_{ab} = –.12, *bootSE* = .05, bias-corrected 95% bootstrap CI [–.26, –.04]). The condition of converging on the threat and communicative preparatory action, compared to the condition of converging on the threat, communicative preparatory action, and sheltering preparatory action, increased the credibility of the NWS message (*B* = –.49, *p* = .01), which, in turn, increased the intention to take communicative preparatory action (*B* = .25, *p* = .00) (Figure 7.1). Also, the indirect effect via the credibility of the broadcast meteorologist's message was significant (B_{ab} = –.06, *bootSE* = .04, bias-corrected 95% bootstrap CI [–.16, –.001]). The convergence on the threat and communicative preparatory action, compared to the convergence on the threat, communicative

Table 7.2 Indirect effects of convergence type on communicative preparatory action

	B	*bootSE*	*Bias-corrected 95% bootstrap CI*	
Total indirect effect	–.20	.07	–.35	–.06
via message credibility of NWS	–.12	.05	–.26	–.04
via message credibility of broadcast meteorologist	–.06	.04	–.16	–.001
via message credibility of social media-orologist	–.02	.03	–.09	.02

Note: The convergence type in this analysis refers to two conditions—the convergence on the threat and communicative preparatory action versus the convergence on the threat, communicative preparatory action, and sheltering preparatory action.

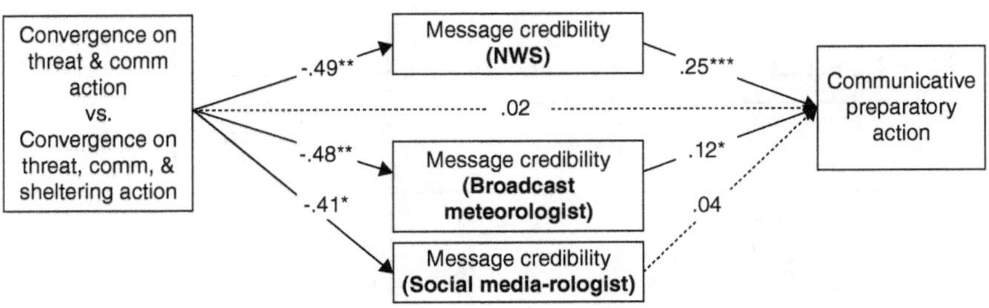

Figure 7.1 Model for communicative preparatory action (RQ2-1).

Note: Convergence on the threat and communicative preparatory action coded as 0; Convergence on the threat, communicative preparatory action, and sheltering preparatory action coded as 1.

preparatory action, and sheltering preparatory action, increased the credibility of the broadcast meteorologist's message ($B = -.48$, $p = .01$), which, in turn, increased the intention to take communicative preparatory action ($B = .12$, $p = .03$). Meanwhile, the indirect effect via the credibility of the social media-rologist's was not statistically significant.

However, the indirect effect of convergence type on the intention to take sheltering preparatory action was statistically significant only via the credibility of the NWS message ($B_{ab} = -.06$, *bootSE* = .04, bias-corrected 95% bootstrap CI [−.17, −.01]). As shown in Figure 7.2, when compared to the convergence on the threat, communicative preparatory action, and sheltering preparatory action, the convergence on the threat and communicative preparatory action increased the credibility of the NWS message ($B = -.38$, $p = .04$), which, in turn, increased the intention to take sheltering preparatory action ($B = .16$, $p = .004$). Neither the credibility of the broadcast meteorologist's message nor the credibility of the social media-rologist's message mediated the relationship between convergence type and the intention to take sheltering preparatory action (Table 7.3).

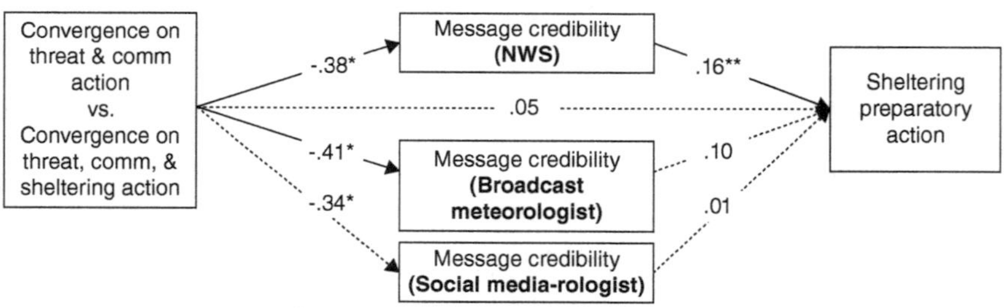

Figure 7.2 Model for sheltering preparatory action (RQ2-1).

Note: Convergence on the threat and communicative preparatory action coded as 0; convergence on the threat, communicative preparatory action, and sheltering preparatory action coded as 1.

Table 7.3 Indirect effects of convergence type on sheltering preparatory action

	B	*bootSE*	*Bias-corrected 95% bootstrap CI*	
Total indirect effect	−.11	.05	−.22	−.02
via message credibility of NWS	−.06	.04	−.17	−.01
via message credibility of broadcast meteorologist	−.04	.03	−.14	.00
via message credibility of social media-orologist	−.00	.02	−.06	.03

Note: The convergence type in this analysis refers to two conditions—the convergence on the threat and communicative preparatory action versus the convergence on the threat, communicative preparatory action, and sheltering preparatory action.

Table 7.4 Indirect effects of convergence type on sharing information with others

	B	*bootSE*	*Bias-corrected 95% bootstrap CI*	
Total indirect effect	–.16	.06	–.28	–.04
via message credibility of NWS	–.08	.04	–.19	–.01
via message credibility of broadcast meteorologist	–.03	.03	–.10	.02
via message credibility of social media-orologist	–.05	.03	–.14	–.004

Note: The convergence type in this analysis refers to two conditions—the convergence on the threat and communicative preparatory action versus the convergence on the threat, communicative preparatory action, and sheltering preparatory action.

Sharing information with others (RQ2-2)

We further explored, as another communication outcome, publics' intentions to share the given weather information with others (RQ2-2). Similar to RQ2-1, the results showed the mediating role of message credibility in the relationships between convergence type and sharing information with others (Table 7.4). However, the indirect effect of message convergence on sharing information was only significant via the credibility of the NWS message or the social media-rologist's message, not via the credibility of the broadcast meteorologist's message. The indirect effect via the credibility of the NWS message was statistically significant (B_{ab} = –.08, *bootSE* = .04, bias-corrected 95% bootstrap CI [–.19, –.01]), as was the effect via the credibility of the social media-rologist's message (B_{ab} = –.05, *bootSE* = .03, bias-corrected 95% bootstrap CI [–.14, –.002]). The condition of converging on the threat and communicative preparatory action, compared to the condition of converging on the threat, communicative preparatory action, and sheltering preparatory action, increased the message credibility of NWS or a social media-rologist, which, in turn, increased the intention to share the given weather information with others (see Figure 7.3). However, the credibility of the broadcast meteorologist's message did not mediate this relationship.

Social media engagement with messages (RQ3)

We also ran the PROCESS macro, using bias-corrected 95% bootstrap confidence intervals with 5,000 bootstrap samples, to answer RQ3. In RQ3, having publics' social media engagement with each actor's message as a communication outcome, we explored the mediating role of message credibility in the relationship between convergence type and social media engagement. Specifically, we examined three models in which the message credibility of the NWS, a broadcast meteorologist, and a social media-rologist respectively

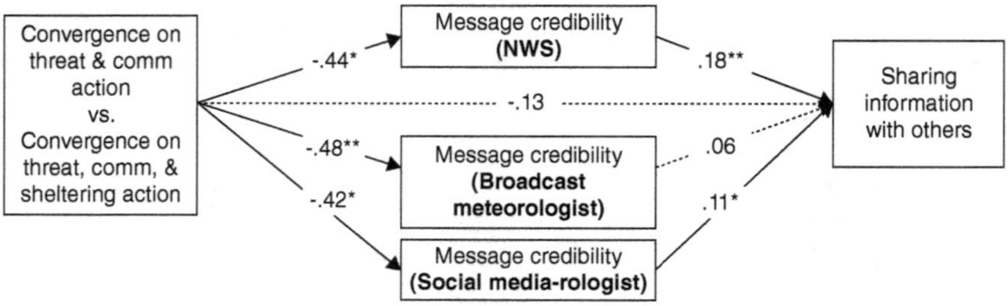

Figure 7.3 Model for sharing information with others (RQ2-2).

Note: Convergence on the threat and communicative preparatory action coded as 0; convergence on the threat, communicative preparatory action, and sheltering preparatory action coded as 1.

serve as a mediator, and social media engagement with the corresponding actor's message is an outcome. All three models showed the same pattern: the convergence on the threat and communicative preparatory action, compared to the convergence on the threat, communicative preparatory action, and sheltering preparatory action, increased the credibility of each actor's message, which, in turn, increased individual's engagement with each actor's message on social media. For example, compared to the condition of converging on the threat, communicative preparatory action, and sheltering preparatory action, the condition of converging on the threat and communicative preparatory action increased the credibility of the NWS message ($B = -.43$, $p = .02$), and this message credibility increased the intention of social media engagement with the NWS message ($B = .32$, $p < .001$) (Figure 7.4). The indirect effect of convergence type on social media engagement via the credibility of the NWS message was statistically significant ($B_{ab} = -.14$, $bootSE = .06$, bias-corrected 95% bootstrap CI [−.27, −.03]) (Table 7.5).

Discussion

In times of a public crisis, multiple actors communicate to help prepare communities for potential devastating consequences, bringing multivocality to crisis communication (Frandsen & Johansen, 2010; Sellnow et al., 2019). Weather communication, in particular, involves a multitude of actors, including the NWS, other organizations like the media, and active individuals (Atwell Seate et al., 2022; Liu et al., 2020a, 2020b), and the field strive for the most effective collection of weather messages from these various actors (Williams & Eosco, 2021). This study provides empirical findings that can guide such multiactor coordination for effective weather communication. In the weather alert context, we explored the

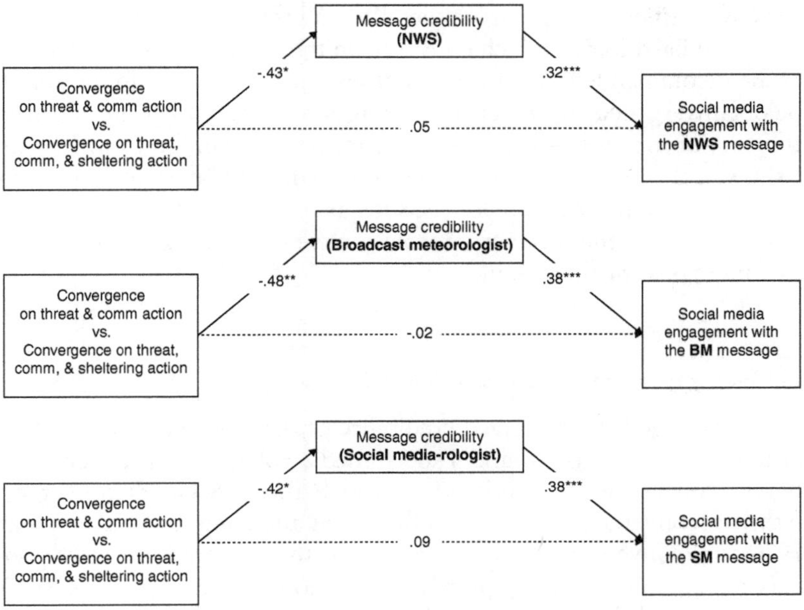

Figure 7.4 Models for social media engagement (RQ3).

Note: Convergence on the threat and communicative preparatory action coded as 0; Convergence on the threat, communicative preparatory action, and sheltering preparatory action coded as 1. (BM stands for broadcast meteorologist; SM stands for social media-rologist).

Table 7.5 Indirect effects of convergence type on social media engagement

	B	*bootSE*	*Bias-corrected 95% CI*	
via message credibility of the NWS (DV: Social media engagement with the NWS message)	–.14	.06	–.27	–.03
via message credibility of broadcast meteorologist (DV: Social media engagement with the broadcast meteorologist's message)	–.18	.07	–.32	–.05
via message credibility of social media-orologist (DV: Social media engagement with the social media-orologist's message)	–.16	.07	–.30	–.04

Note: The convergence type in this analysis refers to two conditions—the convergence on the threat and communicative preparatory action versus the convergence on the threat, communicative preparatory action, and sheltering preparatory action.

effects of weather messages from the NWS, a broadcast meteorologist, and a social media-rologist, which converge on the information about a threat and the recommended preparatory actions. Specifically, we found that the type of convergence—whether the messages converged on a specific preparatory action or more—led to varying message credibility. Furthermore, we showed the mediating role of message credibility between convergence type and communication outcomes, such as intentions to take preparatory actions and share the weather information. The following sections discuss these findings in further detail.

Convergence type and message credibility (RQ1)

RQ1 investigated the perceived credibility of the message from the NWS, a broadcast meteorologist, and a social media-rologist, respectively, under different convergence conditions—in which three messages converge on the threat (convergence type 1), on the threat and communicative preparatory action (convergence type 2), and on the threat, communicative preparatory action, and sheltering preparatory action (convergence type 3). Our findings showed that message credibility varied according to convergence type. The credibility of the message from each actor was the highest when the messages converged on the threat and communicative preparatory action (convergence type 2). Specifically, compared to the convergence on the threat, communicative preparatory action, and sheltering preparatory action (convergence type 3), the convergence on the threat and communicative preparatory action (convergence type 2) led to higher message credibility. In other words, publics perceived each actor's message as more credible when the messages addressed the threat and communicative preparatory action only, than when the messages addressed the threat, communicative preparatory action, and sheltering preparatory action. This suggests that the recommendation of communicative preparatory action served as a more effective converging point for weather messages in the given context, than did the addition of the recommendation of sheltering action. Given that communicative preparatory actions are important during the watch phase (Federal Emergency Management Agency, 2023), these findings have important implications for weather communicators.

This relative lack of prominence in the convergence on the threat, communicative preparatory action, and sheltering preparatory action might be due to "complete convergence" (Anthony et al., 2013, p. 350). MCF scholars note that excessive coherence can cause distrust for message convergence, as such coherence can be seen as contrived or incompatible with the volatile nature of crisis events (Anthony et al., 2013; Perelman & Olbrechts-Tyteca, 1969). While further exploration is necessary to confirm the mechanism underlying complete convergence, our findings add empirical evidence in the weather alert context that messages converging on most elements are not always convincing, leading to lower message credibility.

The effect of converging messages could also depend on the contextual significance. The experimental context of this study assumed a 'slight risk' for severe storms, directing public alertness, which discern from warnings that provide guidance on protective actions to take immediately (Bean et al., 2015; Bean & Hasinoff, 2022; Federal Emergency Management Agency, 2023). In such an alert context with slight risk, messages informing of the threat and recommending attentiveness (i.e., communicative preparatory action) might be most convincing. Higher-level actions, such as taking shelter or evacuating, require perceived severity and imminence of the event (Cuite et al., 2021; Dash & Gladwin, 2007), and sheltering preparatory actions might seem redundant in the slight-risk context and might not serve as the most effective converging point for messages. Meanwhile, the public warning scholarship calls for research to determine the amount of information for effective alert or warning messaging, especially in the brief or limited-text formats (Bean et al., 2015; Bean & Hasinoff, 2022). Our findings suggest that, in an alert context for high-impact weather, multiple actors could coordinate their brief messages to include information about the threat and communicative preparatory action.

These findings reiterate a call for a more critical approach to understand when and how to converge for effective communication (Anthony et al., 2013). Further research needs to explore varying effects of converging messages, considering the contemporary communication ecology of message convergence. For instance, prior ethnographic research found that NWS forecasters believe their tornado risk communication is most effective when individuals receive NWS messages from social media and then share those NWS messages with their offline social networks (Atwell Seate et al., 2022). Longitudinal research may be necessary to clarify varying message credibility and effectiveness in such a two-step convergence flow.

The mediating role of message credibility (RQ2)

RQ2 explored the mediating role of message credibility between convergence type and communication outcomes—i.e., intentions to take preparatory actions (RQ2-1) and to share the information with others (RQ2-2). Overall, the findings demonstrated that message credibility mediated the effects of varying message convergence on communication outcomes, which had only been implicitly suggested in previous qualitative studies (e.g., Anthony et al., 2013; Anthony & Sellnow, 2016).

Specifically, the effects of convergence type on the intention to take preparatory actions were mediated by message credibility (RQ2-1). When the messages converged on the threat and communicative preparatory action (convergence type 2), it led to higher message credibility and, in turn, higher intentions to take preparatory actions, than did the convergence on the threat, communicative preparatory action, and sheltering preparatory action (convergence type 3). Concretely, when the intention to take "communicative" preparatory action came as an outcome, the mediating effect was significant through the credibility of the NWS message or the broadcast meteorologist's message. The credibility of the social media-rologist's message was not a significant mediator. Meanwhile, when the intention to take "sheltering" preparatory action came as an outcome, only the credibility of the NWS message was a significant mediator. Namely, in the given alert context, we found more mediating paths through message credibility in the model on the intention to take communicative preparatory action than in the model on the intention to take sheltering preparatory action (RQ2-1), while messages converging on the recommendation of communicative preparatory action appeared to be more effective than others (RQ1).

The effects of convergence type on the intention to share the information with others were likewise mediated by message credibility (RQ2-2), but through the credibility of the NWS message or the social media-rologist's message. This differs from the results of RQ2-1, where only the credibility of the message from a core weather communicator—either the NWS or a broadcast meteorologist—was a significant mediator. In other words, when the intention to share the information with others came as a communication outcome, the credibility of the message from an active individual—i.e., social media-rologist—also served as a significant mediator.

These mixed findings on varying mediating effects prompt further research on the roles of diverse actors in message convergence. The MCF scholarship has highlighted the importance of credible sources in ensuring the effectiveness of message convergence (Anthony et al., 2013). Yet, the focus has been mostly on formal actors as message sources such as government agencies (Anthony et al., 2013; Soares et al., 2023). As RAT theorizes (Frandsen & Johansen, 2010), the communication ecology is comprised of more than official actors like government agencies. In this study, we tested social media-rologists and found mixed effects of the mediating role of message credibility between convergence type and communication outcomes. More empirical evidence is needed to specify how messages from individual actors can contribute to leading to certain communicative outcomes under the condition of message convergence. Furthermore, future research is needed to test other prominent actors in a variety of crisis communication contexts to better understand the interplay of message credibility and convergence.

Social media engagement with converging messages (RQ3)

RQ3 investigated publics' social media engagement with each actor's message and found that the effect of convergence type on social media engagement was mediated by message credibility. More precisely, as the convergence on the threat and communicative preparatory action (convergence type 2) led to higher credibility of the message from a given actor, the perceived message credibility, in turn, led to publics' social media engagement with that actor's message. This mediating path was significant in all cases—i.e., with the NWS message, the broadcast meteorologist's message, and the social media-rologist's message.

These findings provide one of the first empirical tests on the indirect effects of convergence type on social media engagement. The field of weather communication has been aware of the importance of social media engagement in enhancing the effects of weather communication, as it helps spread the word, clarify information, or even foster community building (e.g., Liu et al., 2020b; Olson et al., 2019; Sutton et al., 2019). The multivocal approach has also highlighted communicative behaviors of publics in an arena addressing the crisis, especially on social media (Coombs & Holladay, 2014; Frandsen & Johansen, 2010). However, the literature lacks studies investigating publics' social media engagement with crisis messages under the condition of message convergence. These findings serve as empirical evidence on how converging messages could engage publics on social media and, therefore, activate an arena to effectively address the crisis, especially in the weather alert context. Additional research is needed to understand any offline effects of these engaging online convergent messages, reflecting the crisis communication ecology proposed by RAT (Frandsen & Johansen, 2010). We suspect that crisis messages may flow among online and offline channels, becoming more powerful as they converge, but to date research has not explored such flow.

Theoretical and practical implications

The study findings have theoretical implications. First, our study extends the micro-level framework of RAT by integrating MCF. As previously reviewed, the RAT literature has provided the overview of multiple actors in crisis communication and highlighted the importance of communicative coordination among them to effectively manage the crisis (Ndlela, 2019; Zhao & Oh, 2021). However, the scholarship lacks micro-level studies to explicate the process of multivocal communication, which can serve as a guidance for strategic multiactor coordination. In the meantime, the MCF research has addressed the mechanism underlying multivocal communication where crisis messages from multiple actors converge (Anthony et al., 2013). Applying MCF, our study has revealed how multiple alert messages from various weather communicators could be processed, adding micro-level findings to the RAT literature as well.

Second, our study serves as one of the first quantitative tests in the scholarship, generalizing qualitative findings on the effects of multiactor communication. Both the RAT and MCF scholarships have uncovered how multivocal communication would work to promote public safety in the crisis context (Frandsen & Johansen, 2010; Ndlela, 2019) using qualitative approaches. However, only recently has quantitative work begun to confirm the cause and effect relationships underlying communicative processes (e.g., Soares et al., 2023; Ye & Ki, 2018) articulated in these lines of scholarship. Our study tested, from an experimental approach, the effects of converging messages on publics' intentions to take safety measures. The findings confirmed not only the association between convergence type and message credibility but also the mediating role of message credibility in leading to taking recommended actions, which had been only implicitly implied in previous qualitative findings (e.g., Anthony et al., 2013; Anthony & Sellnow, 2016).

Our findings also have practical implications for the multiactor coordination in weather crisis communication. First, the study findings showed that the credibility of converging messages could vary depending on the points of convergence, and not necessarily all the converging points lead to the highest credibility. In the slight-risk and alert context of this study, the recommendation of communicative preparatory action serves as an effective converging point that leads to higher message credibility, than with the recommendation of sheltering preparatory action. However, given the duty of weather communicators to include necessary elements for weather messages, ranging from the threat information to safety measures, in their communication (Liu et al., 2020b; Mileti & Sorensen, 1990), the field needs more studies on how to strategize certain information as converging points out of all required elements.

Second, our study showed the need to vary the prominence of each actor in collective communication, depending on targeted communication outcomes. We have mixed findings on the mediating effects of each actor's messages that, for example, the credibility of social media-rologist's messages did not mediate the effect of convergence type on publics' intentions to take preparatory actions but did mediate the effect on the intention to share the information with others. These findings imply that different actors can take a lead role in certain collective communication, depending on the goal of that communication. However, the field needs more empirical findings to specify the roles of various actors in different communication circumstances. Additionally, we call for further research on the communication ecology of message convergence, such as the (longitudinal) flow of converging messages among actors in their on and offline communication.

Limitations and future research

Our study has several limitations. First, our sample was limited to five states in the Southeastern region of the United States. Follow-up studies across other regions and in other countries are needed to confirm if the study's findings apply to other cultural contexts. Second, we tested three convergent messages, respectively, from three actors—the NWS, a broadcast meteorologist, and a social media-rologist. Given the weather communication ecology where more than three actors or three messages come together to address weather information, future research is needed to reflect the complex communication environment. Third, our research operationalized message convergence by exposing multiples messages which share the same points of arguments but with different wording. The MCF scholarship distinguishes convergence from congruence (Anthony et al., 2013), and weather communication research also acknowledges the difference in message features or other elements even among consistent messages (Williams & Eosco, 2021). Thus, future research needs to cover varied convergence conditions where partial divergence or deviation exists. Lastly, the study design can be applied to other public crisis contexts, such as public health emergencies, and compare the findings.

Conclusion

This study explored the effectiveness of converging messages from different crisis actors, ranging from a government agency to an active individual, in the public crisis context. Based on RAT and MCF, this study provides empirical findings to guide multiactor coordination for effective crisis communication during the watch phase of high-impact weather, especially on social media platforms. Specifically, we add the understanding of how converging messages could be processed to promote community members' preparatory actions or communicative behaviors. Through this understanding, we can better strategize the multivocality of public crises and achieve effective crisis communication to ensure public safety.

Appendix A. Message stimuli

1. Convergence on the threat
   Note
   The three tweet messages were presented in a random order.

Appendix A.1 Convergence on the threat.

Note: Organizational logos were removed to be compliant with the publishing guidelines. Participants viewed the message with the corresponding organizational logos when completing the study.

2. Convergence on the threat and communicative preparatory action
   Note
   The three tweet messages were presented in a random order.

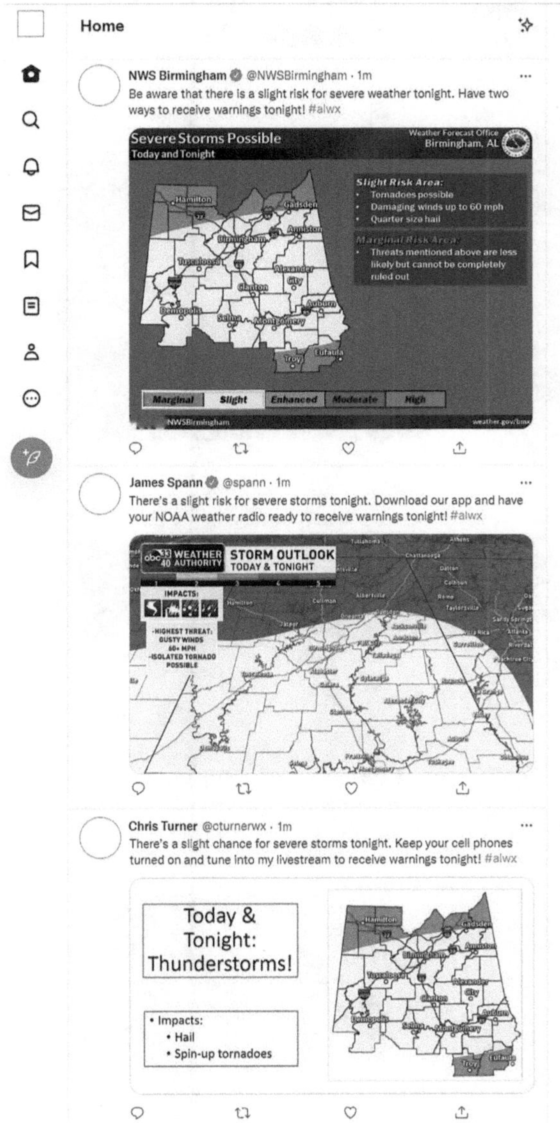

Appendix A.2 Convergence on the threat and communicative preparatory action.

Note: Organizational logos were removed to be compliant with the publishing guidelines. Participants viewed the message with the corresponding organizational logos when completing the study.

3. Convergence on the threat, communicative preparatory action, and sheltering preparatory action
   Note
   The three tweet messages were presented in a random order.

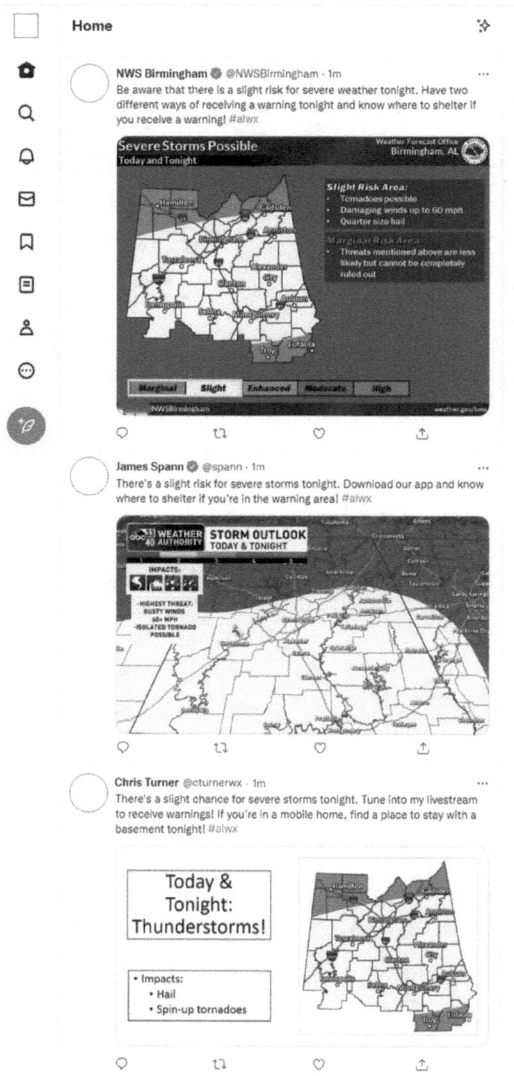

Appendix A.3 Convergence on the threat, communicative preparatory action, and sheltering preparatory action.

Note: Organizational logos were removed to be compliant with the publishing guidelines. Participants viewed the message with the corresponding organizational logos when completing the study.

Appendix B: Measurement items and descriptive statistics

Variable	*Items*	*α*	*M*	*SD*
Message credibility (NWS)	*The message from Birmingham NWS is* - Credible - Believable - Accurate.	.96	6.64	2.21
Message credibility (Broadcast meteorologist)	*The message from James Spann is* - Credible - Believable - Accurate.	.95	6.61	2.15
Message credibility (Social meteorologist)	*The message from Chris Turner is* - Credible - Believable - Accurate.	.94	6.22	2.09
Communicative preparatory action	*If I saw the messages on my Twitter feed, I would* - Ensure I have multiple ways to receive messages about the severe weather (i.e., warnings). - Ensure that I leave my cell phone turned on to receive messages about the severe weather (i.e., warnings). - Ensure that my weather radio is turned on and ready to receive messages about the severe weather (i.e., warnings).	.74	6.67	1.83
Sheltering preparatory action	*If I saw the messages on my Twitter feed, I would* - Change my schedule to ensure that I am in a safe place during the severe weather event. - Leave my residence to stay in a location where sturdy shelter is readily available. - Put lawn furniture, trash bins, etc. in a secure location. - Park my vehicle in a garage.	.73	6.06	1.8
Sharing the information with others	*If I saw the messages on my Twitter feed, I would* - Create my own tweet about the predicted weather. - Tell people I know (family, friends and coworkers, etc.) via in-person face-to-face conversations about the severe weather. - Call people I know (family, friends and coworkers, etc.) via telephone to talk about the severe weather. - Text people I know (family, friends and coworkers, etc.) about the severe weather. - Tell others to follow the local National Weather Service office's instructions about the severe weather. - Knock on my neighbor's door to alert them about the severe weather.	.84	5.43	1.92

Variable	*Items*	*α*	*M*	*SD*
Social media engagement with the NWS message	- I would retweet Birmingham NWS' message. - I would use the like button in response to Birmingham NWS' message. - I would reply with a positive comment to Birmingham NWS' message. - I would reply with a question to Birmingham NWS' message.	.86	5.02	2.28
Social media engagement with the broadcast meteorologist's message	- I would retweet James Spann's message. - I would use the like button in response to James Spann's message. - I would reply with a positive comment to James Spann's message. - I would reply with a question to James Spann's message.	.87	4.98	2.29
Social media engagement with the social media-orologist's message	- I would retweet Chris Turner's message. - I would use the like button in response to Chris Turner's message. - I would reply with a positive comment to Chris Turner's message. - I would reply with a question to Chris Turner's message.	.87	4.76	2.28

References

Anthony, K. E., & Sellnow, T. L. (2016). The role of the message convergence framework in medical decision making. *Journal of Health Communication*, 21(2), 249–256. https://doi.org/10.1080/10810730.2015.1064497

Anthony, K. E., Sellnow, T. L., & Millner, A. G. (2013). Message convergence as a message-centered approach to analyzing and improving risk communication. *Journal of Applied Communication Research*, 41(4), 346–364. https://doi.org/10.1080/00909882.2013.844346

Anthony, K. E., Sellnow, T. L., Venette, S. J., & Fourney, S. P. (2017). Message convergence framework applied to health and risk messaging. *Oxford Research Encyclopedia of Communication*. https://doi.org/10.1093/acrefore/9780190228613.013.540

Appelman, A., & Sundar, S. S. (2016). Measuring message credibility: Construction and validation of an exclusive scale. *Journalism & Mass Communication Quarterly*, 93(1), 59–79. https://doi.org/10.1177/1077699015606057

Atwell Seate, A., Liu, B. F., Stanley, S., Yan, Y., & Chatham, A. (2022). Relational constellations in disasters: Theorizing multiparty relationships through ethnographic research. *Journal of Public Relations Research*, 34(5), 208–226. https://doi.org/10.1080/1062726X.2022.2093203

Bean, H., & Hasinoff, A. A. (2022). The social functions of idle alerts. In Y. Jin & L. Austin, *Social media and crisis communication* (2nd ed., pp. 360–370). Routledge. https://doi.org/10.4324/9781003043409-43

Bean, H., Sutton, J., Liu, B. F., Madden, S., Wood, M. M., & Mileti, D. S. (2015). The study of mobile public warning messages: A research review and agenda. *Review of Communication*, *15*(1), 60–80. https://doi.org/10.1080/15358593.2015.1014402

Coombs, W., & Holladay, S. (2014). How publics react to crisis communication efforts: Comparing crisis response reactions across sub-arenas. *Journal of Communication Management*, 18(1), 40–57. https://doi.org/10.1108/JCOM-03-2013-0015

Cuite, C. L., Morss, R. E., Demuth, J. L., & Hallman, W. K. (2021). Hurricanes vs Nor'easters: The effects of storm type on perceived severity and protective actions. *Bulletin of the American Meteorological Society*, 102(7), E1306–E1316. https://doi.org/10.1175/BAMS-D-19-0043.1

Dash, N., & Gladwin, H. (2007). Evacuation decision making and behavioral responses: Individual and household. *Natural Hazards Review*, 8(3), 69–77. https://doi.org/10.1061/(ASCE)1527-6988(2007)8:3(69)

Federal Emergency Management Agency. (2023, April 5). *Watch vs. warning: What to know before severe storms*. https://www.fema.gov/press-release/20230426/watch-vs-warning-what-know-severe-storms

Frandsen, F., & Johansen, W. (2010). Crisis communication, complexity, and the cartoon affair: a case study. In W. T. Coombs & S. J. Holladay (Eds.), *The handbook of public sector communication* (pp. 425–448). John Wiley & Sons. https://doi.org/10.1002/9781444314885.ch21

Frandsen, F., & Johansen, W. (2018). Voices in conflict? The crisis communication of meta-organizations. *Management Communication Quarterly*, *32*(1), 90–120. https://doi.org/10.1177/0893318917705734

Frandsen, F., & Johansen, W. (2020a). Arenas and voices in organizational crisis communication: How far have we come? In F. Frandsen & W. Johansen (Eds.), *Crisis communication* (pp. 195–212). De Gruyter Mouton. https://doi.org/10.1515/9783110554236-009

Frandsen, F., & Johansen, W. (2020b). Public sector communication: Risk and crisis communication. In V. Luoma-aho & M. J. Canel (Eds.), *The handbook of public sector communication* (pp. 229–244). John Wiley & Sons. https://doi.org/10.1002/9781119263203.ch15

Frandsen, F., & Johansen, W. (2022). Rhetorical arena theory: Revisited and expanded. In W. T. Coombs & S. J. Holladay (Eds.), *The handbook of crisis communication* (2nd ed., pp. 169–181). John Wiley & Sons. https://doi.org/10.1002/9781119678953.ch12

Hayes, A. F. (2022). *Introduction to mediation, moderation, and conditional process analysis: A regression-based approach* (3rd ed.). The Guilford Press.

Heath, R. L. (2006). Onward into more fog: thoughts on public relations' research directions. *Journal of Public Relations Research*, 18(2), 93–114. https://doi.org/10.1207/s1532754xjprr1802_2

Herovic, E., Sellnow, T. L., & Anthony, K. E. (2014). Risk communication as interacting arguments: Viewing the L'aquila earthquake disaster through the message convergence framework. *Argumentation & Advocacy*, 51(2), 73–86. https://doi.org/10.1080/00028533.2014.11821840

Huang, J., Yang, J. Z., & Chu, H. (2022). Framing climate change impacts as moral violations: The pathway of perceived message credibility. *International Journal of Environmental Research and Public Health*, 19(9), 5210. https://doi.org/10.3390/ijerph19095210

Iannacone, J. I. (2021). Negotiating crises interpretations: The global rhetorical arena of the 2018 migrant caravan "crisis." *Public Relations Review*, 47(2), 102034. https://doi.org/10.1016/j.pubrev.2021.102034

Johansen, B. F., Johansen, W., & Weckesser, N. M. (2016). Emotional stakeholders as "crisis communicators" in social media: The case of the Telenor customer complaints crisis. *Corporate Communications: An International Journal*, *21*(3), 289–308. https://doi.org/10.1108/CCIJ-05-2015-0026

Kim, J., Lee, S., Wang, Y., & Leach, J. D. (2023). The power of moral words in politicized climate change communication. *Environmental Communication*, 1–15. https://doi.org/10.1080/17524032.2023.2227771

Lee, Y. (2022). An examination of the effects of employee words in organizational crisis: Public forgiveness and behavioral intentions. *International Journal of Business Communication*, *59*(4), 598–620. https://doi.org/10.1177/23294884 19877236

Liu, B. F., & Atwell Seate, A. (2021). The evolving weather service: forecasters' perceptions of their relationships with core partners. *Weather, Climate, and Society*, 13(3), 437–448. https://doi.org/10.1175/WCAS-D-20-0097.1

Liu, B. F., Atwell Seate, A., Iles, I., & Herovic, E. (2020a). Eyes of the storm: How citizen scientists contribute to government forecasting and risk communication. *Weather, Climate, and Society*, 12(2), 263–277. https://doi.org/10.1175/WCAS-D-19-0131.1

Liu, B. F., Atwell Seate, A., Iles, I., & Herovic, E. (2020b). Tornado warning: Understanding the National Weather Service's communication strategies. *Public Relations Review*, 46(2), 101879. https://doi.org/10.1016/j.pubrev.2019.101879

Liu, B. F., Fraustino, J. D., & Jin, Y. (2016). Social media use during disasters: How information form and source influence intended behavioral responses. *Communication Research*, 43(5), 626–646. https://doi.org/10.1177/0093650 214565917

Maier, C. D., Frandsen, F., & Johansen, W. (2022). Understanding the arena of smoldering crises: A longitudinal study of discursive struggles after implementing a new IT health care platform. *Journal of Communication Management*, 27(3), 329–344. https://doi.org/10.1108/JCOM-12-2021-0136

Mayer, M., Vega, J., Demarco, I., Eicher, R., Flores Molina, D., Lee, C., Perez Naufel, J., Sheng, X., Sublette, J., Freihaut, R., & Sellnow, T. L. (2023). Message convergence as reassurance about the safety of the food supply concerning African swine fever virus. *Animal Health and Therapy Reports*, *2*(1), 2–11. https://doi.org/10.31491/AHTR.2023.02.002

Mileti, D., & Sorensen, J. (1990). *Communication of emergency public warnings: A social science perspective and state-of-the-art assessment* (No. ORNL-6609). Oak Ridge National Laboratory. https://doi.org/10.2172/6137387

Morss, R. E., Demuth, J. L., Lazo, J. K., Dickinson, K., Lazrus, H., & Morrow, B. H. (2016). Understanding public hurricane evacuation decisions and responses to forecast and warning messages. *Weather and Forecasting*, 31(2), 395–417. https://doi.org/10.1175/WAF-D-15-0066.1

National Severe Storms Laboratory. (n.d.). VORTEX Southeast. https://www.nssl.noaa.gov/projects/vortexse/

Ndlela, M. N. (2019). Stakeholder communications during a crisis. In M. N. Ndlela (Ed.), *Crisis communication: A stakeholder approach* (pp. 131–150). Springer International Publishing. https://doi.org/10.1007/978-3-319-97256-5_7

Nedelcu, D., & Balaban, D. C. (2021). The role of source credibility and message credibility in fake news engagement. Perspectives from an experimental study. *Journal of Media Research*, 14(3), 42–62. https://doi.org/10.24193/jmr.41.3

Olson, M. K., Sutton, J., Vos, S. C., Prestley, R., Renshaw, S. L., & Butts, C. T. (2019). Build community before the storm: The National Weather Service's social media engagement. *Journal of Contingencies and Crisis Management*, 27(4), 359–373. https://doi.org/10.1111/1468-5973.12267

Perelman, C., & Olbrechts-Tyteca, L. (1969). *The new rhetoric: A treatise on argumentation*. University of Notre Dame Press. https://doi.org/10.2307/j.ctvpj74xx

Ploran, E. J., Trasciatti, M. A., & Farmer, E. C. (2018). Efficacy and authority of the message sender during emergency evacuations: A mixed methods study. *Journal of Applied Communication Research*, 46(3), 291–322. https://doi.org/10.1080/00909882.2018.1464659

Pulos, R. (2020). COVID-19 crisis memes, rhetorical arena theory and multimodality. *Journal of Science Communication*, 19, A01. https://doi.org/10.22323/2.19070201

Rodin, P., Ghersetti, M., & Odén, T. (2019). Disentangling rhetorical subarenas of public health crisis communication: A study of the 2014–2015 Ebola outbreak in the news media and social media in Sweden. *Journal of Contingencies and Crisis Management*, 27(3), 237–246. https://doi.org/10.1111/1468-5973.12254

Sellnow, D. D., Sellnow, T. L., & Martin, J. M. (2019). Strategic message convergence in communicating biosecurity: The case of the 2013 Porcine Epidemic Diarrhea Virus. *Communication Reports*, *32*(3), 125–136. https://doi.org/10.1080/08934215.2019.1634747

Soares, R., Jin, X., Spence, P. R., & Sellnow, T. L. (2023). Interacting arguments in crisis communication: The influence of message convergence on risk and crisis messages. *Journal of Contingencies and Crisis Management*, 31(3), 516–523. https://doi.org/10.1111/1468-5973.12456

Spence, P. R., Edwards, C., Edwards, A., Rainear, A., & Jin, X. (2021). "They're always wrong anyway": Exploring differences of credibility, attraction, and behavioral intentions in professional, amateur, and robotic-delivered weather forecasts. *Communication Quarterly*, 69(1), 67–86. https://doi.org/10.1080/01463373.2021.1877164

Sutton, J., Renshaw, S. L., Vos, S. C., Olson, M. K., Prestley, R., Gibson, C. B., & Butts, C. T. (2019). Getting the word out, rain or shine: The impact of message features and hazard context on message passing online. *Weather, Climate, and Society*, 11(4), 763–776. https://doi.org/10.1175/WCAS-D-19-0021.1

Weyrich, P., Scolobig, A., & Patt, A. (2019). Dealing with inconsistent weather warnings: Effects on warning quality and intended actions. *Meteorological Applications*, 26(4), 569–583. https://doi.org/10.1002/met.1785

Williams, C. A., & Eosco, G. M. (2021). Is a consistent message achievable?: Defining "message consistency" for weather enterprise researchers and practitioners. *Bulletin of the American Meteorological Society*, *102*(2), E279–E295. https://doi.org/10.1175/BAMS-D-18-0250.1

Ye, L., & Ki, E.-J. (2018). Impact of message convergence on organizational reputation: An examination of organizational crisis communication on Facebook. *Corporate Reputation Review*, *21*(1), 1–8. https://doi.org/10.1057/s41299-017-0040-5

Zhang, X., & Chen, A. (2022). The multiplicity and dynamics of functional crisis memories in crisis communication: How Chinese social media users collectively reconstructed SARS during COVID-19. *Journal of Public Relations Research*, *34*(1/2), 45–63. https://doi.org/10.1080/1062726X.2022.2063869

Zhao, X., & Oh, H. J. (2021). What fosters interorganizational frame convergence: Examining a semantic network during the opioid crisis. *Public Relations Review*, *47*(3), 102042. https://doi.org/10.1016/j.pubrev.2021.102042

Zhao, X., Xu, S., & Austin, L. L. (2022). Medium and source convergence in crisis information acquisition: Patterns, antecedents, and outcomes. *New Media & Society*. Advance online publication. https://doi.org/10.1177/14614448221088866

8 Crisis Communication in the Age of AI

Navigating Opportunities, Challenges, and Future Horizons

Yang Cheng, Jaekuk Lee, and Jinzhe Qiao

Introduction

In today's interconnected world, characterized by rapid information dissemination and global interdependence, the demand for swift and effective communication strategies has never been more critical. Crises, whether natural disasters, public health emergencies, or socio-political events, can unfold rapidly, requiring immediate and coordinated responses. The ability to convey timely and accurate information is essential for managing these situations and minimizing their impact on individuals and communities.

Artificial Intelligence (AI) emerges as a game-changing tool in crisis management efforts due to its transformative capabilities. AI technologies, such as natural language processing (NLP), machine learning, and data analytics, empower systems to process vast amounts of information at unprecedented speeds. This enables AI to contribute significantly to various aspects of crisis communication, from early detection and monitoring to response optimization and public engagement. However, AI-powered media tools also introduce challenges. Ethical considerations such as data privacy, algorithmic biases, and the potential for unintended consequences underscore the need for careful integration and regulation of AI tools in crisis management efforts. Striking a balance between leveraging AI's benefits and addressing these ethical concerns remains a critical challenge in harnessing the full potential of AI for effective crisis communication.

To sum up, the evolution of artificial intelligence has significantly impacted contemporary crisis communication, necessitating a dedicated chapter to succinctly capture AI tools' benefits, challenges, and applications in this context. In our interconnected world, where crises unfold rapidly, effective communication plays an increasingly pivotal role. Therefore, a focused chapter offers a comprehensive exploration of how AI tools meet the unique demands of crisis communication, providing valuable insights into their practical applications and relevance.

DOI: 10.4324/9781032619187-9

To fill the gap, the first section of this chapter examines the essentials of crisis communication and the critical components of effective crisis response. It underscores the importance of real-time information dissemination, sentiment analysis, and public engagement to navigate crises successfully. The subsequent part introduces AI and its various technologies, including NLP, machine learning, and data analytics. These tools empower AI systems to process vast amounts of information rapidly and derive valuable insights, making them ideal for handling crisis communication challenges. The central focus of this chapter revolves around the key functions of AI-powered media tools for the crisis communication process. However, the chapter acknowledges that alongside their significant benefits, AI tools in crisis communication pose ethical challenges. Ensuring data privacy, minimizing algorithmic biases, and balancing automation with human intervention are vital concerns that require careful consideration.

Finally, the chapter speculates on the future trends and implications of AI in crisis communication. It discusses emerging AI technologies and their potential to revolutionize crisis response efforts while also urging for continued research to mitigate any adverse impacts on society and communication processes.

Essentials of Crisis Communication

Three Steps of Crisis Communication

Crisis communication entails a deliberate and timely sharing of information during crises, with the objective of managing and mitigating their impact (Alexander, 2014). This facet assumes a pivotal role in the effective navigation of crises, serving to furnish precise and pertinent details to a diverse spectrum of stakeholders, including the general public, employees, and authorities (Coombs, 2014a). At its core, the primary aim is to ensure that stakeholders, on an individual level, possess a lucid understanding of the crisis, its potential ramifications, and the measures being undertaken for its resolution (Cheng et al., 2021).

The crisis communication process unfolds in three basic phases: pre-crisis, crisis event, and post-crisis, involving specific actions and strategies for effective crisis management. The pre-crisis phase emphasizes prevention and preparation, involving actions such as monitoring and scanning various sources like newspapers, TV news, online platforms, and public opinion polls; assessing issues, risks, and stakeholder relationships, and designing tools and crisis communication systems (Coombs, 2014a).

During the crisis management effort, timely detection is essential, requiring continuous monitoring and the persuasion of upper management regarding the crisis's reality. Notably, an important step of crisis management pertains to the analysis of public sentiment and the cultivation of engagement. In the contemporary digital era, where information traverses swiftly across diverse online platforms, comprehending public sentiment is imperative (Cheng et al., 2021). Sentiment analysis, involving the assessment of the emotional tone and subjective information within text data, emerges as a critical tool. Such analytical tools effectively gauge public reactions, concerns, and emotional responses during a crisis (Mirbabaie et al., 2020). Through the utilization of sentiment analysis, crisis communicators can tailor their messages to address specific concerns and emotions, thereby augmenting the overall efficacy of their communication strategies (Mirbabaie et al., 2020).

The significance of sentiment analysis is underscored during crises as it furnishes real-time insights into public reactions. The ability to discern whether the public is experiencing anxiety, fear, anger, or hopefulness empowers organizations and authorities to dynamically adjust their communication strategies (Gruda & Ojo, 2022). Moreover, sentiment analysis plays a pivotal role in identifying emerging issues or concerns that might not be readily apparent through traditional communication channels. This enables a more personalized and empathetic approach to addressing the emotional needs of the affected population (Mirbabaie et al., 2020). Last but not least, ensuring public engagement during a crisis holds equal importance, necessitating active involvement through feedback mechanisms, open forums, and social media interactions. These processes serve a dual purpose by not only facilitating the dissemination of information but also enabling the collection of valuable insights and feedback essential for guiding crisis management strategies (Cheng et al., 2022). Such an approach fosters a sense of community and shared responsibility during challenging times, thereby enriching communication practices (Lerbinger, 2011).

In addition, as a crisis unfolds, information evolves from mere data to a crucial lifeline. Timely communication delineates the distinction between an informed and prepared public and one left in a state of confusion and disarray (Fink, 2000). The provision of regular updates and accurate information plays a pivotal role in assuaging uncertainty, anxiety, and fear—common emotional responses during a crisis, the exacerbation of which could potentially escalate the situation (Gruda & Ojo, 2022). The instantaneous dissemination of real-time information fulfills several crucial functions. Firstly, it facilitates situational awareness, empowering the public to make informed decisions concerning their safety and well-being. Simultaneously, it serves as a countermeasure against the dissemination of misinformation, which, if unchecked, has the potential to escalate the crisis and induce unwarranted panic (Alexander, 2014). Moreover, this real-time distribution of information fosters transparency and engenders trust among authorities, organizations, and the public, further solidifying the foundations of effective crisis communication (Coombs, 2014a).

In the post-crisis stage, the recovery phase of crisis communication involves a comprehensive follow-up to keep stakeholders informed about corrective actions, financial implications, and ongoing compassion (Coombs, 2014a); continuous monitoring of issues, risks, and developments is imperative for a thorough recovery; assessing effectiveness through record examination and phase analysis informs necessary changes for future crises, and learning from the crisis (Coombs, 2014a). In addition, the overall evaluation of the crisis management process contributes to understanding its effectiveness and areas for enhancement (Reynolds & Seeger, 2005).

Crisis Communication Strategies

Termed as both verbal and nonverbal responses utilized by organizations to confront a crisis (Huang et al., 2005), crisis communication strategies (CCS) represent a vital array of approaches indispensable for effective crisis management. Image restoration theory, introduced by Benoit (1995) and now extensively referenced in crisis communication research, posits that a dual-component attack—comprising an offensive act coupled with an accusation of responsibility—jeopardizes the reputation of an organization or individual, prompting the need for a strategic crisis response. The five fundamental strategies within image restoration theory encompass denial, evasion of responsibility, mitigation of offensiveness, corrective action, and mortification. However, Coombs (2014b) noted that not every crisis necessitates reputation repair efforts; in many cases, the provision of instructive information and expressions of concern proves adequate to protect the reputation. To facilitate effective crisis communication, the significance of expeditious information dissemination cannot be overstated. Three primary informational strategies are "instructing information," "adjusting information," and "internalizing information," which serve as indispensable tools ensuring the swift and efficient flow of crucial information during crises (Cheng, 2018).

In the realm of information strategies, instructing information was emphasized, involving the communication of how the crisis might affect stakeholders and what actions they should take to protect themselves physically. Furthermore, the emphasis on instructing information also encompasses guidance on protecting stakeholders financially. This could involve information about available resources, financial assistance programs, or steps individuals can take to secure their financial well-being in the face of economic challenges triggered by the crisis (Coombs, 2014b). Adjusting information emerges as another indispensable strategy within crisis communication, involves a proactive and targeted approach, entailing the rapid and precise dissemination of critical information to stakeholders. This strategy, as outlined by Jin et al. (2014), aims to keep all relevant parties well informed about the evolving crisis, including the general public, employees, and authorities. Its primary objective is to reduce uncertainty and confusion by providing timely updates on crisis developments, safety guidelines, and recommended actions, thereby bridging the gap between the crisis and those affected. This, in turn, enhances the efficiency of crisis management and response (Fink, 2000; Reynolds & Seeger, 2005). Last, internalizing information, as identified by Coombs (2014a), was highlighted as a crucial component for reputation management, encompassing strategies within denial, diminishment, rebuilding, and bolstering clusters.

In the healthcare sector, for instance, effective information instructing and adjusting assumes a critical role in managing public health crises, exemplified by instances of disease outbreaks. Notably, the COVID-19 pandemic underscored the pivotal role of timely and accurate communication to the public (Reddy & Gupta, 2020). Health authorities and organizations globally engaged in extensive crisis communication efforts to disseminate pertinent information regarding the virus, its transmission, safety measures, and vaccination distribution. The integrated crisis communication model, as elucidated by Reynolds and Seeger, accentuates the imperative of a unified approach to managing public health crises (Reynolds & Seeger, 2005). This unified approach not only contributed to mitigating panic but also endorsed crucial public health measures such as mask-wearing and social distancing. Consequently, it enhanced the overall crisis response and management within the healthcare domain, highlighting the indispensable role of crisis communication in saving lives and effectively managing global health crises.

In summary, the three steps of crisis communication, as expounded in the referenced sources, stand as the linchpin of effective crisis management. Its paramount role lies in the expeditious and lucid conveyance of information, thereby diminishing uncertainty and averting panic. The foundational element is the real-time dissemination of information, acting as a bulwark against misinformation and cultivating transparency. Augmented by sentiment analysis and public engagement, this process is enriched, facilitating a more nuanced and responsive approach. Collectively, these integrated elements contribute to the development of a resilient and well-informed community when confronted with crises.

Functions of AI Tools for Crisis Communication

In the realm of AI, its multifaceted applications span technologies like NLP, machine learning, and data analytics. Scholarly interest has grown in exploring AI's functions in crisis communication (Nguyen et al., 2017). AI systems exhibit significant potential in processing vast amounts of unstructured data from diverse sources, such as social media, news outlets, and government alerts. This analytical prowess enables the rapid identification of emerging crises, allowing timely interventions by crisis management authorities (Park & Cho, 2015). The transformative impact of AI on crisis communication strategies extends throughout the crisis lifecycle. AI plays a role in automated information scanning and predictive analytics pre-crisis, real-time engagement, social media monitoring, personalized communication during crises, and assessing and learning in the post-crisis. The following section lists several major AI functions and emphasizes their key roles in the crisis communication process (see Figure 8.1 for more details).

Pre-Crisis: AI-Powered Scanning and Early Detection

Automated Information Scanning

Automated information scanning in crisis communication leverages AI to rapidly process large volumes of diverse data, enabling quick scanning of the situation. This automated data processing has a significant impact on crisis communicators, allowing them to comprehend the evolving nature of the issues, identify trends, and extract actionable insights for effective communication.

For instance, AI-driven chatbots, as highlighted by Yang et al. (2023), play a transformative role in reshaping the landscape of crisis communication. By automating repetitive and time-consuming tasks, AI, as emphasized by Nishant et al. (2020), liberates human resources to engage in higher-value tasks demanding critical thinking and creativity. The benefits

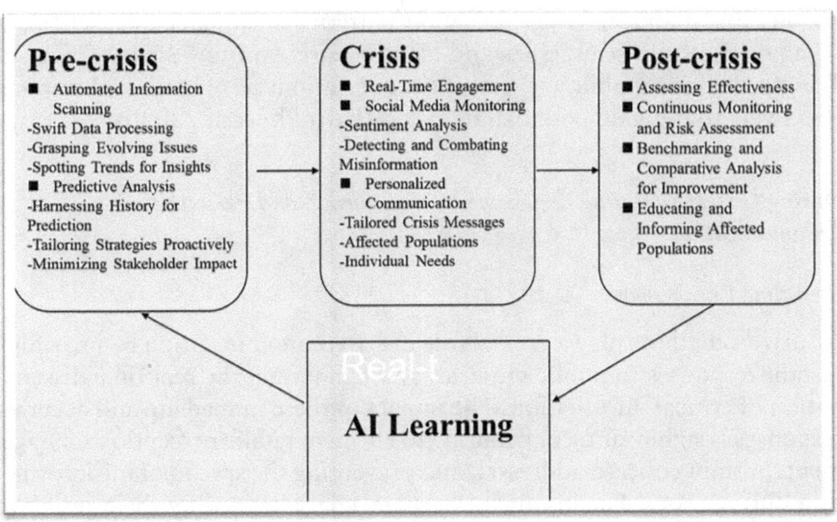

Figure 8.1 Key functions of AI tools across crisis stages.

extend to speed, accuracy, and data-driven decision-making, proving effective in diverse crisis scenarios such as natural disasters, cyberattacks, and global pandemics (Vladu, 2023). Moreover, the automation facilitated by AI enables organizations to predict potential crises, empowering them to make more informed decisions (Farrokhi et al., 2020). For instance, AI techniques, like convolutional neural networks, can automatically scan and detect flooded areas, damaged buildings, and infrastructure from satellite imagery (Fujita et al., 2017). In analyzing emergency communications, AI-powered language processing can rapidly extract threats, location details, and situational information (Aboualola et al., 2023).

Predictive Analytics

AI algorithms leverage historical data to predict potential crisis scenarios, enabling proactive communication planning. This predictive capability empowers organizations to anticipate crises, tailor communication strategies accordingly, and minimize the impact on stakeholders.

AI's ability to develop predictive models, which can foresee potential crisis situations, allows for proactive crisis management. This application of AI is particularly important in predicting natural disasters or other emergencies, enabling authorities to take preemptive action (Vladu, 2023). Techniques like Deep Learning (DL), Long Short-Term Memory (LSTM) networks, and Convolutional Neural Networks (CNNs) are applied to predicting crowd density and movement, enhancing emergency management capabilities (Aboualola et al., 2023). AI's role in predictive analysis is specifically applied to the detection of potential crisis events within organizations. By analyzing communication patterns, such as email exchanges, AI algorithms can scan issues and identify early warning signs of a crisis. This predictive capability is vital for organizations to prepare and respond effectively to mitigate potential damages (Farrokhi et al., 2020).

During Crises: Real-time Engagement, Monitoring, and Personalized Communication

Real-time Engagement

AI-driven chatbots play a crucial role in crisis communication by providing instant responses to public inquiries and facilitating the real-time dissemination of critical information. The impact of these immediate and accurate responses is significant, contributing to effective public perception management, prompt concern addressal, and preventing the spread of misinformation during crises. For instance, chatbots, characterized by their ability to mimic human conversation, have emerged as indispensable tools in crisis communication. With user-friendly interfaces and seamless integration into popular messaging services, these AI-driven programs offer immediate responses, making them effective for information dissemination and public engagement during crises (Cheng & Jiang, 2022). A study by Kim et al. (2022) emphasizes the strategic importance of communication by public health agencies on social media, underscoring the effectiveness of two-way communication strategies. The integration of AI chatbots into these platforms significantly enhances public engagement by providing instant and accurate information, contributing to improved public understanding and response during crises.

Monitoring and Sentiment Analysis

AI, particularly leveraging machine learning techniques, proves instrumental in crisis management, especially in the realm of social media monitoring. Wong (2021) emphasizes its notable advantage in monitoring diverse social media platforms, enabling the anticipation of emerging trends, shifts in public sentiment, and potential issues. This proactive approach allows crisis communicators to stay ahead of developments and adapt strategies in real time, aligning with the dynamic nature of social media conversations. Machine learning techniques, exemplified by the AIDR project (Imran et al., 2015), showcase the ability to scrutinize platforms like Twitter or Facebook, discerning potential threats based on discussions related to key terms, rumors, and misinformation. In crisis scenarios, network data analysis, including messages, emails, and social media interactions, proves invaluable for organizations, offering a comprehensive understanding of both historical and real-time communication for more informed responses (Farrokhi et al., 2020).

Sentiment analysis, as one type of monitoring, benefits emergency agencies in understanding public perception and refining communication strategies (Mirbabaie et al., 2020). By analyzing sentiment, AI provides predictive insights into the emotional state of organizations or stakeholders, which is crucial for anticipating and managing crisis situations (Farrokhi et al., 2020). NRC-based sentiment analysis, as demonstrated by Kaur et al. (2021), explores how leaders portray emotions in crisis communication, highlighting the significance of positive and trust emotions for the effective dissemination of knowledge. Furthermore, Rahman et al. (2023) elaborate on the effectiveness of AI in detecting social crises through Twitter data, emphasizing its potential for real-time understanding of public sentiment during crises.

Detecting and Combating Misinformation

AI's capability to identify and counteract the proliferation of deepfake material is essential in the realm of crisis communication. This function is vital for recognizing and filtering out altered or fabricated content, thus hindering the spread of misleading information that could intensify the crisis situation.

For instance, in response to challenges posed by the COVID-19 pandemic, governments worldwide, including Indonesia and the United Kingdom, along with organizations like the World Health Organization (WHO), have turned to advanced tools such as chatbots to disseminate real-time information, manage public sentiment, and address concerns effectively (Untari, 2020). Chatbots thus play a crucial role in countering misinformation and rumors prevalent in larger communities by offering concise and credible answers (Untari, 2020).

In addition, AI techniques also exhibit promise in detecting the spread of misinformation during crises through content analysis. Computer vision algorithms can filter out irrelevant visual media, while textual anomaly detection can identify suspicious claims lacking evidence (Nguyen et al., 2017). Such capabilities to process social data have the potential to help crisis coordinators pinpoint and respond to misleading narratives that jeopardize response priorities.

Last but not least, in the examination of 112 scholarly articles addressing various approaches to deepfake detection, encompassing deep learning-based techniques, classical machine learning methods, statistical techniques, and blockchain-based methodologies, Rana et al. (2022) observed that deep learning-based methods demonstrated superior efficacy compared to alternative strategies. This underscores the proficiency of artificial intelligence within the domain of deepfake detection.

Personalized Communication to Specific Demographics

The application of AI tools to personalized communication offers significant benefits for crisis management. AI allows organizations to tailor their communication to specific demographics based on individual preferences and behaviors. Personalized means are crucial in preventing the dissemination of false information and managing crises more effectively.

Studies on human-AI interactions acknowledge the capability of AI to adapt to individual needs. Through human-AI interactions, people can achieve a balance that enables personalized outputs without sacrificing productivity (Castro et al., 2023). This finding is particularly inspiring in crisis communication, where there is a great demand for accurate and tailored information. A great potential of AI in personalizing learning experiences to meet individual student's needs and preferences (Pendy, 2021) in terms of education helps us to understand that it is not challenging for AI to analyze individual behaviors and preferences, personalize messages, and ensure that they are relevant and effective.

In particular, AI-powered chatbots and virtual assistants play a crucial role in engaging with affected populations. These tools offer distinct advantages, providing immediate, consistent, and accessible communication during crises. In the realm of digital mental health, a study by Balcombe (2023) highlights the potential of AI chatbots that leverage Big Data, natural language processing, and machine learning algorithms, reshaping interactions with information and responses to crises. In providing social companionship during crises, AI chatbots, acting as conversational agents and social bots, contribute to empathetic and supportive communication, as examined in a study by Chaturvedi et al. (2023).

Post-Crisis: Assessing and Learning with AI Insights

In the post-crisis phase, the role of AI in evaluating the effectiveness of crisis communication strategies is critical. This phase involves a comprehensive follow-up with stakeholders, where AI can significantly contribute to analyzing the impact and effectiveness of communication strategies (Coombs, 2014a). AI's capabilities in data analytics, sentiment analysis, and pattern recognition become invaluable in this context.

One of the key functions of AI in this phase is the analysis of communication reach and engagement. This involves an in-depth evaluation of how effectively the crisis communication strategies have reached and resonated with the intended audiences. For instance, AI's ability to analyze social media data for public sentiment and reactions is pivotal in this regard, as it provides insights into how the public responds to crisis communications. As Nishant et al. (2020) indicate, AI's machine learning algorithms are proficient in processing large volumes of unstructured data, offering insights into public perception and the emotional impact of crisis communications. Bruns and Burgess (2015) further underscore this aspect of AI's functionality and emphasize the importance of analyzing social media data for real-time public sentiment analysis in crisis situations. Stieglitz et al. (2018) highlight the role of AI in identifying patterns and trends in social media data, which can provide valuable feedback on the effectiveness of crisis communications. The importance of AI in evaluating public perception and organizational reputation in the post-crisis stage reinforces the need for a comprehensive and data-driven approach to crisis communication assessment (Schultz et al., 2011). This process is critical not only for evaluating current strategies but also for informing and refining future communication efforts.

Furthermore, AI can assist in benchmarking and comparative analysis. By leveraging advanced AI tools, organizations can dissect complex datasets to unearth nuanced insights into their crisis management strategies. This benchmarking process is crucial for evaluating the overall effectiveness of the crisis management process (Reynolds & Seeger, 2005). AI algorithms can compare real-time crisis response data against a vast repository of historical crisis events and industry benchmarks, providing a deeper understanding of the organization's performance in a crisis context. Such comparative analysis is vital in highlighting areas of strength and pinpointing areas that need improvement. This approach enables organizations to align their crisis communication strategies with the best practices and industry standards (Coombs, 2014a).

AI also plays a vital role in continuous monitoring and risk assessment post-crisis. This ongoing analysis, crucial for a thorough recovery, allows for identifying emerging risks and assessing the ongoing effectiveness of crisis management strategies. AI's capacity for Big Data analytics and pattern recognition allows for detecting subtle changes in public sentiment or operational anomalies that may signal emerging risks or areas of improvement in crisis management. Such capabilities are critical for an organization's adaptability and resilience, as evidenced in research by Dubey et al. (2022), who explore how AI-driven analytics can enhance organizational response to dynamic environments. Furthermore, the role of AI in facilitating organizational learning during the post-crisis stage underscores the importance of leveraging AI's data processing strengths to refine crisis management strategies continually (Gupta & George, 2016). This continuous learning and adaptation process enabled by AI is not only essential for a thorough recovery but is also crucial in preparing organizations for future crises.

Lastly, AI tools, such as chatbots, can be instrumental in the educational aspect of crisis communication. As Essel et al. (2022) indicate, AI chatbots act as virtual teaching assistants, offering conversational capabilities crucial for crisis communications in educating and informing affected populations. The efficacy of chatbots in crisis communication is further explored by Miner et al. (2020), who emphasize their role in providing timely, accurate information and emotional support to individuals in crisis. Additionally, Diederich et al. (2019) highlight the potential of AI chatbots in handling large volumes of inquiries during crises, thereby reducing the burden on human responders and ensuring consistent, reliable communication. The ability to maintain an informed and engaged stakeholder in post-crisis is essential, not only for immediate response but also for long-term trust and relationship building with stakeholders (Van der Meer & Verhoeven, 2013).

In summary, AI's role in the post-crisis phase is multifaceted and crucial for assessing the effectiveness of crisis communication strategies. From analyzing public sentiment and engagement to benchmarking and risk assessment, AI tools offer invaluable insights that help refine and improve future crisis communication strategies.

AI and Crisis Communication Strategies

AI plays a transformative role in crisis communication strategies, particularly in the three types of information strategies (i.e., instructing, adjusting information, and internalizing information). Automation introduced by AI enhances the speed and precision of disseminating critical updates. Through targeted communication, AI tailors messages to specific audiences, optimizing relevance. Furthermore, in the fast-paced and multilingual landscape of global crises, automated translation services, particularly those driven by machine translation by AI, have become indispensable in sending information (O'Brien, 2016). These technologies ensure that crucial information is accurately and promptly disseminated across diverse linguistic groups, enhancing communication and response efforts during emergencies. In crisis situations, automated translation plays an important role in bridging communication gaps across cultures and languages (Ashraf & Ahmad, 2015). Also, the potential of automated translation technologies in emergency medical services (EMS) shows that context-specific automated translation in emergencies could be a preference (Turner et al., 2019). As global crises continue to present complex communication challenges, the importance of advanced automated translation services in crisis management cannot be overstated.

AI-powered chatbots also streamline the forwarding process, providing timely and accurate responses. For instance, social media optimization leverages AI to identify and engage influential figures, amplifying the impact of forwarded information (Karinshak & Jin, 2023). Multilingual forwarding becomes seamless with AI-driven translation services, promoting inclusivity (Turner et al., 2019). Content recommendation algorithms encourage users to forward pertinent crisis-related information. AI aids in detecting and preventing the forwarding of deepfake content, ensuring the dissemination of trustworthy information (Verdoliva, 2022).

In addition, automated information tracking and reporting provide real-time insights, allowing adaptive strategies. Looking ahead, aspirational goals involve crafting crisis communication strategies informed by public reactions from Big Data sources, using sentiment analysis and misinformation detection with AI. Incorporating community feedback loops during disasters can help maintain engagement, debunk false claims, and address stakeholder concerns, ultimately enhancing emergency response outcomes (Vladu, 2023). Compassion should be prioritized in automating communication functions, recognizing the potential for technologically enhanced empathy to positively disrupt crises through caring connections (Cui et al., 2023). With cautious optimism and scientific rigor, AI may expand our collective capacity to comprehend complex contexts and develop impactful crisis communication strategies as emerging tools undergo testing (Cui et al., 2023).

Ethical Considerations in AI for Crisis Communication

Data Privacy and Security

Despite the aforementioned significant benefits of leveraging AI in crisis communication, AI tools also pose ethical challenges. The efficiency of AI in managing, disseminating, and analyzing information during crises is undeniable, yet this utility comes with significant responsibilities. Among these, the concerns for data privacy and security stand out. Jang and Lee (2023) exemplify this in the Lee-Luda, a South Korean AI chatbot case. Lee-Luda sparked controversy due to its use of intimate conversations between couples, collected without proper consent for AI training purposes. The public outcry over this violation of privacy rights underscored the vital importance of ethical AI practices.

Ensuring data privacy in AI-driven crisis communication extends beyond legal obligations; it's a cornerstone of public trust and ethical integrity in AI systems. When individuals trust that their personal data is handled with the utmost care and confidentiality, they are more likely to engage cooperatively in crisis situations, enhancing the effectiveness of the response efforts. Conversely, neglecting data privacy can lead to public mistrust, reduced effectiveness of crisis communication strategies, and potential harm to individuals whose data is mishandled or exposed, like those in the Lee-Luda case.

AI enhances crisis communication through rapid data analysis, predictive modeling, and efficient information dissemination. However, the data used in these processes often includes sensitive personal information, necessitating stringent privacy and security measures. Lee and Meng (2021) emphasize the digital competencies needed by communication professionals in this evolving landscape, including a deep understanding of privacy and security standards within AI systems.

Navigating these challenges involves adhering to regulatory and ethical frameworks that prioritize data privacy and security. This includes compliance with laws like the General Data Protection Regulation (GDPR) and adhering to standards set by international bodies. Shin (2022) discusses the importance of anthropomorphism in AI and how it influences user trust and perception, further highlighting the need for transparency and ethical consideration in AI's interaction with users. Stakeholders must be informed about how AI systems collect, use, and protect data. Clear policies on data usage and regular audits are crucial for maintaining accountability and ensuring compliance with privacy and security standards.

One of the primary challenges here is balancing the need for rapid response during crises with the imperative of data ethics. Future developments in AI for crisis communication must focus on creating systems that inherently prioritize privacy and security. This involves ongoing research into AI ethics, continuous policy development, and active engagement with various stakeholders.

While AI significantly enhances the efficiency and effectiveness of crisis communication, it raises critical ethical concerns, particularly regarding data privacy and security. Addressing these concerns requires a multifaceted approach incorporating technical measures, regulatory compliance, ethical decision-making, and ongoing stakeholder engagement. The future of AI in crisis communication depends on the ability to uphold these high standards of data ethics and security.

Minimizing Algorithmic Biases

Algorithmic biases in AI-driven crisis communication are a critical concern, as they can exacerbate inequalities and lead to misrepresentation or unequal treatment of certain groups. This issue is particularly crucial in crises where equitable access to information and resources is critical. For instance, Laestadius et al. (2022) discuss the emotional dependence on AI chatbots like Replika, highlighting the importance of unbiased AI interactions, especially in sensitive areas like mental health. If an AI system is trained predominantly on data from certain demographics, it may be less effective or accurate for other groups, leading to unequal access to information and assistance. Furthermore, ethical risks emerge when AI is utilized to profile or target marginalized communities based solely on their social media activity, underscoring the importance of proper oversight (Mittelstadt, 2019). The potential for algorithmic analysis of social media content during disasters to disproportionately emphasize areas with higher social media usage raises concerns about neglecting less connected communities (Park & Cho, 2015).

To mitigate these biases, it is essential to diversify training data to ensure AI systems are representative of different demographics, as emphasized by Lee and Meng (2021). Inclusive design principles play a vital role in this process, focusing on creating AI systems that cater to the needs of diverse user groups to minimize biases from sneaking into the system. Continuous monitoring and updating of AI systems are also key to ensuring fairness and accuracy. This involves regularly assessing the performance of the system across various demographics and making necessary adjustments (Shin, 2022). Addressing the root causes of biases present in the data is a broader societal challenge. Collaborative efforts in AI developers, ethicists, sociologists, and other stakeholders are crucial in addressing systemic issues that contribute to these biases.

In addition to these strategies, implementing rigorous testing protocols is vital. This involves testing AI systems under various scenarios and conditions to identify and address potential biases. Furthermore, involving end-users in the development process can provide valuable insights into how different groups may be affected by the AI system. User feedback on the usability can inform more inclusive and equitable AI design.

Minimizing algorithmic biases in AI-driven crisis communication is an ethical imperative that requires a commitment to fairness, inclusivity, and continuous improvement. Employing strategies such as diversifying training data, inclusive design, continuous monitoring, transparency, addressing systemic issues, rigorous testing, user involvement, and ethical training are key to ensuring that AI systems serve all segments of society equitably and effectively.

Balancing Automation and Human Intervention

The integration of AI in crisis response, while offering efficiency in data analysis and decision-making, necessitates a critical balance with human intervention, particularly in addressing ethical implications. AI's capability for processing large data volumes and real-time decision-making is invaluable, as seen in its application for analyzing satellite imagery and monitoring social media sentiments. However, relying solely on AI can be problematic. AI's limitations in understanding human emotions, cultural contexts, and ethical complexities highlight the need for human oversight in crisis situations (Meier, 2015).

Human intervention in crisis response is essential to provide this context and understanding. Human decision-makers can consider ethical implications, cultural sensitivities, and moral judgments that AI systems may overlook. For example, decisions about resource allocation during disasters need to be taken into account not just logistical efficiency but also ethical considerations such as fairness and equity. Notably, AI-based social media monitoring, while valuable, is not without its limitations. The Flint water crisis serves as a poignant illustration of the potential discrimination perpetuated by algorithms reliant on biased data for crisis prediction (Liao et al., 2020). To navigate the prevalence of false and misleading information online, human verification becomes a necessary layer to avoid misinterpretation (Liao et al., 2020). In the face of a flood of disinformation, the role of human decision-makers in managing risks, as emphasized by Karinshak and Jin (2023), becomes even more pronounced.

The challenge lies in finding the optimal balance between AI automation and human intervention. Over-reliance on AI can lead to ethical oversights, while insufficient can result in inefficiencies and delayed responses. A collaborative approach, where AI provides rapid data analysis and recommendations while humans make the final decisions while considering ethical and cultural factors, seems most effective. To address model limitations, AI predictions should be complemented by experienced human judgment in crisis situations.

One ethical consideration in this balance is accountability. In AI-driven decision-making, it can be challenging to identify who is responsible for the decisions made, especially when they lead to adverse outcomes. Human oversight ensures that there is accountability and that decisions can be explained and justified.

Another consideration is bias in AI algorithms. While AI can help reduce human bias in decision-making, the algorithms themselves can be biased based on the data they are trained on. Algorithms have the potential to be biased against marginalized communities if biased data is used for training, as demonstrated in the mental health chatbot and crisis prediction (Laestadius et al., 2022; Liao et al., 2020). Human intervention is necessary to identify and mitigate these biases, ensuring equitable crisis response.

Transparency in AI decision-making processes is also crucial in AI-driven crisis responses (Gundeti et al., 2024). Stakeholders, including the public and those affected by the crisis, should understand how decisions are being made. A balance between AI automation and human intervention can enhance transparency, as it allows for a clear explanation of how decisions were reached.

The balance between the two in crisis communication not only optimizes efficiency and effectiveness but also ensures that ethical considerations are adequately addressed. Human intervention is vital to provide context, ensure accountability, address biases, and maintain transparency in the decision-making process. As AI continues to evolve, its role in crisis response must be carefully managed to harness its strengths while mitigating its limitations, always with an eye toward ethical implications.

Future Horizons

Emerging AI Technologies

As we look to the future of crisis communication, emerging AI technologies promise to revolutionize how we respond to emergencies. Advancements in predictive analytics, personalized communication via AI chatbots, and novel AI-driven technologies are set to transform crisis response efforts, making them more efficient, responsive, and tailored to individual needs (Cheng & Jiang, 2022; Syvänen & Valentini, 2020; Vladu, 2023).

Predictive analytics is one of the most promising AI technologies in crisis communication. By analyzing vast amounts of data, AI can predict the onset, progression, and impact of various crises, from natural disasters to health emergencies. For instance, AI systems can analyze weather patterns to predict natural disasters or track the spread of diseases to anticipate healthcare needs. These predictive capabilities enable more proactive and prepared responses, potentially saving lives and reducing the impact of crises.

Personalized communication through AI chatbots represents another significant advancement. In future crisis scenarios, AI chatbots could provide real-time, personalized guidance and support to each individual affected by a crisis. These chatbots could deliver critical information tailored to the specific needs and circumstances of each person, such as medical advice. Xu and Li (2022) highlight the role of AI voice assistants like Siri and Alexa, demonstrating this potential and indicating a future where AI could offer personalized advice during crises. The ability to communicate on a personal level at scale could significantly enhance the effectiveness of crisis communication.

Emerging AI technologies hold immense potential for transforming crisis communication. However, as these technologies evolve, it will be crucial to navigate their ethical implications carefully, ensuring that crisis response efforts remain equitable, secure, and respectful of individual privacy. The future of crisis communication in the AI era is bright, with the promise of a more proactive, personalized, and effective response to emergencies.

Responsible AI Implementation

The integration of AI in crisis communication necessitates responsible implementation, prioritizing not only technical excellence but also ethical considerations. Responsible AI in crisis scenarios involves ethical design, development, and deployment, ensuring privacy, security, and bias mitigation. AI adoption in communication management requires adherence to ethical standards and awareness of potential challenges and risks (Zerfass et al., 2020). AI systems used in crisis situations must protect the sensitive personal data they collect or process, adhering to stringent data protection standards.

Transparency is another crucial aspect of responsible AI. Stakeholders should understand how AI systems operate and make decisions. This transparency helps build trust in the AI systems and ensures that users can rely on them during crises (Gundeti et al., 2024). Additionally, there should be clear accountability in the decision-making processes of AI systems. When AI is used to make or support decisions during crises, it should be clear who is responsible for those decisions, especially if they lead to negative outcomes.

Mitigating the potential adverse impacts of AI on society and communication processes requires ongoing research and development. This research should focus not only on improving the technical capabilities of AI but also on understanding and addressing the ethical, social, and cultural implications of AI in crisis communication. For example, studies could explore how AI systems might inadvertently amplify misinformation during a crisis and develop strategies to prevent such outcomes.

Continued research is also needed to address the challenge of biases in AI algorithms. AI systems must be trained on diverse datasets to ensure they do not perpetuate existing inequalities or discriminate against certain groups during crisis response. Collaborations between AI developers, ethicists, sociologists, and other stakeholders are crucial in this endeavor to ensure that AI systems are fair and equitable.

The responsible implementation of AI in crisis communication is essential to ensure that these powerful technologies are used in ways that benefit society as a whole. This involves a commitment to ethical practices, transparency, accountability, and continuous research and development. By navigating these challenges responsibly, we can harness the potential of AI to revolutionize many aspects of crisis communication while safeguarding the values and principles that are fundamental to a just and equitable society.

Conclusion

In conclusion, the integration of AI in crisis communication signifies a shift in crisis management, offering transformative capabilities to enhance real-time insights, public engagement, and emergency response optimization. As we explore the potential implications of AI in crisis communication, several key takeaways emerge.

Firstly, the profound impact of AI tools in enhancing crisis communication cannot be overstated. From predictive analytics to personalized communication through AI chatbots, emerging technologies promise more proactive, efficient, and tailored crisis response efforts. These advancements hold the potential to save lives and mitigate the impact of various crises, from natural disasters to health emergencies. The primary benefit underscored across studies is the enhancement of stakeholder communication. AI-driven tools, like chatbots, significantly improve interaction efficiency during crises (Syvänen & Valentini, 2020). These technologies enable rapid information dissemination and real-time engagement, which is crucial for maintaining trust and transparency (Cheng & Jiang, 2020). Another key advantage of AI identified in the literature is its strategic role in information management, particularly in countering misinformation and managing public relations (Karinshak & Jin, 2023). AI's capacity for large-scale data analysis aids in identifying and addressing misinformation quickly, an essential capability in the digital information age.

However, these advancements come with challenges. Ethical considerations and potential biases in AI algorithms are a significant concern. The reliance on AI for decision-making raises questions about the objectivity of these systems, especially in handling sensitive data and privacy issues (Lee & Meng, 2021). Another notable limitation is the need for specialized skills to implement and manage AI technologies effectively. This challenge is evident in the gap between AI expertise and the understanding of crisis communication principles (Zerfass et al., 2020). Moreover, while AI excels in handling volume, it lacks the nuanced understanding and empathy crucial in certain crisis communication aspects. This limitation suggests the necessity for a hybrid approach, combining AI efficiency with human sensitivity.

In summary, this chapter highlights AI as a potent but complex tool in crisis communication. Its benefits in communication efficiency and strategic information management are counterbalanced by ethical, technical, and practical challenges. Looking forward, a comprehensive understanding of these dual aspects is essential for organizations to leverage AI effectively in crisis contexts.

References

Aboualola, M., Abualsaud, K., Khattab, T., Zorba, N., & Hassanein, H. S. (2023). Edge technologies for disaster management: A survey of social media and artificial intelligence integration. *IEEE Access*, *11*, 73782–73802. https://doi.org/10.1109/access.2023.3293035

Alexander, D. E. (2014). Social media in disaster risk reduction and crisis management. *Science and Engineering Ethics*, *20*, 717–733. https://doi.org/10.1007/s11948-013-9502-z

Ashraf, N., & Ahmad, M. (2015). Machine translation techniques and their comparative study. *International Journal of Computer Applications*, *125*(7), 25–31. https://doi.org/10.5120/ijca2015905955

Benoit, W. L. (1995). *Accounts, excuses, and apologies: A theory of image restoration*. State University of New York Press.

Balcombe, L. (2023). AI Chatbots in digital mental health. *Informatics*, *10*(4), 82. https://doi.org/10.3390/informatics10040082

Bruns, A., & Burgess, J. (2015). Twitter hashtags from ad hoc to calculated publics. In: Rambukkana N (ed.) *Hashtag Publics: The Power and Politics of Discursive Networks*. Bern: Peter Lang Publishing, pp. 13–27.

Castro, F., Gao, J., & Martin, S. (2023). Human-AI interactions and societal pitfalls. *ArXiv, abs/2309.10448*. https://doi.org/10.48550/arXiv.2309.10448

Chaturvedi, R., Verma, S., Das, R., & Dwivedi, Y. K. (2023). Social companionship with artificial intelligence: Recent trends and future avenues. *Technological Forecasting and Social Change*, *193*, 122634. https://doi.org/10.1016/j.techfore.2023.122634

Cheng, Y., & Cameron, G. T. (2022). Contingent organization-public relationships and their application in organizational crises. In W.T. Coombs & S.J. Holladay (Eds.), *The Handbook of Crisis Communication* (pp. 113–126). John Wiley & Sons Ltd.

Cheng, Y., Funkhouser, C., Raabe, T., & Cross, R. (2021). Examining organization-public relationships in crises: A thematic meta-analysis of updated literature from 1997 to 2019. *Journal of Contingencies and Crisis Management*, 2, 148–160.

Cheng, Y., & Jiang, H. (2020). AI-Powered mental health chatbots: Examining users' motivations, active communicative action and engagement after mass-shooting disasters. *Journal of Contingencies and Crisis Management*, *28*(3), 339–354. https://doi.org/10.1111/1468-5973.12319

Cheng, Y., & Jiang, H. (2022). Customer-brand relationship in the era of artificial intelligence: understanding the role of chatbot marketing efforts. *Journal of Product & Brand Management*, *31*(2), 252–264.

Cheng, Y., Wang, Y., & Kong, Y. (2022). The state of social-mediated crisis communication research through the lens of global scholars: An updated assessment. *Public Relations Review*, 2, 102172. https://doi.org/10.1016/j.pubrev.2022.102172

Cheng, Y. (2018). How social media is changing crisis communication strategies: Evidence from the updated literature. *Journal of Contingencies and Crisis Management*, 26(1), 58–68. https://doi.org/10.1111/1468-5973.12130

Coombs, W. T. (2014a). *Ongoing Crisis Communication: Planning, Managing, and Responding* (Fifth Edition, pp. 165–176). SAGE Publications, Inc.

Coombs, T. (2014b). *The state of crisis communication: Evidence and the bleeding edge*. Retrieved from https://instituteforpr.org/state-crisis-communication-evidence-bleeding-edge/

Cui, J., Wang, Z., Ho, S. B., & Cambria, E. (2023). Survey on sentiment analysis: Evolution of research methods and topics. *Artificial Intelligence Review*, *56*, 8469–8510.

Diederich, S., Brendel, A. B., & Kolbe, L. M. (2019). Towards a taxonomy of platforms for conversational agent design. *Proceedings of 14th International Conference on Wirtschafsinformatik*, pp. 1100–1114.

Dubey, R., Bryde, D. J., Dwivedi, Y. K., Graham, G., & Foropon, C. (2022). Impact of artificial intelligence-driven big data analytics culture on agility and resilience in humanitarian supply chain: A practice-based view. *International Journal of Production Economics*, *250*(1), 108618. https://doi.org/10.1016/j.ijpe.2022.108618

Essel, H. B., Vlachopoulos, D., Tachie-Menson, A., Johnson, E. E., & Baah, P. K. (2022). The impact of a virtual teaching assistant (chatbot) on students' learning in Ghanaian higher education. *International Journal of Educational Technology in Higher Education*, *19*(1), 1–19.

Farrokhi, A., Shirazi, F., Hajli, N., & Tajvidi, M. (2020). Using artificial intelligence to detect crisis related to events: Decision making in B2B by artificial intelligence. *Industrial Marketing Management*, *91*, 257–273.

Fink, S. (2000). *Crisis Management: Planning for the Inevitable*. iUniverse.

Fujita, I., Sakurada, K., Imaizumi, T., Ito, R., Hikosaka, S., & Nakamura, R. (2017). Damage detection from aerial images via convolutional neural networks. In *Proceedings of the 35th ISARC* (pp. 574–579).

Gruda, D., & Ojo, A. (2022). All about that trait: Examining extraversion and state anxiety during the SARS-CoV-2 pandemic using a machine learning approach. *Personality and individual differences*, *188*, 111461.

Gundeti, R., Vuppala, K., & Kasireddy, V. (2024). The future of AI and environmental sustainability: Challenges and opportunities. In H. Kannan, R. Rodriguez, Z. Paprika, & A. Ade-Ibijola (Eds.), *Exploring Ethical Dimensions of Environmental Sustainability and Use of AI* (pp. 346–371). IGI Global. https://doi.org/10.4018/979-8-3693-0892-9.ch017

Gupta, M., & George, J. (2016). Toward the development of a big data analytics capability. *Information & Management*, *53*(8), 1049–1064. https://doi.org/10.1016/j.im.2016.07.004

Huang, Y. H., Lin, Y. H., & Su, S. H. (2005). Crisis communicative strategies in Taiwan: Category, continuum, and cultural implication. *Public Relations Review*, *31*(2), 229–238.

Imran, M., Castillo, C., Lucas, J., Meier, P., & Vieweg, S. (2015). AIDR: Artificial intelligence for disaster response. In *Proceedings of the 23rd International Conference on World Wide Web* (pp. 159–162).

Jang, H. & Lee, S.M. (2023). Introducing the Co-oriented Scansis (CoS) model: A case of chatbot, Lee-Luda. *Public Relations Review*, *49*(4). https://doi.org/10.1016/j.pubrev.2023.102360

Jin, Y., Liu, B. F., & Austin, L. L. (2014). Examining the role of social media in effective crisis management. *Communication Research*, *1*, 74–94. https://doi.org/10.1177/0093650211423918

Karinshak, E. & Jin, Y. (2023). AI-driven disinformation: a framework for organizational preparation and response. *Journal of Communication Management*, *27*(4), 539–562. https://doi.org/10.1108/JCOM-09-2022-0113

Kaur, M., Verma, R., & Otoo, F. N. K. (2021). Emotions in leader's crisis communication: Twitter sentiment analysis during COVID-19 outbreak. *Journal of Human Behavior in the Social Environment*, *31*(1–4), 362–372.

Kim, H. M., Saffer, A. J., Liu, W., Sun, J., Li, Y., Zhen, L., & Yang, A. (2022). How public health agencies break through COVID-19 conversations: A strategic network approach to public engagement. *Health communication*, *37*(10), 1276–1284.

Laestadius, L., Bishop, A., Gonzalez, M., Illenčík, D., & Campos-Castillo, C. (2022). Too human and not human enough: A grounded theory analysis of mental health harms from emotional dependence on the social chatbot Replika. *New Media & Society*. https://doi.org/10.1177/14614448221142007

Lee, J.J. & Meng, J. (2021). Digital competencies in communication management: a conceptual framework of readiness for industry 4.0 for communication professionals in the workplace. *Journal of Communication Management*, *25*(4), 417–436. https://doi.org/10.1108/JCOM-10-2020-0116

Lerbinger, O. (2011). *The Crisis Manager: Facing Disasters, Conflicts, and Failures (Routledge Communication Series)* (Second Edition). Routledge.

Liao, Q. V., Gruen, D., & Miller, S. (2020). Questioning the AI: Informing design practices for explainable AI user experiences. *Proceedings of the 2020 CHI Conference on Human Factors in Computing Systems*, 1–15.

Meier, P. (2015). *Digital Humanitarians: How BIG DATA is Changing the Face of Humanitarian Response*. CRC Press.

Miner, A. S., Laranjo, L., & Kocaballi A. B. (2020). Chatbots in the fight against the COVID-19 pandemic. *NPJ Digital Medicine*, *3*(65). https://doi.org/10.1038/s41746-020-0280-0

Mirbabaie, M., Fromm, J., Löppenberg, S., Meinig, S., & Reuße, M. (2020). The potential of social media analytics for improving social media communication of emergency agencies. *arXiv preprint arXiv*:2004.08570.

Mittelstadt, B. (2019). *Principles alone cannot guarantee ethical AI. Nature Machine Intelligence*, *1*(11), 501–507.

Nguyen, D. T., Alam, F., Ofli, F., & Imran, M. (2017). Automatic image filtering on social networks using deep learning and perceptual hashing during crises. *arXiv preprint arXiv*:1704.02602.

Nishant, R., Kennedy, M., & Corbett, J. (2020). Artificial intelligence for sustainability: Challenges, opportunities, and a research agenda. *International Journal of Information Management*, *53*, 102104.

O'Brien, S. (2016). Training translators for crisis communication: Translators without borders as an example. In F. M. Federici (Ed.), *Mediating Emergencies and Conflicts: Frontline Translating and Interpreting* (pp. 85–111). Palgrave Macmillan UK. https://doi.org/10.1057/978-1-137-55351-5_4

Park, H.W. & Cho, J.Y. (2015). Social media use during Japan's 2011 earthquake: how Twitter transforms the locus of crisis communication. *Media International Australia, Incorporating Culture & Policy*, *157*, 28–40.

Pendy, B. (2021). Artificial intelligence: The future of education. *Jurnal Indonesia Sosial Sains*, 2(11), 17.

Rahman, S., Jahan, N., Sadia, F., & Mahmud, I. (2023). Social crisis detection using Twitter based text mining-a machine learning approach. *Bulletin of Electrical Engineering and Informatics*, *12*(2), 1069–1077.

Rana, M. S., Nobi, M. N., Murali, B., & Sung, A. H. (2022). Deepfake detection: A systematic literature review. *IEEE Access*, *10*, 25494–25513.

Reddy, Bv., & Gupta, A. (2020). Importance of effective communication during COVID-19 infodemic. *Journal of Family Medicine and Primary Care*, *8*, 3793. https://doi.org/10.4103/jfmpc.jfmpc_719_20

Reynolds, B., & Seeger, M. W. (2005). Crisis and emergency risk communication as an integrative model. *Journal of Health Communication*, *10*(1), 43–55. https://doi.org/10.1080/10810730590904571

Schultz, F., Utz, S., & Göritz, A., (2011). Is the medium the message? Perceptions of and reactions to crisis communication via twitter, blogs and traditional media. *Public Relations Review*, *37*(1). 20–27. https://doi.org/10.1016/j.pubrev.2010.12.001

Shin, D. (2022). The perception of humanness in conversational journalism: An algorithmic information-processing perspective. *New Media & Society*, *24*(12), 2680–2704. https://doi.org/10.1177/1461444821993801

Stieglitz, S., Mirbabaie, M., Ross, B., & Neuberger, C. (2018). Social media analytics - challenges in topic discovery, data collection, and data preparation. *International Journal of Information Management*, *39*(1), 156–168. https://doi.org/10.1016/j.ijinfomgt.2017.12.002

Syvänen, S., & Valentini, C. (2020). Conversational agents in online organization-stakeholder interactions: a state-of-the-art analysis and implications for further research. *Journal of Communication Management*, *24*(4), 339–362. https://doi.org/10.1108/JCOM-11-2019-0145

Turner, A. M., Choi, Y. K., Dew, K., Tsai, M. T., Bosold, A. L., Wu, S., ... & Meischke, H. (2019). Evaluating the usefulness of translation technologies for emergency response communication: a scenario-based study. *JMIR public health and surveillance*, *5*(1), e11171.

Untari, I. M. (2020). Chatbots and government communications in covid-19 pandemic. *Jurnal Komunikasi Indonesia*, IX(2), 98–109.

Van der Meer, T. G. L. A., & Verhoeven, P. (2013). Public framing organizational crisis situations: social media versus news media. *Public Relations Review*, *39*(3). 229–231. https://doi.org/10.1016/j.pubrev.2012.12.001

Verdoliva, L. (2022, June). Towards Generalization in Deepfake Detection. In *Proceedings of the 1st International Workshop on Multimedia AI against Disinformation* (pp. 1–1).

Vladu, O. M. (2023). Digital transformation in crisis management: The key role of artificial intelligence. *Scientific Research & Education in the Air Force-AFASES*, *24*, 103–110. https://doi.org/10.19062/2247-3173.2023.24.15

Wong, Y. K. (2021, September). Dealing Crisis Management using AI. In *CS & IT Conference Proceedings* (Vol. 11, No. 14).

Xu, S., & Li, W. (2022). A tool or a social being? A dynamic longitudinal investigation of functional use and relational use of AI voice assistants. *New Media & Society*. https://doi.org/10.1177/14614448221108112

Yang, L. W. Y., Ng, W. Y., Lei, X., Tan, S. C. Y., Wang, Z., Yan, M., ... & Ting, D. S. W. (2023). Development and testing of a multi-lingual Natural Language Processing-based deep learning system in 10 languages for COVID-19 pandemic crisis: A multi-center study. *Frontiers in public health*, *11*, 1063466.

Zerfass, A., Hagelstein, J., & Tench, R. (2020). Artificial intelligence in communication management: a cross-national study on adoption and knowledge, impact, challenges and risks. *Journal of Communication Management*, *24*(4), 377–389. https://doi.org/10.1108/JCOM-10-2019-0137

9 Checking the Pulse of Stakeholders through the Eyes of the Media

Examining Publics' Emotions in COVID-19 Management and Communication

Augustine Pang, Jerena C.K. Ng, and Ryan Lim

Introduction

In times of a pandemic or health crisis, health authorities have the responsibility to regularly disseminate and update health messages to safeguard the publics, guided by the twin objectives of consistent messaging and reinforcement of key messages (Coombs, 2023). One of the key instruments used would be the mainstream media (Seeger, 2006).

The memory of the COVID-19 crisis from 2020 to 2022 is still fresh in the minds of many. Much of how we understood the crisis and the communication of it came through the media. A 2020 survey by the Reuters Institute for the Study of Journalism at the University of Oxford showed that almost two-thirds of the respondents said mainstream media had helped them understand the pandemic, and explained what they could do in response (Rekhi, 2020b). In a discussion on the role of the media in times of pandemic, several insights on the media were consistently discussed. The media must:

- Play a role in communicating during a pandemic;
- Ensure good quality journalism to help combat fake news;
- Gatekeep information in an era where information overload is rife;
- Ensure credible information is reported to fight misinformation (Koh, 2020).

According to Garnett and Kouzmin (2007), crises are "media events" (p. 175) and as such, Pang et al. (2013) contended that how the media frame the crises could influence how stakeholders perceive the crisis. A study examining how the views of readers were shaped by any given topic found that they formed their opinions and viewed the importance of these articles based on what they had read in the media (Durant et al., 2003).

DOI: 10.4324/9781032619187-10

Given the importance of the media, for COVID-19, while many studies have examined government crisis communication through the media (see for instance, Sanjeev et al., 2021), this study adds another dimension of analysis and examines audience reactions—the emotions that were displayed and how they were exhibited behaviorally—as reported in the media, in the government/health authorities' management and communication of the pandemic.

This study examines Singapore, a city state near the equator. Pang et al. (in press) described it as a developed business and financial hub with high economic growth and social achievements. It has strong development of infrastructure, low corruption, and strong investments (Lim et al., 2005). Boasting one of the world's highest gross domestic product and recognized as one of the four Asian Tigers (Han, 2023) along with Taiwan, Hong Kong, and South Korea, Singapore consistently retains its position as the world's leading business environment and the best place for foreign companies to operate. With a population of 5.64 million, Singapore is a multi-ethnic society consisting of 74.1% Chinese, 13.6% Malays, 9% Indians, and 3.3% made up of other races (Department of Statistics Singapore, 2023) with English its lingua franca (Lim et al., 2005).

Singapore is studied because the authorities have been consistently lauded for the way it managed COVID-19. It was ranked one of the best places to be during the pandemic by Bloomberg (Hong, 2021). The US Center for Disease Control and Prevention (CDC) ranked it lowest for COVID-19 risks in June 2021 (Shepardson, 2021). The theoretical lens this study uses is the Integrated Crisis Mapping Model (ICM) (Jin et al., 2012), which is constructed to understand the emotional upheavals publics face in times of crises.

This study is significant for three reasons. First, it addresses the call by Coombs (2010) to understand reactions to crisis response. "We know very little about how people react to crisis response strategies," argued Coombs (2010, p. 722). Second, it further builds on the Integrated Crisis Mapping (ICM) model (Jin et al., 2012). ICM, thus far, has only identified emotions of stakeholders. This study examines behavioral manifestation of the emotions exhibited, as reported in the media. Third, it is hoped that this study can add further insights on the continuing importance of mainstream media even as social media dominate discussions.

Context: What Singapore went through

The novel coronavirus reached the shores of Singapore not long after word got out that China's Wuhan was battling a new deadly disease. On January 23, 2020, Singapore confirmed its first case of the virus when a

66-year-old Wuhan resident who arrived on the island state tested positive at the Singapore General Hospital (SGH) the day before.

Singapore has had first-hand experience in dealing with a contagious disease, namely the SARS (severe acute respiratory syndrome) outbreak in 2003. At that time, Singapore had never encountered such a virulent disease, and health institutions were unprepared for it, and there was little or no information on the virus. The lack of sharing of information between healthcare institutions exacerbated the crisis (Ooi & Phua, 2009).

Among the steps taken were the issuance of travel advisory for those who had traveled to areas with the disease, like China and Hong Kong; at immigration checkpoints, infrared fever scanning systems went into effect, while thermometers were distributed to homes, schools, and workplaces (Chua, 2004). Schools were closed and places like market wholesale center, where an outbreak was suspected, were shutdown (Ooi & Phua, 2009). In sum, 238 were infected and 33 died (Straitstimes.com, 2016).

The lessons learnt from SARS would inform the government how to manage COVID-19. The government quickly implemented the measures to tackle transmission of the disease, including temperature screening, quarantine for those who returned from overseas, and DORSCON (disease outbreak response system condition) alert, developed after SARS to contain the spread of the virus, was activated (Chen et al., 2020). Despite that, many took to social media platforms like Facebook and WhatsApp to rant, with comments like the medical system would break down; that they could not control the spread of the virus (CNA Facebook, 2020); some even petitioned the government to ban the Chinese from entering the country (Kim, 2020). Emotions like fear, paranoia, uncertainty, and anxiety were palpable.

On March 30, 2020, reports of a surge in the wave of infection in a foreign workers' dormitory sent further fears across the island state. Bilahari Kausikan, a former diplomat wrote: "We did drop the ball on foreign workers" (Sim & Kok, 2020). On April 3, 2020, Prime Minister Lee Hsien Loong announced that the country would enter a lockdown called a circuit breaker to limit the spread of the virus, leading many to rush to stock up food—and toilet paper. When the government announced that they would distribute masks to all households, they added that the public need not wear them if they were well (Zhang, 2020). Many were confused by the directive. However, in an about-turn on April 14, the government announced that those caught not wearing would be fined (Tay, 2020). As stated in a government White Paper on the pandemic, the new rule contradicted the government's earlier instruction and "affected public trust and confidence" in their management of the situation (Tham, 2023). Another issue that dented trust and "caused unhappiness" with the authorities was the disclosure that the data from the contact-tracing app called TraceTogether could be used by the police for their investigations (Tham, 2023).

Although the pandemic showed no signs of abating, the government started to scale down restrictions in phases. From lockdown, two in a family, later five, would be allowed to visit their elderly members; group size of ten people were allowed to meet (Tan, 2022). Mask wearing was also eased for those outdoors; 75% of workers could return to the office; public events were allowed to resume, safe-distancing measures would still be in effect; routine testing would be lifted and vaccinated travelers could enter the country (Tan, 2022).

Lifting of restrictions, in effect, led to the endemic phase. On March 24, 2022, Prime Minister Lee announced that Singapore would move into "living with the virus." However, this was contingent on the fact that 70% of the population had to be vaccinated; the healthcare system had to remain robust to anticipate the resurgence of the virus (Khalik, 2021). To do so, the government introduced the vaccination-differentiated safe management measures (VDS) where business owners could adopt specific "instructions relevant for staff or customers or for workers who are unvaccinated" (Ministry of Health, 2022). Another key concern was that citizens must practice self-responsibility such as wearing masks, keeping a safe distance, etc. (Mathews et al., 2023).

The government also announced that they would set aside $11 billion called the COVID-19 Resilience Package to protect public health, support workers, and industries and businesses badly affected by the virus. This financial support was on top of an earlier one at the start of the pandemic. Called Stabilisation and Support Package and Care and Support Package with an amount of $5.6 billion (Government of Singapore, 2020a) budgeted to support the economy and to help relieve the financial burdens that families were facing; many commended the government for its efforts in helping residents weather the pandemic (Loke, 2020).

Literature Review

Emotions in crisis situations

In a crisis, the public experience a multitude of emotions, as can be seen from COVID-19. It is thus imperative for studies to be conducted to identify what these emotions are and the specific ways to help the public cope (Jin & Pang, 2010). According to Carver and Blaney (1977), the public's reaction to a crisis is based on their perception of the event, and the resulting emotion they experience is the interpretation of that crisis event, how it developed and how it changed.

To understand the emotional upheavals of stakeholders in a crisis, Jin et al. (2007) developed the Integrated Crisis Mapping model (ICM). Two constructs formed the basis of the model: the stakeholders and the emotions they face in a crisis, how they cope, and organizational involvement.

The model was premised on two foundational ideas: in times of crises, who are the stakeholders involved, and what emotional upheavals they are likely to experience. Based on the literature, Jin et al. (2007) identified critical stakeholders as primary publics who share three key characteristics:

- They are most affected by the crisis;
- They share common interests, and destiny, in seeing the crisis resolved;
- They have long-term interests, and influences, on the organization's reputation and operation.

Informed by research in psychology and crisis, a range of emotions are plotted on a continua in the ICM model. How the public cope—cognitively and conatively—are set on the *X*-axis. The two coping strategies includes the cognitive and behavioral processes in a crisis situation. Jin et al. (2007) examined two types of coping:

1 "problem-focused coping"—where steps are taken to change the relationship between stakeholders and organization.
2 "cognitive-focused coping"—where steps are initiated to only change how the public view the relationship.

The authors contended that the public's form of coping is their way of managing the crisis through: (1) cognitive coping, where the stakeholders try to understand the crisis and how it affects them, or (2) conative coping, where the stakeholders attempt to take action in order to change the situation. Based on these two strategies, stakeholders experiencing crises may decide on one that best help them to cope.

Organizational engagement, from high to low, lies on the *Y*-axis. When engagement is high, the organization would devote more resources to manage the crises (Jin et al., 2007). When the organization finds itself unable to do much to mitigate the crisis, the level of engagement would be low or reduced; instead, it may turn to external parties for help.

Emotions and publics' coping mechanism. In the crisis matrix, the two axes divide the four quadrants. Quadrant 1 is made up of high engagement/conative coping; Quadrant 2 has high engagement/cognitive coping; Quadrant 3 is made up of low engagement/cognitive coping. Quadrant 4 is made up of low engagement/conative coping. Given the interplay of stakeholders' coping strategy and organizational engagement, both primary and secondary emotions are found in all four quadrants.

Based on Lazarus' (1991) appraisal model of emotion, the authors identified four emotions predominant in crisis situations, namely anger, anxiety, fright, and sadness. (See Jin, Pang & Cameron [2007] for a visual presentation of the quadrants.)

Anger—stakeholders are likely to experience anger in a crisis as they see an offense made against them or is a threat to them.
Anxiety—when stakeholders feel threatened and are profoundly affected by the crisis and seek to resolve the crisis as quickly as possible.
Fright—uncertainty and fear of the situation plague stakeholders, especially toward the organization and their handling of the crisis.
Sadness—when stakeholders' survival is threatened and their experience of loss result in sadness.

In the appraisal model of emotion, stakeholders experienced different levels of emotions. The first emotion they experience in a crisis is known as the primary emotion. Emotions experienced after the first wave and depending on how the organizations manage the crisis are known as secondary emotions. Secondary emotions can also be a result of primary emotions or transferred from dominant emotions. For instance, in the second quadrant, for crises related to economic/hostile takeovers, natural disasters and accidents, sadness is the primary emotion and fright the secondary.

Revised Integrated Crisis Mapping model

The Integrated Crisis Mapping (ICM) has been systematically tested, presented, and published, and has been refined since 2006 to ensure it is robust and ecologically valid (see Jin et al., 2007/2010). Thus far, empirical tests have refined key emotions (Jin et al., 2012). Here are the key findings:

Quadrant 1: Five crises are posited here, i.e., crises that entail publics' conative coping and high-organizational engagement, namely reputational damage, technological breakdown, industrial crisis, labor unrest/protest, and regulatory/legislative minefield, where the primary emotions identified are anger, followed by anxiety. Findings showed the presence of anger and anxiety, as posited. Additionally, the emotion of sadness was also found to co-exist with anger and anxiety. The primary publics seemed to engage more in conative than cognitive coping (Jin et al., 2012).
Quadrant 2: Three crises are posited here, i.e., crises that entail the public's cognitive coping and high-organizational engagement, namely hostile takeovers, accidents, and natural disasters, where the primary emotions identified are sadness, followed by fright. Findings showed variations of

sadness, anger, and fright. The primary publics seemed to engage more in conative coping (Jin et al., 2012).

Quadrant 3: Three crises are posited here, i.e., crises that entail public's cognitive coping and low-organizational engagement, namely CEO retirement, rumor, and psychopathic acts, where the primary emotions identified are fright, followed by sadness. Findings showed fright and anger. Conative rather than cognitive coping was evident (Jin et al., 2012).

Quadrant 4: Three crises are posited here, i.e., crises that entail public's conative coping and low organizational engagement, namely transport failure, security issues and human resource problems, where the primary emotions identified are anxiety, followed by anger. Findings showed variations of sadness and anger. Conative coping was evident (Jin et al., 2012). (See Jin, Pang and Cameron [2012] for a visual presentation of the quadrants.)

In the four quadrants, the researchers observed two key trends. First, anxiety is the default emotion that publics feel in crises. Second, evidence suggests strong merit that conative rather than cognitive coping to be present. Conative coping is argued to be the external manifestation of the internal cognitive processing that has already taken place, the *antecedent* of conative coping (Jin et al., 2012).

Since this study seeks to examine the emotions of stakeholders in the COVID-19 crisis, which is classified as a natural disaster (i.e., quadrant 2), this study poses three research questions:

RQ1: Based on the ICM model, what were the emotions exhibited by the publics?
RQ2: What were other emotions exhibited but not captured in the ICM model?
RQ3: How were these emotions manifested behaviorally?

Method

Textual analysis

This study employs textual analysis of news reports, which has been the prevalent and primary method of analysis in Integrated Crisis Mapping studies (Jin et al., 2007, 2010, 2012). This qualitative method allows the researcher to assess the interpretation of the text (Garyantes, 2006) to understand the impact of the COVID-19 pandemic on the emotions of the public. In this study, we sought to identify and analyze the meaning in the texts. In such a study, the researchers are guided by the Integrated Crisis

Mapping (ICM) model and analyze the data as closely as possible based on the theoretical lens (Hsieh & Shannon, 2005; Croucher & Cronn-Mills, 2019).

Media in Singapore

Mainstream media was identified as the source of the study as they have reported content pertinent to the pandemic, the stakeholders, and the evolving situation at the time. News reports were primarily collected from the three key mainstream media outlets in Singapore, *The Straits Times*, *Channel NewsAsia*, and *TODAY*.

In Singapore, there are two prominent mainstream media players. Singapore Press Holdings (SPH), owned by non-profit entity SPH Media Trust (SMT), which owns an array of news publications, chief of which is *The Straits Times*. Started in 1845, it is Singapore's newspaper of record and is the most widely read newspaper in the country (Tandoc Jr, 2022). It continues to be distributed countrywide in print, digital, and social media formats. Its online version, *Straitstimes.com* has 42% of the market share. Mediacorp, which started in 1936, is owned by Temasek Holdings, the government's investment arm. An English language Asian news network, it is positioned as a lens to understand global events with an Asian perspective, and it is Singapore's largest media platform operator (Mediacorp Pte Ltd., 2023a). Besides its selection of radio and television channels, it runs the popular website *Channel NewsAsia*, which has an online share of 46%, and *TODAY*. Both are prestige publications in Singapore.

The mainstream media have remained a key source of news in helping citizens navigate the pandemic, according to the Reuters Institute for Journalism at the University of Oxford (Tang, 2022). In Singapore, the trust level of the media has remained consistently high. During COVID-19, trust in media was at an all-time high (Rekhi, 2020a). In 2023, the Reuters Institute Digital News Report found that *Channel NewsAsia* recorded 75% trust while *The Straits Times* came in second at 73%.

The Singapore government has repeatedly maintained the importance of mainstream media. Minister for Communications and Information Josephine Teo said the government's support for the local media is so that they would continue to "provide trusted news as a public good" and explained how during the COVID-19 pandemic the government engaged the media by holding press conferences to update the public and to front "tough and inconvenient" questions from the media. As a result, she pointed out, "Singaporeans did not become divided along ideological lines about mask-wearing, vaccinations, or safe-distancing measures" (Tham, 2023). Prime Minister Lee said government support mainstream media as they see the "importance of having high-quality, authoritative and influential mainstream media." The mainstream media, the Prime Minister reiterated, help "Singaporeans dissect and make better sense of complex issues, as well as domestic policies or external developments" and to "fight the spread of fake news online" (Businesstimes.com.sg, 2023).

The case to access only prestige publications is further argued by Krippendorff (2004). He stated that "this choice is grounded on the assumption that political agendas are set and public debates are led by these so-called prestige papers rather than by local newspapers, which are less likely to reproduce what the prestige papers print and are, hence, less informative" (p. 348). Riffe et al. (1998) argued that prestige newspapers are valid instruments for analysis because they play a "key role in history" (p. 86).

Data collection

Data come from media reports from April 2020 to 2021 (N = 126). This study draws data primarily from the two prestige media in Singapore—*The Straits Times* and *Channel NewsAsia.* A third source was accessed to provide supplemental data. News articles were retrieved from TODAY, a fully digital newspaper, a prestige and sister publication owned by Mediacorp, and the second-most read news platform (Mediacorp Pte Ltd., 2023b).

The analyzed data was published between April 2020 and May 2021. This time period was significant for Singapore's pandemic response as it saw the implementation of the first Circuit Breaker, a series of extensive safe-distancing measures to limit local transmission of the virus (Ministry of Health, 2020, para. 1). The measures had a drastic impact on day-to-day living as most people were confined to their place of residence. Initially scheduled to last for two incubation cycles or for four weeks, the Multi-Ministry Taskforce on COVID-19 imposed tighter measures on movement and extended the Circuit Breaker period until June 1, 2020 (Government of Singapore, 2020b, para 1.) It is also worth noting that this was the first time that similar measures were implemented after the outbreak of SARS between February and May 2003, which saw the revision of the Infectious Diseases Act (Ooi et al., 2005). At the end of the Circuit Breaker, the Multi-Ministry Taskforce announced that a re-opening would be done in three phases (Lai, 2020, para. 1). The relaxation of safe-distancing measures, which saw frequent violations and growing paranoia, lasted until May 2021 when the government re-imposed stricter measure to curb the resurgence in COVID-19 cases (Lai, 2021b, para. 1)

Data analysis

The data analysis was carried out in three stages, guided by and adapted from Low et al.'s (2011) study. The first stage was identifying the key issues and how the crises developed. Issues form the researcher's theme (Stake, 1998). The key issues were identified through a careful examination of news articles. The stories were read to understand the general issues present. In this study, we sought to understand issues that were covered: adapting to new safe-distancing or Circuit Breaker measures, flouting of safe-distancing measures, mental fatigue, and exclusive behavior toward certain groups of people.

Once the issues were identified, the second stage involved examining the emotions that the public exhibited in these articles, guided by theory. This involved examination of the cause of these emotions, and to whom or what were these emotions directed at. As priorities varied across members of the public, so would their trigger factors and the extent of their reaction toward such issues. For example, business owners may express anxiety over an unknown time period where their businesses cease to operate, whereas members of the public may express anger toward one another as some failed to comply with safe-distancing measures. Emotions not identified in ICM were also examined.

The third stage involved identifying how the emotions were manifested behaviorally. Examples of such manifestations included fraudulent flouting of safe-distancing measures such as the illegal operation of nightlife establishments or breaching the maximum number of individuals gathered together, violent actions carried out against individuals of a different ethnicity or nationality due to misinformation and perpetuated stereotypes, as well as increased enrollment in wellness workshops or a spike in the number of calls reported by counselling hotlines, which highlighted the public's attempt to deal with growing fatigue, anxiety, and isolation.

Guided by Low et al. (2011), throughout the three stages, close attention was paid to patterns of consistency and contradictions. This would ensure what Plowman et al. (1995) described as systematic analysis of data.

Findings

The first research question sought to examine the emotions exhibited by the public as evident in news reports. Four emotions were evident: anger, sadness, anxiety, and fright.

Anger

Anger was directed at the Singapore government's stop-gap measures. During a parliamentary debate, Pritam Singh, the leader of the Worker's Party, an opposition party, argued the measures were "piecemeal announcements, u-turns and positions that did not gel intuitively" (Kurohi, 2020b, para. 3). One such instance was the lifting of safe-distancing rules on public transport, but the two-person limit on household visits to loved ones remained. Moreover, the sudden closure of businesses, the implementation of safe-distancing measures without any proper support or transition, as well as an unclear rationale behind some of these measures made it frustrating for business owners to adapt, especially during such times of uncertainty. Doubt was cast over the Singapore government's policymaking as "... at times it felt as if no one in government was taking ownership of how COVID-19 directives would be perceived, interpreted and understood on the ground" (Kurohi, 2020a, para. 5).

The public also expressed anger toward the authorities' use of location data that has been collected from the TraceTogether mobile application or token, a national contact tracing tool that was implemented during the pandemic. All members of the public were required to use TraceTogether should the authorities need to contain community outbreaks and quarantine-affected individuals. However, the Singapore government did not reveal that members of the public could be ordered by the police to produce their TraceTogether history to assist with police investigations (Tang, 2021, para. 2). This mistake led to a public outcry, which prompted the introduction of a Bill to restrict the use of TraceTogether data for selected serious crimes (Chee, 2021, para. 2)

Specific groups also expressed their anger toward certain ethnic groups. At the start of the pandemic, the public was angry with Chinese nationals who were still traveling overseas and spreading the virus that originated in Wuhan, China (Matthews & Zainuddin, 2021, para. 6). At the same time, migrant workers were at the brunt of public anger after several community outbreaks were reported in their dormitories (Matthews & Zainuddin, 2021, para. 8). Public anger was fueled by the circulation of videos and images that falsely depicted the living conditions of migrant worker dormitories, which aimed to stoke greater anger toward and among the migrant worker population (Ng, 2020a, para. 1).

Anxiety–Sadness

The public also exhibited *sadness* and anxiety as they coped with the loss and stresses that came with the pandemic. In a survey conducted in early 2020, many Singaporeans expressed their anxiety about the economic fallout that the pandemic would bring (Kurohi, 2020a, para. 2). Some had also expressed bleak outlook on their employment as they had lost their jobs, while graduating students were anxious about their job prospects (Phua & Ang, 2020, para. 16). Anxiety was palpable from the calls for help. Counselling hotlines experienced a surge in calls from the public as they struggled to deal with uncertainty. Tai (2020) reported that in a month since the National Care hotline was established in April 2020, trained volunteers and professionals received more than 6,600 phone calls (para. 6). From its set-up to July 2020, more than 23,000 phone calls were made (Choo, 2020, para. 7). Similar public sentiment was echoed in an online poll conducted by Silver Ribbon, a mental health charity, which found that a quarter of respondents were experiencing greater levels of anxiety (Tai, 2020, para. 17). In addition, some turned to alcohol and drugs to manage their emotions during the pandemic (Teo, 2020, para. 18). Students also exhibited anxiety as they struggled to adapt to home-based learning. Cheow (2020) wrote that students sitting for major examinations during the pandemic had to manage higher levels of stress, compounded by the uncertainty of pandemic restrictions (para. 10). Even younger students were anxious as they "want to know if they will lose their friends whom they have not seen in weeks, and how to manage their online schoolwork. They also worry if their parents or they themselves will fall ill" (Goh, 2020, para. 3). From the reports, it appeared that many of these anxieties led to sadness.

Fright

Fright was evident when confronted with the unknown dangers of the pandemic and a disruption to their daily lives. In response to lockdown measures implemented by the Singapore government, members of the public were afraid that they would lose access to daily necessities, prompting hoarding behavior at supermarkets across the country (Loke, 2020, para. 1). This panic-buying behavior was exhibited again during the second round of measures in May 2021, despite calls from executives and the authorities (Ong, 2021, para. 1). There was also a general sense of fright observed during the early stages of the pandemic, as asymptomatic transmission of the virus meant that there was no certainty on how to stop the spread of the virus (Tan & Kurohi, 2020, para. 26).

The second research question examined what other emotions were exhibited by the public but not captured in the ICM model, as evident in news reports.

Fear

Reports found the exhibition of fear. Contrary to anxiety, which is generally described as the feeling of worry, fear is an intense emotional response to a known threat.

Fear was evident in response to several issues. First, the public was fearful of the increasing number of community cases, especially after a prolonged period where the daily number of new cases had stabilized. This was prevalent when clusters of community transmissions were found, including Tan Tock Seng Hospital, the epicenter of Singapore's COVID-19 efforts (Tan, 2021b, para. 2). Another cluster was identified at the Singapore police force's K-9 Unit, and Ang (2021a) reported that several infected patients did not seek medical treatment even though they had flu-like symptoms (para. 5).

Second, fear was evident at the community settings. The mandatory COVID-19 tests that were carried out in the community generated fear. On May 22, 2021, for the first time, the Ministry of Health announced that all residents living in a specific residential block were required to be tested after new cases were detected (Chong, 2021, para. 4). Accompanying fear was anxiety, and the situation was tense as "people around me [an interviewed resident] also seem to be getting more nervous" (Chong, 2021, para. 12).

Third, fear was also evident in reports of authorities clamping down on unauthorized operation of public and private entertainment establishments that breached safe-distancing measures (Ng, 2020b, para. 1; Kamil, 2021a, para. 4; Wong, 2021, para. 1). There was a fear that community transmitted cases would spike as the nightlife scene prepared for recovery after a prolonged period of enhanced measures.

Four, in response to the pandemic, the public was fearful of certain population demographics as they were perceived as the cause of the increased rate of transmission of the virus. As mentioned earlier, in addition to anger directed at Chinese nationals, there was also fear that traveling Chinese nationals were responsible for spreading the virus. Similar situations occurred with other communities in Singapore.

Five, fear was evident when the strains were reported to be more infectious. During a press conference hosted by the COVID-19 task force, Minister Lawrence Wong, who was the co-chair of the task force, said that "the new variant strains have higher attack rates, they are more infectious, they are causing larger clusters than before...." (Chew, 2021b, para. 5). It is also worth noting that new sub-variant strains were found in the cluster at Tan Tock Seng Hospital, which exacerbated fear of potential exposure to the virus. This resulted in a fear of frontliners, especially healthcare workers, whom the Healthcare Services Employees' Union reported have faced greater discrimination after the news of the Tan Tock Seng Hospital cluster broke (Ang, 2021b, para. 1).

Six, fear was evident in the new vaccines. The public was reported to be fearful of receiving the vaccine as it was a relatively new formulation that was produced in an expedited time frame and not much was known about its potential side effects. The Senior Minister of State for Health, Dr. Janil Puthucheary, responded to questions posed on the side effects of the vaccine after four patients experienced severe allergic reactions (Koh, 2021, para. 1). He assured Members of Parliament, as well as the public, that "the benefits of getting vaccinated to protect oneself... far outweigh the risk of any potential adverse events known to be associated with vaccination" (Koh, 2021, para. 12). To allay public fear, former President Halimah Yacob had her vaccination completed alongside a group of senior citizens, and assured Singaporeans that "only vaccines that meet strict standards of safety, quality and effectiveness will be used" (Lai, 2021a, para. 1).

The third research question examined how the emotions were manifested behaviorally, as evident in news reports.

News reports across the three main publications reported extensively on newly coined buzzwords such as pandemic fatigue or shifted the spotlight on emerging topics such as mental health. In response to various issues, the behaviors of the public can be categorized into the following: paranoia, fatigue, racism, and discrimination.

Paranoia

Paranoia was manifested as a result of fear. One of the main manifestations came in response to the increasing number of community cases. Many residents were confined in their homes, constantly barraged with negative news reports, and dealing with new living arrangements. Paranoia was also fueled by "the fear of being infected, having no control over the situation and the potential financial insecurity over a prolonged period of time..." (Tan & Kurohi, 2020, para. 8). As the public prepared itself to be confined to their homes, as mentioned earlier, individuals and families started panic-buying groceries at supermarkets, out of fear that they would lose access to necessities (Loke, 2020, para. 1). Even as community cases started to spike in April and May 2021, the public reactively reduced their frequency of attending social gatherings or eating out.

Fatigue

Fatigue, also known as pandemic fatigue, was the manifestation of anxiety and anger. This was manifested as the public went through an extensive period of safe-distancing measures without any certainty or knowledge of when measures would be lifted. Pandemic fatigue refers to "a mental state where a prolonged, heightened state of fear and caution leads to a form of burnout" (Kaur, 2020a, para. 8). The first signs of pandemic fatigue were observed as counsellors, social organizations, and experts reported an increase in mental health enquiries. Phua and Ang (2020) reported shortly after an extension of the circuit breaker was announced, "calls from new clients to mental hotlines have gone up, while existing clients have expressed fresh worries about their health and the economic fallout" (para. 4). The barrage of announcements regarding a phased reopening of the economy made it "hard for people to keep up, and even more so with no clear end in sight" (Kaur, 2020a, para. 15). To cope with the fatigue, as well as an overwhelming sense of anxiety, members of the public were reportedly signing up for mindfulness and mental wellness programs (Chew, 2021a, para. 18). The level of fatigue was compounded with the use of video conferencing, also known as "Zoom fatigue," as students and employees could only interact with their peers virtually (Kaur, 2020a, para. 21). Binge eating also became increasingly prevalent, as the change in living arrangements and daily routines resulted in greater anxiety. Food became "the fastest and most convenient way [to destress]" (Kaur, 2020b, para. 10).

Fatigue was also manifested in an increased sense of complacency, as members of the public became desensitized to the need for safe-distancing measures such as a limit of large gatherings, wearing of masks, or visiting nightlife establishments. Chong (2020) wrote that upon the start of Phase 2 of the reopening of Singapore as it exited the first Circuit Breaker, "crowds here [in Singapore] are still lowering their masks and inhibitions for long makan [eating] sessions and aimless strolls in shopping centres," despite warnings that a resurgence in community cases was around the corner (Chong, 2020, para. 11). Kaur (2020a) reported that according to a *Sunday Times* survey, 44% of respondents were weary of adhering with safe-distancing measures (para. 28). For example, Ang (2021b) reported in May 2021 that six men were investigated for failing to wear their surgical masks properly in public, out of which three of them were aggressive toward the authorities (para. 1).

Fatigue was evident in how the public coped with prevailing measures—by going against recommended practices in their attempts to, for want of a better word, to rebel out of anger. For instance, in early 2021, it was reported that more patients were seeing doctors for the treatment of flu-like symptoms, a sign that people were less compliant with safe-distancing measures (Tan, 2021a, para. 1). Operators of dining establishments and entertainment venues also failed to comply with measures by allowing groups of people to mingle with each other, or by serving alcohol past 10:30 pm. This included a report where restaurant staff "had transferred the alcoholic beverages into teapots and empty green tea bottles to avoid detection" (Wong, 2020, para. 4). The authorities also clamped down on karaoke lounges, which were not allowed to operate under COVID-19 restrictions (Iau, 2021, para. 10). Several members of the public hosted large parties that exceeded the cap on the number of people allowed. A notable incident was the suspension of a yacht's license after a group of ten were filmed hosting a party near an offshore island the day after Christmas in 2020 (Lim, 2021, para.1). There were also several illegal parties that the authorities raided, especially around celebratory periods such as New Year's Day or the school holidays. In a series of arrests, the police arrested 44 individuals who were present at a New Year's Day party in an industrial building (TODAY, 2021, para. 1). During the first half of the March 2021 school holidays, enforcement officers caught 165 individuals and families flouting safe-distancing measures at parks and beaches (Sun et al., 2021, para. 1). Psychologically speaking, these acts of complacency are reflective of the effects of pandemic fatigue, and that "people are desperate to reclaim personal control" after months of restrictive measures (Seah, 2021, para. 25).

Pandemic fatigue was also prevalent among healthcare workers in the form of burnout. Nationwide, doctors, nurses, and volunteers worked round the clock to provide medical care for patients, and were at the risk of being infected as well. Oh (2021) wrote that "not only are they working longer hours to contain the far-from-tamed outbreak, they also shoulder the mental stressors of being away from loved ones, getting infected or passing on the infection to those around them" (para. 8). On top of that, healthcare workers were managing the uncertainty that "comes from not knowing what to expect when dealing with an unpredictable disease" (Oh, 2021, para. 14).

Racism

Racism was the manifestation of anger and fear. As reports of new and foreign strains of the virus found in Singapore were published, irrational behavior in the form of racism was exhibited toward segments of the community. Racist acts became more frequent after reports of new variants that originated in other countries such as India were found in the island state (Chew, 2021b, para. 2). In May 2021, a 47-year-old man was being investigated after he "allegedly uttered offensive remarks toward an Indian family, and confronted a male member of the family for not wearing his mask at Pasir Ris Beach Park" (Ganapathy, 2021, para. 2). In a video uploaded online, the man was seen saying, "you [the male member of the family] are spreading the virus" (Ganapathy, 2021, para. 7). In the same month, an Indian Singaporean lady was attacked by a Chinese male for not wearing a mask while exercising outdoors (Menon, 2021, para. 1). Although she explained that she was brisk walking, which was considered a form of strenuous exercise that permitted her to not wear a mask, "the man allegedly uttered a racial slur and assaulted her, causing her to fall" (Kamil, 2021b, para. 5). This particular incident prompted several Singaporean leaders, including Prime Minister Lee, to speak out against such acts. Being a multi-racial society, the Prime Minister said that "it [the incident] goes against everything that our multiracial society stands for, and the mutual respect and racial harmony that we hold so dear" (Cheng, 2021, para. 4).

Discrimination

Discrimination was manifested as a result of fear and anxiety. The fear of potential exposure to the virus, coupled with the anxiety caused by the growing number of community transmissions and local clusters, resulted in healthcare workers being shunned. The level of discrimination felt by healthcare workers was evident in a report featuring Nigel Rankine, a staff nurse at Tan Tock Seng Hospital, who commented that "I don't expect people to treat us differently or put us on a pedestal just because we are healthcare workers. But they should at least speak to us like we're human and not some kind of parasite" (Tan & Tan, 2021, para. 11). Following the outbreak of a virus cluster at Tan Tong Seng Hospital, several nurses, who had taken on temporary living arrangements to protect their family members, were told by their landlord to vacate their rented accommodation at short notice (Ang, 2021a, para. 6). Additionally, hotel operators turned away healthcare workers from booking accommodation in their premises (Tan & Tan, 2021, para. 7). Several hospital staff also experienced difficulties getting to and from their homes and the hospital as cab drivers refused to accept their bookings (Kurohi, 2021, para. 6). Several healthcare workers had to change out of their uniforms before taking public transport as members of the public would distance themselves from them (Tan & Tan, 2021, para. 19). The discriminatory behavior was widespread and prompted leaders like the Minister for Health Gan Kim Yong and the Prime Minister to address the discrimination toward healthcare workers. In response to healthcare workers being evicted from their homes, Minister Gan firmly stated that it was the government's "preference to encourage our landlords to understand the situation, to play their part to support our healthcare workers, and the work that we do" (Ang, 2021a, para. 11).

Discussion

Drawing from the significance of the study as argued earlier, three observations can be made from this study.

Explicating emotions

The ICM model had posited four emotions in a crisis like COVID-19: anxiety, anger, sadness, and fright. In the model, anxiety was the default emotion, followed by variants of sadness and fright, and anger as secondary emotion (Jin et al., 2012). This study found the presence of all four emotions as posited in the model. In doing so, it further explicated and validated the emotions posited in the model. However, it is not able to establish if anxiety was the default emotion, as posited in the model, or which emotions superseded the other emotions. What we could surmise were first, the emotions displayed were targeted at the different issues over the period of analysis; second, anxiety and fright were evident in news reports throughout the duration of analysis; third, anger was manifested when the public perceived lack of consistency or competency in management of certain issues.

Given that understanding stakeholders' perspectives would increasingly dominate crisis (see for instance, Wei & Kim, 2021), it would be valid to assume that in crises relating to economic/hostile takeovers, natural disasters or accidents, stakeholders would experience anxiety, sadness, fright and anger, with anxiety and fright evident dominating. Coombs (2010) argued this should inform crisis managers how to fine tune their strategies to meet the demands of the evolving situations. While stakeholders could accept how challenging COVID-19 was, would there be ways to reduce the negative emotions they face? For instance, in this study, one issue where the public was angry pertained to the use of TraceTogether as a form of contact tracing for the authorities to contain community outbreaks and quarantine-affected individuals. However, when it was revealed that the data could also be used in police investigations, it generated public unhappiness. Questions asked were why were this information not released earlier? Singapore's Foreign Minister, Dr. Vivian Balakrishnan, who oversaw the provisions of usage of data collected from TraceTogether, apologized, stating that "...what I said in June was wrong, because, in a sense, my own enthusiasm for the technology blindsided me" (Tang, 2021, para. 43).

Expounding behavioral manifestations

While the ICM model has been found to be useful in identifying emotions of stakeholders, it has not examined how emotions are manifested in behavioral manifestations. This study is a nascent attempt to do so. What this study has found are:

- Fear can lead to paranoia;
- Anxiety and anger can lead to fatigue;
- Anger and fear can lead to racism;
- Fear and anxiety can lead to discrimination.

Paranoia had been examined. Tay et al. (2010) argued that fear could influence paranoia (Corr, 2006; Kantor, 2004). Environmental cues, including communication, may facilitate paranoia. Fatigue was found to be present in a health pandemic (Menon, 2008). The Singapore leaders were cognizant of this. They wrote in June 2021, "But it has been 18 months since the pandemic started, and our people are battle-weary. All are asking: When and how will the pandemic end?" (Gan et al., 2021).

Discrimination was evident in how Singapore managed SARS. Healthcare professionals like nurses were discriminated for the erroneous belief that they would carry the disease from the workplace to the community then

(Jin et al., 2006), it was evident again in this crisis. Racism was a behavioral manifestation that had not been studied. It could be argued as an irrationality borne out of ignorance.

Encapsulating the essentiality of the media in crisis communication

During SARS, the government communicated efficiently and effectively through the mainstream media (Jin et al., 2006). "Government crisis communication was disseminated through the media, and it was evident that, in this regard, *The Straits Times* had performed its role as supporting the government in crisis governance with aplomb. This development journalism approach, where there is a co-operative relationship between the media and the government, is a situation, in most parts, accepted and preferred by the Singapore public" (p. 96).

Crisis communication with the mainstream media as a key anchor is also evident in other contexts. Miller and Goidel (2009), in their study of crisis communication in Hurricane Katrina, argued that the media kept stakeholders informed and the authorities in check. Zafra and Maydell (2018) argued that the mainstream media were among the "most important publics during a crisis" (p. 44). A study of European communication practitioners found that they regarded the mainstream media as the "most important communication channel" (Verhoeven et al., 2014, p. 164).

What this means is that first, in government crisis communication, media scrutiny is a given and will continue to increase (Liu & Horsley, 2007). Yet they argued, citing Allison (2004), the relationship between the government and the media is "mutually dependent" (p. 404) not afforded to private entities. The government would need to enhance that engagement. Second, the media are often reliant on government for information. The government would do well in greater information subsidy. Third, explore all channels of communication to complement and supplement efforts on mainstream media (Pang et al., 2018). Social media have been used (see, for example, Yeo et al., 2020), but communicating via the mainstream media adds a layer of credibility.

Conclusion

This chapter has explored how stakeholder emotions could be examined through mainstream media coverage. The media's role in reflecting public sentiments remains important. This study concludes with three key ideas about the media in times of crises:

- The media have the capacity to frame issues that reflect public opinion (Pang et al., 2013);

- The media can be used as a resource manager in crisis response, and at the same time, be an information resource to understand the pulse of society (Veil & Ojeda, 2010);
- Engagement with the media remain one of the fundamental tasks of crisis managers (Seeger, 2006; Pang, 2010/2013; Veil & Ojeda, 2010).

In the age of information explosion and social media use, the mainstream media's role in crisis communication has not diminished, but has intensified (Supa & Zoch, 2021).

References

Allison, G. T. (2004). Public and private management: Are they fundamentally alike in all unimportant aspects? In J. M. Shafritz, A. C. Hyde & S. J. Parkes (Eds.), *Classics of public administration* (pp. 396–413). Belmont, CA: Wadsworth.

Ang, H. M. (2021a, May 11). Healthcare workers being asked to move out, shunned in public a 'very worrisome trend': Gan Kim Yong. *Channel NewsAsia*. https://www.channelnewsasia.com/singapore/ttsh-covid-19-cluster-nurses-asked-to-move-out-shunned-1356371

Ang, H. W. (2021b, May 17). Many TTSH staff members face discrimination after COVID-19 cluster emerged: Union. *Channel NewsAsia*. https://www.channelnewsasia.com/singapore/covid-19-ttsh-cluster-discrimination-against-healthcare-workers-1372301

Ang, Q. (2021c, May 3). Covid-19 cluster linked to police para-vet is reminder to be vigilant about symptoms, urge experts. *The Straits Times*. https://www.straitstimes.com/singapore/covid-19-cluster-linked-to-police-para-veterinarian-is-a-reminder-to-be-vigilant-say

Ang, Q. (2021d, May 12). 6 men investigated for allegedly not wearing mask properly, 3 also probed over verbal abuse. *The Straits Times*. https://www.straitstimes.com/singapore/courts-crime/6-men-investigated-for-allegedly-not-wearing-masks-properly-3-also

Businesstimes.com.sg. (2023, September 29). PM Lee highlights importance of high-quality, authoritative mainstream media at Zaobao centennial celebrations. *Businesstimes.com.sg*. https://www.businesstimes.com.sg/singapore/pm-lee-highlights-importance-high-quality-authoritative-mainstream-media-zaobao

Carver, C. S., & Blaney, P. (1977). Perceived arousal, focus of attention, and avoidance behavior. *Journal of Abnormal Psychology*, *86*, 154–162.

Chee, K. (2021, February 2). Bill limiting police of TraceTogether data to serious crimes passed. *The Straits Times*. https://www.straitstimes.com/singapore/politics/bill-limiting-use-of-tracetogether-for-serious-crimes-passed-with-govt-assurances

Chen, J.I.-P., Yap, J.C.H., Li Yang Hsu, L.Y., & Teo, Y.Y. (2020, August). COVID-19 and Singapore: From early response to circuit breaker. *Annals, Academy of Medicine, Singapore*, *49*(8). https://annals.edu.sg/pdf/49VolNo8Aug2020/V49N8p561.pdf

Cheng, I. (2021, May 10). PM Lee Hsien Loong and other ministers speak out against racism after alleged attack. *Channel NewsAsia* https://www.channelnewsasia.com/singapore/lee-hsien-loong-ministers-alleged-racism-man-racial-slur-kick-1376766

Cheow, S. (2020, April 1). Covid-19 could take toll on people's mental health, say experts. *The Straits Times*. https://www.straitstimes.com/singapore/health/covid-19-could-take-toll-on-peoples-mental-health-say-experts

Chew, H. M. (2021a, January 9). More turn to mindfulness, mental wellness programmes to cope with stress from COVID-19. *Channel NewsAsia*. https://www.channelnewsasia.com/singapore/mental-wellness-programmes-mindfulness-courses-covid-19-stress-388291

Chew, H. M. (2021b, May 5). COVID-19 virus variants from India detected in Singapore: What you need to know. *Channel NewsAsia*. https://www.channelnewsasia.com/singapore/covid-19-virus-variants-india-singapore-what-you-need-know-1402601

Chong, C. (2021, May 22). Jitters among Hougang HDB block residents as Covid-19 testing continues on second day. *The Straits Times*. https://www.straitstimes.com/singapore/jitters-among-hougang-hdb-block-residents-on-second-day-of-covid-19-testing

Chong, D. (2020, July 24). Covid-19 crisis fatigue: 'We forgot about Dorscon orange'. *The Straits Times*. https://www.straitstimes.com/opinion/covid-19-crisis-fatigue-we-forgot-about-dorscon-orange

Choo, D. (2020, July 10). Society must recognise potential mental health crisis following Covid-19, says Singapore doctor. *Today*. https://www.todayonline.com/singapore/society-must-recognise-potential-mental-health-crisis-following-covid-19-says-singapore

Chua, M. H. (2004). *A defining Moment: How Singapore Beat Sar*. Institute of Policy Studies.

Coombs, W. T. (2010). Parameters for crisis communication. In W. T. Coombs & S. J. Holladay (Eds.), *Handbook of Crisis Communication* (pp. 17–53). Malden, MA: Wiley-Blackwell.

Coombs, W. T. (2023). *Ongoing crisis communication* (6th ed.). Thousand Oaks, CA: Sage.

Corr, P. J. (2006). *Understanding biological psychology*. Oxford: Blackwell.

CNA Facebook (2020, March 21). Just in: The new imported cases of COVID-19 in Singapore had travelled to Australia, Europe, North America, ASEAN and other parts of Asia. *CNA*. https://m.facebook.com/ChannelNewsAsia/posts/10157231801222934/

Croucher, S. M. & Cronn-Mills, D. (2019). *Understanding communication research methods: A theoretical and practical approach* (2nd ed.). New York, NY: Routledge.

Department of Statistics Singapore. (2023). Population dashboard. Retrieved April 27, 2023, from https://www.singstat.gov.sg/find-data/search-by-theme/population/population-and-population-structure/visualising-data/population-dashboard

Durrant, R., Wakefield, M., McLeoud, K., Clegg-Smith, K., & Chapman, S. (2003). Tobacco in the news: An analysis of newspaper coverage of tobacco issues in Australia, 2001. *Tobacco Control*, *12*(Suppl.II), 75–81.

Ganapathy, K. (2021, May 13). Man investigated for public nuisance, intent to wound racial feelings over Pasir Ris Beach Park incident. *Channel NewsAsia*. https://www.channelnewsasia.com/singapore/pasir-ris-beach-park-public-nuisance-wound-racial-feelings-1362191#:~:text=%E2%80%9CPreliminary%20investigations%20revealed%20that%20on,said%20in%20a%20news%20release

Gan, K.Y., Wong, L. & Ong, Y. K. (2021, June 21). Living normally, with Covid-19: Task force ministers on how S'pore is drawing road map for new normal. *Straitstimes.com*. https://www.straitstimes.com/opinion/living-normally-with-covid-1

Garnett, J. L., & Kouzmin, A. (2007). Communicating throughout Katrina: Competing and complementary conceptual lenses on crisis communication. *Public Administration Review, December*, 171–188.

Garyantes, D. (2006). *Coverage of the Iraqi elections: A textual analysis of Al-Jazeera and the New York Times*, ICA: Dresden, Germany.

Goh, Y. H. (2020, May 9). COVID-19 SPECIAL; Anxiety may cause kids to 'misbehave'. *The Straits Times*, p. B4.

Government of Singapore. (2020a, February 20). Cushioning the impact of COVID-19. *Gov.sg.* https://www.gov.sg/article/cushioning-the-impact-of-covid-19

Government of Singapore. (2020b, April 21). Circuit breaker extension and tighter measures: What you need to know. *Gov.sg.* https://www.gov.sg/article/circuit-breaker-extension-and-tighter-measures-what-you-need-to-know

Han, D. (2023, January 14). Economic grrrowth in the East: Asian Tiger economies. *JSTOR Daily.* https://daily.jstor.org/economic-grrrowth-in-the-east-asian-tiger-economies/

Hong, J.S. (2021, April 27). Singapore is now the world's best place to be during Covid. *Bloomberg.com.* https://www.bloomberg.com/news/newsletters/2021-04-27/singapore-is-now-the-world-s-best-place-to-be-during-covid

Hsieh, H.-F., & Shannon, S.E. (2005 November). Three approaches to qualitative content analysis. *Qualitative Health Research 15*(9), 1277–1288. DOI: 10.1177/1049732305276687

Iau, J. (2021, April 3). 8 arrested in raids on unlicensed KTV joints near Jalan Besar. *The Straits Times.* https://www.straitstimes.com/singapore/courts-crime/8-arrested-in-raids-on-unlicensed-ktv-joints-near-jalan-besar#:~:text=They%20allegedly%20housed%20karaoke%20lounges,of%20arrest%2C%20was%20also%20arrested

Jin, Y., & Pang, A. (2010). Future directions of crisis communication research: Emotions in crisis – The next frontier. In W. T. Coombs & S. J. Holladay (Eds.), *Handbook of Crisis Communication* (pp. 677–682). Malden, MA: Wiley-Blackwell.

Jin, Y., Pang, A., & Cameron, G. T. (2006). Strategic communication in crisis governance: Singapore's management of the SARS crisis. *Copenhagen Journal of Asian Studies*, 23, 81–104.

Jin, Y., Pang, A., & Cameron, G. T. (2007). Integrated crisis mapping: Towards a publics-based, emotion-driven conceptualization in crisis communication. *Sphera Publica*, 7, 81–96.

Jin, Y., Pang, A., & Cameron, G.T. (2010). The role of emotions in crisis responses: Inaugural test of the Integrated Crisis Mapping (ICM) model. *Corporate Communications: An International Journal*, *15*(4), 428–452.

Jin, Y., Pang, A., & Cameron, G. T. (2012). Toward a publics-driven, emotion-based conceptualization in crisis communication: Unearthing dominant emotions in multi-staged testing of the Integrated Crisis Mapping (ICM) model. *Journal of Public Relations Research*, *24*, 266–298.

Kamil, A. (2021a, January 21). 52 people who gathered at unit in Sin Ming industrial building under police probe for breach of Covid-19 laws. *Today.* https://www.todayonline.com/singapore/52-people-who-gathered-unit-sin-ming-industrial-building-under-police-probe-breach-covid

Kamil, A. (2021b, May 11). Man, 30, arrested for alleged racist attack on woman along Choa Chu Kang Drive. *Today.* https://www.todayonline.com/singapore/man-30-arrested-alleged-racist-attack-woman-choa-chu-kang-drive

Kantor, M. (2004). *Understanding paranoia: A guide for professionals, families, and suffers.* Westport: Praeger Press.

Kaur, A. (2020a, September 13). Battling pandemic fatigue: Some feel burned out as Covid-19 outbreak drags on with no end in sight. *The Straits Times*. https://www.straitstimes.com/lifestyle/battling-pandemic-fatigue-some-feel-burned-out-as-the-covid-19-outbreak-drags-on-with-no

Kaur, A. (2020b, October 18). More people overeating or binge eating to cope with greater stress during pandemic. *The Straits Times*. https://www.straitstimes.com/life/more-people-are-overeating-or-binge-eating-to-cope-with-greater-stress-during-pandemic

Khalik, S. (2021, July 3). Moving from Covid-19 pandemic to endemic: Singapore's strategy and how it can unfold. *Straitstimes.com*. https://www.straitstimes.com/singapore/health/moving-from-covid-19-pandemic-to-endemic

Kim, S. (2020, January 26). Ban travellers from China entering Singapore! *Change.org* https://www.change.org/p/lee-hsien-loong-ban-travellers-from-china-entering-singapore

Koh, F. (2020, September 29). Media showcases role in helping to tackle Covid-19 crisis. *The Straits Times*, p. A9

Koh, F. (2021, February 2). Coronavirus Singapore vaccination; benefits of jab outweigh risks — 4 who had severe allergic reactions have recovered. *The Straits Times*. Retrieved on 27 May 2021.

Krippendorff, K. (2004), *Content analysis: An introduction to its methodology* (2nd ed.), Thousand Oaks, CA, Sage.

Kurohi, R. (2020a, April 6). Coronavirus pandemic; Most S'poreans think recession likely, will spend less: Survey. *The Straits Times*. Retrieved on 26 May 2021.

Kurohi, R. (2020b, June 5). Pritam Singh calls for review of Govt's Covid-19 response, citing confusion over measures. *The Straits Times*. https://www.straitstimes.com/politics/parliament-pritam-singh-calls-for-review-of-govts-covid-19-response-citing-confusion-over

Kurohi, R. (2021, May 7). Discrimination against TTSH staff fighting Covid-19 'distressing', says PM Lee. *The Straits Times*. https://www.straitstimes.com/singapore/discrimination-against-tan-tock-seng-hospital-staff-distressing-says-pm-lee

Lai, L. (2020, May 19). Singapore's Covid-19 circuit breaker ends on June 1; economy to reopen in three phases. *The Straits Times*. https://www.straitstimes.com/singapore/singapores-covid-19-circuit-breaker-ends-on-june-1-economy-to-reopen-in-three-phases

Lai, L. (2021a, January 28). President Halimah gets Covid-19 jab, reassures public of S'pore's strict safety standards for vaccines. *The Straits Times*. https://www.straitstimes.com/singapore/president-halimah-gets-covid-19-jab-reassures-on-spores-strict-safety-standards-for

Lai, L. (2021b, May 8). Back to phase 2: Cap of 5 people for social gatherings from May 8 amid rising Covid-19 cases. *The Straits Times*. https://www.straitstimes.com/singapore/health/singapore-to-cut-social-gathering-size-from-8-to-5-amid-rising-covid-19-cases

Lazarus, R. S. (1991). *Emotion and adaption*. New York: Oxford University Press.

Lim, M. Z. (2021, January 23). Licence of pleasure craft suspended after group filmed partying near Lazarus Island on Boxing Day. *The Straits Times*. https://www.straitstimes.com/singapore/licence-of-pleasure-craft-suspended-for-30-days-after-boxing-day-party-onboard-mpa

Lim, S., Goh, J., & Sriramesh, K. (2005). Applicability of the generic principles of excellent public relations in a different cultural context: The case study of Singapore. *Journal of Public Relations Research*, *17*(4), 315–340. DOI: 10.1207/s1532754xjprr1704_1

Liu, B.F., & Horsley, J. S. (2007). The Government communication decision wheel: Toward a public relations model for the public sector. *Journal of Public Relations Research*, *19*(4), 377–393. DOI: 10.1080/10627260701402473

Loke, L. (2020, April 4). Long queues at supermarkets after announcement of 'circuit breakers' to contain Covid-19. *Today*. https://www.todayonline.com/singapore/long-queues-supermarkets-after-announcement-circuit-breakers-contain-covid-19

Low, Y., Varughese, J., & Pang, A. (2011). Communicating crisis: How culture influences image repair in Western and Asian governments. *Corporate Communications: An International Journal*, *16*(3), 218–242.

Mathews, M., Hou, M., & Tan, W (2023, April). Satisfaction with government's handling of Covid-19 in Singapore. *Institute of Public Policy*, IPS Working Papers No. 50. https://lkyspp.nus.edu.sg/docs/default-source/ips/ips-working-paper-no-50_satisfaction-with-governments-handling-of-covid-19-in-singapore.pdf

Matthews, M., & Zainuddin, S. (2021, May 2). Commentary: Worries over rising COVID-19 cases are fuelling racially charged comments. *Channel NewsAsia*. https://www.channelnewsasia.com/commentary/covid-19-racist-remarks-racially-charged-xenophobia-1336716#:~:text=commentary%20Commentary-,Commentary%3A%20Worries%20over%20rising%20COVID%2D19%20cases%20are%20fuelling%20racially,Mathew%20Mathews%20and%20Shamil%20Zainuddin

Mediacorp Pte. Ltd. (2023a). About CNA. https://www.channelnewsasia.com/about-us#:~:text=CNA%20brings%20its%20audience%20not,current%20affairs%20and%20documentary%20programming

Mediacorp Pte. Ltd. (2023b). About TODAY. https://www.todayonline.com/about-us

Menon, K. U. (2008). Risk communications: In search of a pandemic. *Annals of the Academy of Medicine*, *37*(6), 525–534.

Menon, M. (2021, May 10). Police investigating man accused of using racial slur and kicking 55-year-old woman. *The Straits Times*. https://www.straitstimes.com/singapore/police-investigating-man-accused-of-using-racial-slur-and-kicking-55-year-old-woman

Miller, A., & Goidel, R. (2009). News organizations and information gathering during a natural disaster: Lessons from Hurricane Katrina. *Journal of Contingencies and Crisis Management*, *17*(4), 266–273.

Ministry of Health. (2020, April 3). Circuit breaker to minimise further spread of COVID-19. https://www.moh.gov.sg/news-highlights/details/circuit-breaker-to-minimise-further-spread-of-covid-19

Ministry of Health. (2022, September 17). Vaccination-differentiated safe management measures still needed in living with Covid-19. Ministry of Health. https://www.moh.gov.sg/news-highlights/details/vaccination-differentiated-safe-management-measures-still-needed-in-living-with-covid-19/

Ng, C. (2020a, April 29). Some spreading fake news about foreign worker dorms to incite violence: Shanmugam. *The Straits Times*. https://www.straitstimes.com/singapore/some-people-spreading-fake-news-about-foreign-worker-dorms-to-incite-violence-shanmugam

Ng, K. G. (2020b, July 21). Coronavirus: 28 people at two social gathering to be charged with flouting safe distancing rules. *The Straits Times*. https://www.straitstimes.com/singapore/coronavirus-18-people-at-social-gathering-in-compassvale-home-to-be-charged-with-flouting

Oh, T. (2021, May 17). The Big Read: Frontline healthcare workers pushed to limits by non-stop, never-ending COVID-19 fight. *Channel NewsAsia*. https://www.channelnewsasia.com/singapore/covid-19-the-big-read-frontline-healthcare-workers-1373811

Ong, J. (2021, May 14). NTUC FairPrice and Sheng Shiong urge customers not to panic buy in wake of enhanced Covid-19 restrictions. *Today*. https://www.todayonline.com/singapore/ntuc-fairprice-and-sheng-siong-urge-customers-not-panic-buy-wake-enhanced-covid-19

Ooi, G. L. & Phua, K. H. (2009). SARS in Singapore—challenges of a global health threat to local institutions. *National Hazards (Dordr)*, *48*(3). DOI: 10.1007/s11069-007-9194-2

Ooi, P. L., Lim, S., & Chew, S. K. (2005). Use of quarantine in the control of SARS in Singapore. *American Journal of Infection Control*, *33*(5), 252–257. https://doi.org/10.1016%2Fj.ajic.2004.08.007

Pang, A. (2010). Mediating the Media: A journalist-centric model in managing the media by corporate communication practitioners. *Corporate Communications: An International Journal*, *15*(2), 192–204.

Pang, A. (2013). Dealing with external stakeholders during the crisis: Managing the Information Vacuum. In A. J. DuBrin (Ed.). *Handbook of Research on Crisis Leadership in Organizations* (pp.209–229). Northampton, MA: Edward Elgar Publishing.

Pang, A., Kim, H. J., Chaidaroon, S. (2013). Dealing with emotions of stakeholders during crises: Why should leaders care? In A. J. DuBrin (Ed.), *Handbook of Research on Crisis Leadership in Organizations* (pp.127–147). Northampton, MA: Edward Elgar Publishing.

Pang, A., Mak, A., & Shin, W. (2018). Integrated CSR communication: Toward a model encompassing media agenda building with stakeholder dialogic engagement. In A. Lindgreen, J. Vanhamme, F. Maon & R. Mardon. (Eds.), *Communicating Social Responsibility in the Digital Era* (pp. 158–175). London, UK: Routledge.

Pang, A., Ng, J., & Lim, J. (in press). Risk and crisis communication research in Singapore. In Schwarz, A., Seeger, M, & Kim, S (eds), *Handbook of International Risk & Crisis Communication Research* (2nd ed.). Wiley-Blackwell.

Phua, R., & Ang, H. W. (2020, April 15). COVID-19: Worries about pandemic see more calls to mental health helplines. *Channel NewsAsia*. https://www.channelnewsasia.com/singapore/covid-19-fear-toll-mental-health-hotline-anxiety-singapore-763336

Rekhi, S (2020a, June 22). Trust in government surges during pandemic, survey shows. *The Straits Times*, p. A9.

Rekhi, S. (2020b, April 16). Coronavirus: Survey shows people rely on trustworthy news organisations for information. *The Straits Times*. https://www.straitstimes.com/world/coronavirus-survey-shows-people-rely-on-trustworthy-news-organisations-for-information

Riffe, D., Lacy, S., & Fico, F. G. (1998), *Analyzing media messages*, Mahwah, NJ: Lawrence Erlbaum.

Sanjeev, M.A., Pande, N., & Santosh Kumar, P.K. (2021). Role of effective crisis communication by the government in managing the first wave Covid-19 pandemic — a study of Kerala government's success. *Journal of Public Affairs*. DOI: 10.1002/pa.2721

Seah, V. (2021, May 13). Commentary: Flaring tempers and public incidents — are we losing it because of COVID-19? *Channel NewsAsia*. https://www.channelnewsasia.com/commentary/losing-temper-lau-pa-sat-covid-19-coronavirus-mask-wear-mrt-1364226

Seeger, M. (2006, August). Best practices in crisis communication: An expert panel process. *Journal of Applied Communication Research* *34*(3), 232–244.

Shepardson, D. (2021, June 9). U.S. CDC eases travel recommendations on some 110 countries, territories including Japan. *Reuters.com*. https://www.reuters.com/world/us/us-cdc-eases-travel-recommendations-61-countries-including-japan-2021-06-08/

Sim, D. & Kok, X.H. (2020, April 17) How did migrant worker dormitories become Singapore's biggest coronavirus cluster? *South China Morning Post*. https://www.scmp.com/week-asia/explained/article/3080466/how-did-migrant-worker-dormitories-become-singapores-biggest

Stake, R E (1998). Case studies. In Norman K Denzin & Yvonna S Lincoln (Eds.), *Strategies of qualitative inquiry* (pp. 86–109). Thousand Oaks, CA: Sage.

straitstimes.com. (2016, January 19). Sars: 10 years on Sars in Singapore: Timeline. *The Straits Times*. https://www.straitstimes.com/singapore/sars-in-singapore-timeline

Supa, D. W., & Zoch, L. M. (2021). *Strategic media relations in the age of information*. Oxford: UK.

Sun, D., Fang, Y., & Kwee, I. (2021, March 19). 165 caught breaching Covid-19 rules as families flock to parks and beaches. *The Straits Times*. https://www.straitstimes.com/singapore/165-caught-breaching-covid-19-rules-as-families-flock-to-parks-and-beaches

Tai, J. (2020, May 9). Mental health fallout: How Covid-19 has affected those in Singapore. *The Straits Times*. Retrieved on 26 May 2021.

Tan, C. (2021a, February 2). GPs, polyclinics seeing rise in patients with flu-like symptoms as some let guard down. *The Straits Times*. https://www.straitstimes.com/singapore/gps-and-polyclinics-seeing-rise-in-patients-with-flu-like-symptoms-as-some-let-guard-down

Tan, C. (2021b, May 5). Don't shun TTSH healthcare workers as hospital Covid-19 cluster grows, urges MOH's Kenneth Mak. *The Straits Times*. https://www.straitstimes.com/singapore/dont-shun-ttshs-healthcare-workers-urges-professor-kenneth-mak

Tan, C., & Tan, N. (2021, May 18). TTSH healthcare workers refused by cab drivers, turned away by some hotels. *The Straits Times*. https://www.straitstimes.com/singapore/ttsh-healthcare-workers-refused-by-cab-drivers-turned-away-by-some-hotels#:~:text=TTSH%20healthcare%20workers%20refused%20by%20cab%20drivers%2C%20turned%20away%20by%20some%20hotels,-A%20nurse%20told&text=SINGAPORE%20%2D%20On%20May%205%2C%20a,staff%20nurse%20works%20at%20TTSH

Tan, S-A. (2022, April 16). Singapore eases Covid-19 rules: What you need to know — from mask wearing to gathering rules. *Straitstimes.com*. https://www.straitstimes.com/singapore/outdoor-mask-wearing-not-mandatory-from-march-29-gatherings-allowed-for-up-to-10

Tan, T., & Kurohi, R. (2020, April 5). Anxiety and worry amid Covid-19 uncertainty. *The Straits Times*. Retrieved on 26 May 2021.

Tandoc Jr, E. C. (2022, June 15). Singapore. *Reuters Institute for the Study of Journalism*. https://reutersinstitute.politics.ox.ac.uk/digital-news-report/2022/singapore

Tang, S. K. (2021, February 2). Bill restricting use of TraceTogether for serious crimes passed by Parliament. *Channel NewsAsia*. https://www.channelnewsasia.com/singapore/bill-restrict-tracetogether-to-serious-crimes-passed-parliament-297611#:~:text=SINGAPORE%3A%20Parliament%20on%20Tuesday%20(Feb,crimes%2C%20including%20murder%20and%20terrorism)

Tang, S. K. (2022, June 15). CNA remains most trusted news brand in Singapore: Reuters Institute report. *Channel NewsAsia*. https://www.channelnewsasia.com/singapore/cna-most-trusted-news-brand-reuters-institute-news-report-2747566

Tay, K., Agatha, R. R., Lwin, M. O., & Pang, A. (2010). *Crisis preparedness versus paranoia: Testing the crisis message processing model on the effects of over communication of crisis preparedness messages by governments*. Denver, CO: 93rd Annual Association for Education in Journalism and Mass Communication Conference.

Tay, T.T. (2020, April 14). Coronavirus: Mandatory for all in Singapore to wear mask when out, except for kids under 2 and those doing strenuous exercise. *Straitstimes.com*. https://www.straitstimes.com/singapore/coronavirus-mandatory-for-all-to-wear-a-mask-when-out-with-exceptions-for-kids-under-2-and

Teo, J. (2020, August 10). Covid-19 can give rise to mental health stresses, say experts. *The Straits Times*. https://www.straitstimes.com/lifestyle/covid-19-can-give-rise-to-mental-health-stresses-say-experts

Tham, Y.C., (2023, May 17). Mutual trust and respect vital between government and media, says Josephine Teo. *Straitstimes.com*. https://www.straitstimes.com/singapore/politics/mutual-trust-and-respect-vital-between-government-and-media-says-josephine-teo

Today. (2021, January 2). Police investigating 44 people who took part in New Year's Day gathering at industrial building. https://www.todayonline.com/singapore/police-investigating-44-people-who-took-part-new-years-day-gathering-industrial-building

Veil, S. R., & Ojeda, F. (2010). Establishing media partnerships in crisis response. *Communication Studies*, *61*(4), 412–429.

Verhoeven, P., Tench, R., Zerfass, A., Moreno, A., & Vercic, D. (2014). Crisis? What crisis? How European professionals handle crises and crisis communication. *Public Relations Review*, *40*, 107–109.

Wei, L. & Kim, N. (2021). Within- and between-person(s) emotional reactions toward crisis communication. *Corporate Communications: An International Journal*, 1356–3289. DOI 10.1108/CCIJ-06-2020-0096

Wong, C. (2020, August 31). Restaurants and bar shut for flouting Covid-19 rules, including pouring alcohol into teapot to avoid detection. *The Straits Times*. https://www.straitstimes.com/singapore/two-restaurants-and-a-bar-shut-for-flouting-covid-19-measures-staff-at-s-tripes-hotpot

Wong, P. T. (2021, March 22). Police investigating 83 people for allegedly flouting Covid-19 safe-distancing rules to sing, drink and socialise. *Today*. https://www.todayonline.com/singapore/police-investigating-83-people-allegedly-flouting-covid-19-safe-distancing-rules-sing

Yeo, S. L., Pang, A., Cheong, M., & Yeo, J. (2020). Emotions in social media: An analysis of tweet responses to MH370 search suspension announcement. *International Journal of Business Communication*, *57*(2), 194–211.

Zafra, N., & Maydell, E. (2018). Facing the information void: A case study of Malaysia Airlines' media relations and crisis communication during the MH370 disaster. *Asia Pacific Public Relations Journal*, *19*, 41–65.

Zhang, J. (2020, April 16). How S'pore went from 'wear a mask only if you are sick' to 'it is a must to wear masks' in 3 months. *Mothership.com* https://mothership.sg/2020/04/covid-19-mask-wearing-explainer-singapore/

10 Cloaking through Crisis Communication

Hiding Uncomfortable Information

W. Timothy Coombs

Since its early days, Wikipedia has been concerned about companies editing their Wikipedia pages to reflect only positive information. This problem was intensified when groups claiming to be public relations practitioners offered services for sanitizing Wikipedia pages—removing negative content that could damage a corporate reputation. These types of problems resulted in the "Brightline Rule" that precludes public relations practitioners from directly editing the pages of clients (DiStaso, 2013). The Wikipedia editing is one example of how organizations are concerned about how people remember them. We can think of a reputation as a form of public memory. Crises are a direct threat to the reputation/public memory of an organization because they generally create negative associations for the organization (Barton, 2001). Stakeholders link the organization to a negative situation such as a harmful product or an industrial accident. Hence, organizations do not want to be remembered for their crises. Volkswagen does not want to be remembered for the emission cheating crisis nor does Wells Fargo want to be remembered for secretly opening accounts for its customers. In fact, references to crises were some of the negative information being edited from Wikipedia entries. The concern about reputational damage from a crisis is the reason reputation plays a prominent role in image repair theory (IRT) and situational crisis communication theory (SCCT), the two dominant theories in crisis communication research.

This chapter introduces the new concept of cloaking in crisis communication. *Cloaking* refers to the ability to hide or to disguise something. Those familiar with Star Trek franchise know that Klingons were one of the alien races that could cloak their ships, effectively hiding them from the Federation. Cloaking in the crisis context is concerned with concealing uncomfortable (negative) crisis information from future stakeholders while simultaneously helping current stakeholders to forget that information. For instance, a company that recalled a vehicle over a safety issue does not want current and potential new customers to think about that safety flaw

DOI: 10.4324/9781032619187-11

when considering the purchase of a new vehicle. Though stakeholders typically forget about a crisis over time, cloaking is a much more active effort to remove uncomfortable crisis information from public memory. We explore the concept of cloaking by first examining the crisis concerns of responsibility and accountability as forms of uncomfortable crisis information and fusing crisis communication with organizational secrecy to create cloaking. Next, we elaborate on cloaking in crisis through the lens of public memory. Finally, we examine a case study to illustrate how cloaking can be executed effectively through post-crisis communication.

Responsibility, Accountability, and Organizational Secrecy

In crisis communication, responsibility has been an important concept. Both image repair theory (Benoit, 1995) and situational crisis communication theory (Coombs, 1995; Coombs & Holladay, 2002) include responsibility as a key concept. More specifically, many theories utilized in crisis communication research are concerned about the degree to which an organization is perceived as responsible for a crisis, or what is known as *crisis responsibility* (Coombs, 2007). Not all crisis communication theories embrace responsibility. Discourse of renewal (DR), for instance, tends to equate responsibility with blame and argues to focus on a positive future rather than responsibility: "We suggest organizations consider emphasizing a more prospective vision of the future in their crisis communication rather than focusing retrospectively on responsibility for the event" (Ulmer et al., 2010, p. 692). We argue that responsibility is a critical element for crisis management and communication but needs to be expanded to the broader concept of accountability.

Accountability is more than responsibility. *Accountability* is about taking ownership of one's actions and being answerable for those actions. Responsibility is just one aspect of accountability. Wood and Winston (2005) studied the accountability of organizational leaders and found it had three components: (1) responsibility, (2) openness, and (3) answerability. Responsibility is the willingness to own an action or decision. Openness is the expectation a leader will be linked to decisions and actions and should model the values advocated by the organization. Answerability is the expectation a leader will be called upon to explain actions and decisions. Though developed for individual leaders, we can adjust the three factors for organizations. Organizations can accept responsibility, organizations can model their values and stakeholders will associate an organization with its actions and decisions, and stakeholders will expect organizations to be answerable for its actions and decisions.

The three components of accountability are intricately linked to one another. Openness links an organization to actions and decisions which creates a need for answerability, and responsibility is an essential aspect of any answer. Accountability applies to all actions and decisions, not merely those related to a crisis. However, a crisis creates unique demands because being accountable during a crisis requires ownership of actions and behaviors that produced negative effects for stakeholders and the organization (Coombs, 2019). Organizations, like leaders, can distinguish themselves by being accountable during negative situations (Wood & Winston, 2005; 2007). Leaders and organizations in crisis might attempt what is termed a "political explanation" rather than being accountable. Political explaining seeks to avoid "personal disfavor" by obscuring or avoiding responsibility (Wood & Winston, 2007, p. 91). Many crisis response options can seek to minimize or shift blame (Benoit, 1995; Hearit, 2001), and while discourse of renewal recognizes the value of accountability to some extent, DR's focus on the positive future can be a means of skirting accountability through the suppression of responsibility. The discussion of political explanations in crisis communication will be considered in greater detail in the discussion of cloaking.

The position in this chapter is that accountability should be paramount in crisis communication, not a concern that is marginalized or ignored. To be more precise about the use of the term *crisis*, this manuscript is concerned with operational crises, those that present a threat to the safety and well-being of stakeholders (Coombs, 2019). For example, imagine there is an explosion at a manufacturing facility that releases some hazardous chemicals. There are threats to the safety of employees, first responders, and people living in the nearby community. Moreover, the accident is likely to disrupt operations creating financial losses for the organization and perhaps some employees as well as suppliers and clients. Accountability does not mean an exclusive focus on culpability (blame) but rather a concern with responsibility. Crisis responsibility should not be viewed as negative. You need to understand the cause of the problem before you can effectively develop a solution to the problem. It follows that organizations must understand how a crisis occurred to create effective corrective action and that would include wrestling with who was responsible for the crisis.

Moreover, accountability is more than responsibility. Regardless of the cause, the organization can hold itself accountable for any crisis that transpired at its facility. Stakeholders are likely to hold the organization accountable (the organization is linked to its decision and actions) and expect answerability for the crisis. *Crisis communication is the manifestation of answerability driven by needs created by openness.* Accepting responsibility as part of being accountable is not the same as being culpable. Rather, responsibility, as a core element of accountability, is used more broadly as being *answerable* for one's actions. The industrial accident in our example might have been caused by a faulty part from a supplier.

However, the organization holds itself *accountable* because the crisis occurred at its facility and as a result of the decisions and actions of its employees. Furthermore, there are expectations from stakeholders that an organization will hold itself accountable for a crisis. As one prominent crisis professional has observed, accountability is both the right and the smart response during a crisis (Dilenschneider, n.d.).

Certain crisis response strategies allow for the suppression of responsibility and the circumvention of accountability. These strategies appear to be addressing the problems that created the crisis but do so in a way that obscures responsibility and avoids accountability. There are two processes that can explain how crisis response strategies circumvent accountability: organizational secrecy and cloaking.

Organizational Secrecy: Hiding Management Responsibility

Organizational secrecy is a concept developed by Costas and Grey (2014) and is defined as "the ongoing formal and informal social processes of intentional concealment of information from actors by actors in organizations" (p. 1423). Organizational secrecy is a *process* and not an outcome. Secrets are an outcome. Managers purposely take actions to prevent others from learning certain information. This can mean preventing others inside the organization as well as external stakeholders from learning about the information. The key is that the salient information remains known to only a few, select actors. Stealing thunder is based on the idea that the organization should be the first actor to disclose the existence of a crisis. Yet many managers are reluctant to disclose the existence of a crisis, preferring instead to keep that negative information from stakeholders (Claeys & Opgenhaffen, 2016). Not engaging in stealing thunder is a form of organizational secrecy.

Crisis response strategies can be used to conceal crisis responsibility from stakeholders. Such strategies prevent a careful analysis of responsibility and accountability. The individual-group dissociation is a crisis response that is a form of organizational secrecy. The individual-group dissociation response argues that it is just a few individuals, not the organization, that are responsible for the crisis. In this way the individual-group dissociation can conceal that the crisis was a result of larger, systemic concerns and not just the actions of a few individuals. In 2010, BP had a deadly explosion at its Texas City refinery. Initially BP used an individual-group dissociation arguing a few employees were responsible for the blast because they did not follow the proper restart protocols at the facility. The news media and the government both questioned BP's assessment of responsibility. A governmental and BP's own independent analysis found systemic problems were responsible for the deadly blast, not a few workers (US Chemical

Safety Board, 2007). In 2015, Volkswagen (VW) blamed the emission cheating crisis on a few rouge engineers. Again, the news media and various government found it difficult to believe a few engineers were responsible for software that would trick emission testing machines in a number of diesel Volkswagen vehicles. Eventually, the emission crisis was found to be a systemic problem at the company (Leggett, 2018).

In both crises, the individual-group dissociation was used to actively conceal the true responsibility for the crisis. Managers knew the actual cause of the crisis but sought to keep that information from other stakeholders. The process involved identifying a few employees as the problem. The implication is that removing or retraining these problem employees would then fix the problem. Organizational accountability would be circumvented because individuals, not the organization, were responsible for the crises. The organization has identified the guilty parties, thus there is no need to consider organizational accountability. There is no need for managers to own the crisis because the scapegoats take the fall for the crisis.

Cloaking: The Basics

Cloaking is when a crisis response is used to mask responsibility and to circumvent difficult discussions of accountability. Cloaking is inspired by Costas and Grey's (2014) concept of organizational secrecy. However, unlike organizational secrecy, cloaking is concerned with information that *was* known at some point. *Cloaking seeks to obscure the once-known information.* Cloaking seeks to facilitate stakeholders forgetting about information they know and/or to prevent additional stakeholders from learning about the information. Hence, because cloaking is not truly organizational secrecy, we need to use a different term to capture the concept. Cloaking is challenging because it takes what was once known and conceals it. Accountability is avoided because the organization cloaks the discussion and considerations of responsibility, and thus removes the need to be answerable.

Cloaking in Crises: The Power of Narratives

Cloaking is a complex communicative challenge. Organizational actors must remove uncomfortable information from public view and devise a means by which it does not re-emerge. Crises can create uncomfortable information for organizations especially when it is linked to a negative event that might have harmed or killed stakeholders. As noted earlier, the dominant theories of crisis communication focus on responsibility and accountability for the crisis. In most instances, the organization bears some or all the responsibility for a crisis and is held accountable for the crisis. Crisis information is uncomfortable information because it can damage an organization's reputation. In fact, there is a strong correlation between perceptions of crisis responsibility and reputational decline (Coombs, 2007; Stockmyer, 1996). Obviously, managers would prefer stakeholders not recall the crisis when thinking about the organization. For instance, United Airlines would prefer people not think about a passenger being dragged from a plane when they plan air travel. How might organizational management devise a means of concealing this negative information? Public memory, the discourse of renewal, and memorials can be combined to explain a process of cloaking.

Terministic Screens and Public Memory: The Power of Narratives

In 1966, Kenneth Burke expanded upon his concept of terministic screens. Terministic screens are the language (symbols) we use the describe events. Language directs our attention and action to certain information while encouraging us to neglect other information. Entman (2012) discusses a similar process in his concept of framing. Terministic screens allow people to "notice parts of our experience while encouraging us to neglect others" (Stob, 2008, p. 137). How we label "things," including events, permits the reflection, selection, and deflection of realities. Put another way, "language choices reflect and construct particular realities while abandoning alternatives" (Heiss, 2015, p. 537). Terministic screens are far from neutral. Rather, "language is a site of struggle for competing representations of reality" (Fox, 2002, p. 368). Narratives function as terministic screens that use language to shape how a situation is viewed. Narratives have power because these terministic screens create a vision of the future that influences behaviors (Heath, 1993).

One school of thought in crisis communication is that a crisis creates a struggle over the narrative for the situation. We find this line of thought in both corporate apologia (Hearit, 2006) and discourse of renewal (Ulmer et al., 2010). The crisis narrative has implications for how an organization is remembered as well as what about a crisis is forgotten. Thus, the crisis narrative as a terministic screen tells us what is important about a crisis (what to remember) and what is irrelevant (what to forget). It is through the crisis narrative that crisis communicators seek to construct the public memory of the crisis—how the crisis is both remembered and forgotten.

Public memory is central to the cloaking process and fits nicely with terministic screens. Memory is a complex notion within communication, but particularly underdeveloped in the field of crisis communication. While memory can be both individual and collective, Halbwachs and Coser (1992) argue individual memory is a rarity in society in that once a memory is spoken out loud to another person, their responses change/alter that memory such that individual memory is no longer pure and entirely individualistic in nature. The collective society in which conversations of memories occur largely informs individual memory. Public memory is akin to reputation because it affects how stakeholders perceive and react to organizations. This chapter posits that the crisis narrative can function as a terministic screen that creates specific public memories of a crisis.

Bodnar (1991) posits that public memory is a body of beliefs a group holds that informs their past, present, and by implication, their future. Halbwachs and Coser (1992) argue historical memories of the past are stored and interpreted within social structures. These notions of "stored" and "interpreted" prove useful when addressing issues of social and/or bureaucratic structures and their role in the memory and recall process. Particularly in crisis communication, crisis managers seek to strategically interpret the events surrounding an organizational crisis in order to ultimately craft the dominant crisis narrative as favorably as possible for the organization (Hearit, 2006).

Though memory is constructed by structures within society, that does not mean it is completely severed from the actual past or that public memory is entirely fictional. Dickinson, Blair, and Ott (2010) argue public memory must contain traces of actual events (there must be some historicity) but is "invented" and "constructed" and thus serves as a rhetorical resource or tool. This is consistent with Halbwach's notion of historical memory. For public memory to become the dominant narrative, there must be a degree of adherence to that constructed memory by group members (Blair, 2006).

If we view public memory as a dominant narrative created by the few to guide the many (Casey, 2004), we can draw parallels to how crisis communicators craft a narrative to guide conversations surrounding organizational crises to influence the public memory of the crisis. Blight (1989) explains the strategic aspects of memory construction when he argues, "as a culture, we choose which footprints from the past will best help us walk in the present" (p. 1169). The "footprints" of an important event, such as an organizational crisis, are chosen wisely, chosen carefully, and chosen with future interests in mind—to help an organization move past a crisis most effectively. We believe the discourse of renewal is a theory of crisis communication that is concerned with footprints and the utilization of crisis narratives as both terministic screens and public memory.

Discourse of Renewal

Arguing that crisis-related discourse is "most often about an organization or industry absolving itself from guilt and repairing its image" (p. 362),

Ulmer and Sellnow (2002) proposed the discourse of renewal as an alternative approach. Ulmer, Sellnow, and Seeger (2007) explain, "Grounded in the larger framework of organizational rhetoric the renewal model focuses on the provisional responses of organizational leaders to devastating disasters, such as fires and floods, and the leaders' natural impulse to rebuild and move beyond the crisis" (p. 131). Post-crisis discourse of renewal works best when the organization or the community can be seen (defined) as a victim of the crisis (Cotton, Veil, & Iannarino, 2015).

Ulmer et al. (2007) argue that when using a renewal approach, organizations attempt to "rhetorically structure reality" in a way that stakeholders might view favorably (p. 131). This rhetorical construction is consistent with Casey's (2004) notions of public memory as created by the dominant few (organizational managers) to guide the masses (stakeholders). However, using public memory and renewal strategies in post-crisis discourse are only a viable option in certain circumstances. From a public memory perspective, dominant narratives are generally "handed-down" narratives, but they can be challenged. Challenges are likely to occur if the crafted narrative contains glaringly obvious falsities and can be proven to be an inaccurate representation of the events that transpired (Casey, 2004). Consider the earlier examples where BP and VW failed with their initial crisis narratives. The discourse of renewal is limited to crises that allow for dominant narratives that can shift the focus from the present to the future because of the theory's focus on the bright future of the organization.

The renewal discourse is likely to flourish when four criteria are met within the crisis context: (1) crisis type, (2) stakeholder relationships, (3) corrective action and change, and (4) public versus private organizations. For renewal, certain conditions (crisis types) can create a more favorable outcome for post-crisis management. Particularly where natural disasters and crises of destruction are concerned, discourse of renewal is a more viable option because the organization is defined as a victim. Stakeholders are more willing to ignore issues of responsibility and consider the future when the organization is suffering from the crisis as well. Secondly, stakeholder relationships are important when using renewal as a strategy because organizations with strong and positive pre-crisis relationships with stakeholders may be able to tap into a "reservoir of goodwill" to gain support and financial backing to rebuild (Ulmer et al., 2007). Third, similar to other image repair strategies, discourse of renewal must include corrective action and plans for change after the crisis. The most successful uses of renewal have "followed it up with meaningful action and observable change" (Ulmer et al., 2007, p. 133). Corrective action is a rather vague concept in the discourse of renewal. Managers can argue almost any change is a corrective action, including creating memorials for the victims of the crisis. Additionally, too much discussion about corrective action may raise questions of accountability and responsibility. Hence, corrective action is a minor criterion. Fourth, research thus far has demonstrated private organizations tend to be more successful using renewal as a response to crises than public organizations, most likely because, "there is often more of an entrepreneurial spirit and greater autonomy exercised by private owners of companies" (Ulmer et al., 2007, p. 133). The private-public distinction seems important because it reflects the greater discretion with which management of private organization can commit financial resources after a crisis.

In addition to the four conditions that can create an opportunity for renewal discourse, Seeger and Ulmer (2002) posit four aspects of renewal discourse that can serve as effective renewal strategies: provisional discourse, rebuilding, communicate optimism, and ability of organizational leadership to frame the crisis. To begin with, renewal discourse is a unique image restoration strategy in that the goal is first and foremost to create a provisional narrative (Ulmer et al., 2007). Instead of dwelling on the past (the crisis event(s), corporate apologia, who is to blame, etc.) as is the case with much post-crisis discourse, renewal discourse targets the present and the future (Seeger & Ulmer, 2002; Cotton, et al., 2015). Secondly, the focus of renewal discourse is on rebuilding (Ulmer & Sellnow, 2002; Cotton et al., 2015). Rebuilding might include physical rebuilding as was the case with Seeger and Ulmer's (2002) analysis of the textile firm, Malden Mills, whose CEO successfully used renewal discourse to promise to rebuild the organizational facility that was lost during a fire. However, more universal in post-crisis discourse is the need to rebuild confidence—to communicate growth and signal the organization is working to move past deficiencies (Ulmer & Sellnow, 2002). Growth also signifies that as an organization rebuilds, it will also become better than it was before the crisis occurred (Cotton et al., 2015). Rebuilding has the implications of corrective action minus the need to address responsibility or accountability. The focus is the rebuilding itself, a symbolic action, not the reasons there was a need to rebuild or whether the rebuild addresses the underlying problems that propagated the crisis.

A third aspect of renewal discourse is to communicate optimism, which means emphasizing the positive while in turn downplaying the negative (Cotton et al., 2015). The consistent use of positive discourse is not always a viable option in post-crisis; it only works when an organization can be seen as not at fault (Reierson, Sellnow & Ulmer, 2009). When creating a discourse of renewal, a new dominant narrative is being carefully constructed, but with that construction comes the possibility for organizational leadership to disagree and not adhere to the narrative being created, thus potentially halting renewal for the organization. The last element of renewal is "associated with the ability of an organization's leader to enact and frame the meaning of a crisis" (Reierson et al., 2009). Individuals within organizational leadership are often viewed as the faces of the company—they are representatives and ones that stakeholders deem as most trustworthy (Cotton et al., 2015). As such, it is imperative that there is a shared vision of leadership values and a focus on progress in the future (Cotton et al., 2015). These four elements are necessary if crisis managers wish to be successful in the use of renewal as a discourse strategy following an organizational crisis. These four characteristics also reflect public memory. In essence, managers are trying to create a public memory about the crisis that envisions an optimistic future while ignoring the problems of the past that contributed to the crisis. The discourse of renewal includes the creation of memorials, thus linking it to the literature on memorials that also has ties to public memory.

Memorials

After a crisis, the physical crisis space can be used by an organization to remember the crisis through a particular frame: "In the case of renewal, an organization seeks to rhetorically structure reality so that its crisis response is portrayed in a manner stakeholders view favorably" (Ulmer et al., 2007, p. 131). Memorials are built to remember—things a society honors, people who are no longer alive, or tragedy that a collective has face. Haskins and DeRose (2003) argue, "A memorial is by definition a material expression of mourning for lost lives and opportunities, but it can be more than petrified grief. It can be a stage for cathartic closure and critical reckoning" (p. 381). This closure and the opportunity for a community to move on is exactly what renewal seeks to evoke after a crisis within memorial spaces.

When organizations choose to memorialize physical spaces of tragedy as spaces of renewal, they are acting in a way that recognizes those individuals impacted, recognizes the loss that has occurred and that these are things worth memorializing, which allows for these spaces to be "transformed into places of peace and healing in the wake of the violence for which they will always be remembered" (Veil et al., 2011, p. 168). By creating a memorial, a visual element is added into the memory of an event such as a crisis. Physical spaces of renewal can make rhetorical arguments in that, "a memorial illustrates the significance of a tragedy and establishes guidelines for how future generations should remember the event" (Veil et al., 2011, p. 168). Thus, memorials of renewal recognize not only what was lost through a crisis event, but also the way in which people should remember the event itself—memorials serve as physical spaces of public memory enactment. It is through public memory that memorials become salient to cloaking.

Memorials are powerful because they exude an air of impartiality. "The subtle power of memorials is that they often communicate seemingly authentic and unproblematic representations of history" (Dwyer & Alderman, 2008). In reality, memorials are a selective representation of events. "Simply put, the ability (or even desire) to 'make sense' of the past is fraught with present (and future) contestations over meaning" (Tyner, Inwood & Alderman, 2014, p. 3). Memorials seek to "narrate history in selective and controlled ways—hiding as much as they reveal" (Dwyer & Alderman, 2008, p. 168). A memorial can be as much about forgetting as it is about remembering. To create a specific memory requires other information to be forgotten. Memorials can be a way to forget elements of the past (Tyner et al., 2014). As Dwyer and Alderman (2008) note, "memorials hide uncomfortable truths behind platitudes and puffery" (p. 27).

With the need to carefully craft the discourse of renewal comes the opportunity for much to be excluded within the memorializing process. Mandzuik (2003) explains, "public memory is an ideological process, one that will privilege some meanings over others and functions to exclude and forget as much as it included and remembers" (p. 289). Memorials function as rhetorical arguments of the past and how it is to be remembered. While every crisis brings with it its own challenges, the use of renewal discourse brings with it the potential of silencing many voices as it gives hope and healing to other voices. Renewal is a form of public memory-making, particularly when organizations decide to create physical spaces to memorialize crises, as those memorials becomes physical spaces to activate the dominant narrative of the event.

The discourse of renewal is selective in what is remembered about the crisis and what is forgotten. The crisis communication focuses on the promise of the future while suppressing discussions of crisis responsibility and accountability concerns about the present or past (the uncomfortable information). The presence of a memorial enhances the long-term effect of the discourse of renewal. The memorial is a representation of the selective memories for the crisis that future organizational actors will experience because they are removed from direct contact with the crisis. Hence, the memorial as discourse of renewal becomes the point of reference when "new" stakeholders are interpreting the crisis. The memorial institutionalizes the discourse of renewal and a specific interpretation of the crisis. The memorial allows the crisis interpretation to be chronically reproduced (Giddens, 1984). By reproducing a selective memory of the crisis, organizational actors control the scope of the discourse and the interpretation of the crisis—*cloaking occurs*. The uncomfortable issues of crisis responsibility are forgotten while the bright future is reinforced. The once-public discussion of crisis responsibility and accountability is hidden as the memorial reminds other organizational actors of a more positive interpretation/public memory of the crisis for the organization. Organizational managers are much more comfortable discussing a hopeful future than trying to explain how their own failings facilitated a serious crisis. The next section uses a case study to illustrate the process whereby the discourse of renewal can be used to engage in cloaking for an organizational crisis.

Cloaking in Action: The Texas A&M Bonfire

Texas A&M University (TAMU) is steeped in tradition stemming in part from its roots as a military school. At 2:00 am on November 18, 1999, one of those traditions turned deadly. Prior to the annual football game with their rival the University of Texas, Texas A&M students built a massive bonfire. The 1999 bonfire included a 59-foot stack of logs designed to extend the 90-year-old tradition of creating the bonfire for a major sports event. People associated with Texas A&M University are known as Aggies. The term is a reflection of the close, positive ties the university cultivates with and among its stakeholders. That night, 12 students lost their lives and 27 others were injured (Gaffey & Jones Barbour, 2018). The bonfire crisis response fits the four criteria of the discourse of renewal. First, TAMU was portrayed as a victim of a tragic event. Second, the university had strong, positive pre-crisis relationships with key stakeholders (students, families of students, and alumni). Third, the university took corrective action by suspending future bonfires. And fourth, the university leadership had the autonomy to take quick action during the crisis.

While an investigation was launched, the university focused the immediate and long-term response on grieving for the victims, "For the Texas Aggie family and the world, this has been a day of unspeakable grief and sorrow," A&M President Ray Bowen (At, 1999). The Special Commission on the 1999 Texas A&M Bonfire, the body charged with investigating the situation, reported five months later. Here is a statement from page four of the report about the cause of the bonfire collapse:

> The physical failure and causal factors were driven by an organizational failure. This failure, which had its roots in decisions and actions by both students and University officials over many years, created an environment in which a complex and dangerous structure was allowed to be built without adequate physical or engineering controls. This organizational failure is complex but includes such things as the absence of an appropriate written design or design process, a cultural bias impeding risk identification, and the lack of a proactive risk management approach.
> (Special, 2000, p. 4)

Though no specific responsibility was assigned, the lax supervision by TAMU was noted and the report does hold TAMU accountable for decisions made in regard to the bonfire (Special, 2000). One member of the

Special Commission noted the role of alcohol and general failure of TAMU to properly evaluate the hazards of the bonfire. Biology Professor Hugh Wilson led a group called "Aggies against Bonfire" that claimed warning signs had been ignored for years and that the deaths were avoidable (Gaffey & Jones Barbour, 2018). Two competing narratives emerge about the bonfire memory. The tragedy narrative suggests concerns about responsibility or answerability are moot, it was simply a horrible accident. The negligence narrative in the report holds TAMU accountable and demands answerability. The report also references TAMU's culture (values explicitly or implicitly associated with bonfire) as a contributing factor.

The following year, 2000, the first memorial event was held for Bonfire Tragedy. Each year the day is marked and remembered on the TAMU campus. In 2001, construction began on the Bonfire Memorial, a physical space dedicated to the memory of the victims and the bonfire itself. The Bonfire Memorial was dedicated in 2004. It is through the Bonfire Memorial that TAMU officials extend their use of the discourse of renewal for cloaking. As is often the case with the discourse of renewal, the focus was on the future and not accountability. The dedication remarks and official Bonfire Memorial page are silent about accountability while talking about renewal of spirit. A&M President Robert Gates offered this dedication:

> This memorial is a special place where Aggies always will remember those lost and injured in the tragedy of 1999 and throughout the history of Bonfire. We celebrate their lives and the unique Aggie Spirit represented by Bonfire: a Spirit that gave light to our darkest hours; a Spirit that unites the Texas A&M family; a Spirit that will endure in all those who come here; a Spirit that must burn brightly forever.
>
> (Bonfire, 2004)

Note how the spirit will "endure" and "burn brightly forever" focuses on the future. Note too that the event is a "tragedy." His remarks are about renewal of the Aggie spirit and remembering those that were lost. There is no mention of accountability or TAMU's role in the tragedy.

The home page of the Bonfire Memorial states:

> The Bonfire Memorial embodies many layers of meaning associated with the Aggie Spirit—a deep sense of belonging, a strong spirit of teamwork, and leadership and an enduring sense of tradition that unites thousands. The Bonfire Memorial celebrates the tradition, history, and spirit of Texas A&M and the dedication of those involved in the tragic collapse of the 1999 Bonfire.
>
> (2015)

Again, the interpretation is reinforced: the spirit is renewed and must be "enduring" while the event is "the tragic collapse." The dominant narrative is tragedy, an unavoidable accident that tested the Aggie spirit but that spirit must endure (Gaffey & Jones Barbour, 2018). The dominant narrative remains about the future, not about accountability for the event.

On November 18, 2019, the twentieth anniversary of bonfire was held under the title of "Bonfire Remembrance." The statement about the twentieth anniversary begins as follows:

"The lives of 12 Aggies who died in the Bonfire collapse were honored by thousands who gathered at the site early Monday, the 20th anniversary of the tragedy." Again, the event is remembered as a tragedy. The current Texas A&M President Michael K. Young made the following statement:

> In times of great misfortune and great tragedy we are reminded how fragile and fleeting our lives can be but, at the same time, we know that the memories are eternal. The wounds from that night will never fully heal. But we remember, we cherish, we honor and we hope that for at least a moment you find some solace that soothes the terrible grief. The legacy left by the 12 extraordinary men and women is that of service, which is shown through the thousands of acts of service performed daily by Aggies across the globe. Every time we build a medical clinic and place it somewhere around the world to serve those in need, we remember. Every time we plant a tree, a tree that reminds us, creates that memory, we remember.
>
> (2019)

Young repeats the narrative of the tragedy and renewal of spirit. The memory is eternal and the legacy of the 12 who died endures through the service of other Aggies. Almost immediately after the collapse, officials at Texas A&M University constructed a public memory around tragedy. Officials continue to reinforce that public memory of tragedy thereby *cloaking* concerns about the university's accountability for the event. The counter-narrative concerning the need for the university to be held accountable for the deaths is eclipsed by the dominant narrative. The Special Report and Professor Wilson's anti-bonfire group, the primary voices for the accountability counter-narrative, are quickly "forgotten" through the focus on the bonfire renewal discourse. In their analysis of the Bonfire Memorial, Gaffey and Jones Barbour (2018) noted the Bonfire Memorial's role in "obviating institutional responsibility and protecting the memory of the Bonfire tradition" (p. 78). Moreover, future Aggies only learn of the bonfire through the dominant narrative of tragedy promoted through a discourse of renewal.

The dominant tragedy narrative singularly appears at the physical memorial and in later Bonfire Remembrance days. The negligence counter-narrative is cloaked and lost to stakeholders. The memorial and the Remembrance Day are the two primary ways that "new" Aggies learn about the 1999 bonfire event. Hence, TAMU continues to promote the tragedy narrative and reinforce it as the dominant narrative for interpreting the bonfire event.

The bonfire discourse is the discourse of renewal used to cloak uncomfortable crisis information. The organizational leaders frame the crisis as a tragedy. The discourse reinforces rebuilding and communicating optimism, not addressing TAMU's accountability for the crisis. The bonfire discourse about a brighter future and the need to rebuild the Aggie spirit embodies three of the four aspects of the discourse of renewal: focus on rebuilding, emphasis on optimism, and ability of leaders to frame (define) the crisis.

The argument is that by silencing concerns over accountability through the focus on the future (renewal), the TAMU Bonfire case illustrates the process of cloaking. Intentional or unintentional, the discourse of renewal promotes dominant narratives that allow managers to avoid being accountable for the reasons a crisis occurred. Uncomfortable crisis information becomes lost behind the discourse that seeks to emphasize the future and not fully answer for the problems of the past. By continually repeating the discourse of renewal through the memorial, its website (bonfire.tamu.edu/memorial) (complete with Bonfire Memorial photos, videos, downloadable brochure and poster, and a link for scheduling Bonfire Memorial tours), and annual events, TAMU officials essentially hide the discussion of negligence and accountability from future Aggies and influence how new members of the organization remember and interpret the bonfire. Memorials hold a special power as dominant narratives. Dwyer and Alderman (2008) noted, "Memorials influence how people remember and interpret the past, in part, because of the common impression that they are impartial recorders of history" (p. 167). The process of silencing one counter-narrative also serves to cloak that counter-narrative. The failures of TAMU noted in the Special Report and others claiming past warning signs were missed are lost and eclipsed by the tragedy narrative/public memory. TAMU officials are using selective forgetting about the bonfire to cloak uncomfortable information about the bonfire. When current students are asked about the bonfire, negligence by TAMU is not part of their response (Tachkova, 2020). This application of the discourse of renewal provides insights into the process of cloaking by explaining how public knowledge of uncomfortable information might become a secret. Perhaps more importantly, it questions the claim that the discourse of renewal is inherently ethical.

Conclusion

The concern in crisis communication over what crisis information is shared with stakeholders began with the very early crisis writings by crisis professionals (e.g., Kaufmann, Kesner & Hazen, 1994). The focus was on what crisis information should be disclosed to stakeholders. Cloaking elevates concerns over crisis information presentation by illustrating how cloaking, along with public memory, can shape what stakeholders remember and forget about a crisis. Cloaking seeks to have stakeholders remember only select information about the crisis and to forget the troubling information raised by the crisis. The TAMU Bonfire was used to illustrate how cloaking is accomplished through the utilization of discourse of renewal and the manifestation of discourse of renewal in a memorial. Discourse of renewal leverages the power of terministic screens by seeking to dictate what becomes the dominant crisis narrative. The crisis narrative tells people what information is salient in the crisis situation and what information can be discarded. For DR, the focus on the positive future is what to remember while concerns about responsibility and accountability are to be marginalized and forgotten.

Discourse of renewal focuses on crises that have an element of tragedy and situations where stakeholders have strong, favorable pre-crisis relationships (Ulmer et al., 2007). Cloaking co-opts and leverages these and other aspects of discourse of renewal to craft crisis narratives that promote the forgetting of troubling information related to accountability. The TAMU Bonfire narrative, embodied in the Bonfire Memorial, emphasizes tragedy and the desire to honor victims while ignoring the university's negligence and accountability for the deaths. Stakeholders were willing to embrace the tragedy narrative because of the strong, positive pre-crisis relationship with the university. The tragedy narrative quickly overwhelmed and marginalized the negligence narrative. Later messaging by TAMU demonstrated how the tragedy narrative became the public memory for TAMU Bonfire. Not only were those who knew about the negligence encouraged to forget it, future stakeholders learn only about the tragedy narrative from the public memory that was created and continually re-created by the university through the Bonfire Memorial and Remembrance Day celebrations.

Critical views of crisis communication is an established line of research (e.g., Fredriksson, 2014). This manuscript adds to the critical views of crisis communication by unpacking one of the dangers associated with the use of the discourse of renewal. The discourse of renewal offers itself as an alternative to crisis communication theory that focuses too much on responsibility and blame. However, the discourse of renewal ignores how the approach facilitates skirting accountability for crises. Cloaking, through the lens of terministic screens and public memory, reveals how building a dominant narrative around a better future can serve to mask uncomfortable crisis information and counter-narratives that cry out for answerability for a crisis.

References

At least 9 die 28 injured as bonfire structure collapses. (1999). Retrieved from: https://www.poconorecord.com/story/news/1999/11/19/at-least-9-die-28/51094232007/

Barton, L. (2001). *Crisis in organizations II* (2nd ed.). Cincinnati, OH: College Divisions South-Western.

Benoit, W. L. (1995). *Accounts, excuses, and apologies: A theory of image restoration*. Albany: State University of New York Press.

Blair, C. (2006). Communication as Collective Memory. In G. Shepherd, J. St. John, and T. Striphas (Eds.), *Communication As …: Perspectives on theory* (pp. 51–59). Thousand Oaks: Sage.

Blight, D. W. (1989). 'For Something beyond the Battlefield': Frederick Douglass and the Struggle for the Memory of the Civil War. *The Journal of American History*, (4). 1156.

Bodnar, J. E. (1991). *Remaking America: Public memory, commemoration, and patriotism in the twentieth century. John Bodnar*. Princeton, N.J.: Princeton University Press.

Bonfire Memorial (2015). Retrieved from https://bonfire.tamu.edu/89

Bonfire memorial dedication remarks (2004). Retrieved from https://bonfire.tamu.edu/memorialdedication/

Burke, K. (1966). *Language as symbolic action: Essays on life, literature and method*. Berkeley, CA: University of California Press.

Casey, E. (2004). "Public Memory in Place and Time." *Framing public memory* edited by Kendall R. Phillips. Tuscaloosa: University of Alabama Press.

Claeys, A. S., & Opgenhaffen, M. (2016). Why practitioners do (not) apply crisis communication theory in practice. *Journal of Public Relations Research*, *28*(5–6), 232–247.

Coombs, W. T. (1995). Choosing the right words: The development of guidelines for the selection of the "appropriate" crisis response strategies. *Management Communication Quarterly*, *8*, 447–476.

Coombs, W. T. (2007). Attribution theory as a guide for post-crisis communication research. *Public Relations Review*, *33*, 135–139.

Coombs, W. T. (2019). *Ongoing Crisis Communication: Planning, Managing, and Responding* (5th ed.). Thousand Oaks: Sage Publications.

Coombs, W. T., & Holladay, S. J. (2002). Helping crisis managers protect reputational assets: Initial tests of the situational crisis communication theory. *Management Communication Quarterly*, *16*, 165–186.

Costas, J., & Grey, C. (2014). Bringing secrecy into the open: Towards a theorization of the social processes of organizational secrecy. *Organization Studies*, *35*(10), 1423–1447.

Cotton, A., Veil, S., & Iannarino, N. (2015). Contaminated Communication: TEPCO and Organizational Renewal at the Fukushima Daiichi Nuclear Power Plant. *Communication Studies*, *66*(1), 27–44.

Dickinson, G., Blair, C., & Ott, B. L. (2010). *Places of public memory: The rhetoric of museums and memorials*. Tuscaloosa: University of Alabama Press.
Dilenschneider Group (n.d.). Why accountability matters. Retrieved from https://www.dilenschneider.com/files/why_accountability_matters.pdf
DiStaso, M.W. (2013). Rules for Wikipedia Editing for Public Relations. Retrieved from https://instituteforpr.org/rules-wikipedia-editing-public-relations/
Dwyer, O. J., & Alderman, D. H. (2008). *Civil rights memorials and the geography of memory*. Athens, GA: University of Georgia Press.
Entman, R.M. (2012). *Scandal and silence: Media responses to presidential misconduct*. Malden, MA: Polity Press.
Fox, C. (2002). Beyond the "Tyranny of the Real": Revisiting Burke's Pentad as research method for professional communication. *Technical Communication Quarterly*, *11*(4), 365–388.
Fredriksson, M. (2014). Crisis communication as institutional maintenance. *Public Relations Inquiry*, *3*(3), 319–340.
Gaffey, A. J., & Barbour, J. L. J. (2018). "A Spirit That Can Never Be Told": Commemorative Agency and the Texas A&M University Bonfire Memorial. *Rhetoric & Public Affairs*, *21*(1), 75–116.
Giddens, A. (1984). *The Constitution of Society*. Cambridge, UK: Polity Press.
Halbwachs, M., & Coser, L. A. (1992). *On collective memory. Maurice Halbwachs; edited, translated, and with an introduction by Lewis A. Coser*. Chicago: University of Chicago Press.
Haskins, E., & DeRose, J. (2003). Memory, visibility, and public space: Reflections on commemoration(s) of 9/11. *Space and Culture*, *6*, 377–393.
Hearit, K. M. (2001). Corporate apologia: When an organization speaks in defense of itself. In R. L. Heath, (Ed.), *Handbook of public relations* (pp. 501–511). Thousand Oaks, CA: Sage.
Hearit, K.M. (2006). *Crisis management by apology: Corporate response to allegations of wrongdoing*. Mahwah, NJ: Lawrence Erlbaum Associates.
Heath, R. L. (1993). A rhetorical approach to zones of meaning and organizational prerogatives. *Public Relations Review*, *19*(2), 141–155.
Heiss, S. N. (2015). A "naturally sweet" definition: An analysis of the sugar association's definition of the natural as a terministic screen. *Health Communication*, *30*(6), 536–544.
Kaufmann, J. B., Kesner, I. F., & Hazen, T. L. (1994, July/August). The myth of full disclosure: A look at organizational communications during crises. *Business Horizons*, *37*, 29–39.
Leggett, T. (2018). How VW tried to cover up the emission scandal. Retrieved from https://www.bbc.com/news/business-44005844
Mandziuk, R. M. (2003). Commemorating sojourner truth: Negotiating the politics of race and gender in the spaces of public memory. *Western Journal of Communication*, *67*(3), 271–291.
Reierson, J. L., Sellnow, T. L., & Ulmer, R. R. (2009). Complexities of crisis renewal over time: Learning from the case of tainted Odwalla apple juice. *Communication Studies*, *60*, 114–129.
Seeger, M.W., & Ulmer, R.R. (2002). A post-crisis discourse of renewal: The cases of Malden Mills and Cole Hards. *Journal of Applied Communication Research*, *30*(2), 126–142.
Special commission report on the 1999 Texas A&M bonfire (2000). Retrieved from http://csel.eng.ohio-state.edu/productions/pexis/readings/submod3/TAMU bonfire.pdf

Stob, P. (2008). "Terministic Screens," Social Constructionism, and the Language of Experience: Kenneth Burke's Utilization of William James. *Philosophy & Rhetoric*, *41*(2), 130–152.
Stockmyer, J. (1996). Brands in crisis: consumer help for deserving victims. *Advances in Consumer Research*, *23*, 429–435.
Tachkova, E. R. (2020). Enhancing post-crisis communication through memorials: the case of the bonfire crisis at Texas A&M. *Corporate Communications: An International Journal*, *25*(3), 395–411.
Tyner, J. A., Inwood, J. F., & Alderman, D. H. (2014). Theorizing violence and the dialectics of landscape memorialization: a case study of Greensboro, North Carolina. *Environment and Planning D: Society and Space*, *32*(5), 902–914.
Ulmer, R. R., Seeger, M. W., & Sellnow, T. L. (2007). Post-crisis communication and renewal: Expanding the parameters of post-crisis discourse. *Public Relations Review*, *33*(2), 130–134.
Ulmer, R. R., & Sellnow, T. L. (2002). Crisis management and the discourse of renewal: Understanding the potential for positive outcomes of crisis. *Public Relations Review*, *28*(4), 361–365.
Ulmer, R. R., Sellnow, T. L., & Seeger, M. W. (2010). Considering the future of crisis communication research: Understanding the opportunities inherent to crisis events through the discourse of renewal. In W.T. Coombs and S.J. Holladay (Eds), *The handbook of crisis communication* (pp. 691–697). Malden, MA: Wiley.
Veil, S., Sellnow, T., & Heald, M. (2011). Memorializing Crisis: The Oklahoma City National Memorial as Renewal Discourse. *Journal of Applied Communication Research*, *39*(2), 164–183.
Wood Jr, J. A., & Winston, B. E. (2005). Toward a new understanding of leader accountability: Defining a critical construct. *Journal of Leadership & Organizational Studies*, *11*(3), 84–94.
Wood, J. A. A., & Winston, B. E. (2007). Development of three scales to measure leader accountability. *Leadership & Organization Development Journal*, *28*(2), 167–185.
Young, M.K. (2019). We remember. Retrieved from https://today.tamu.edu/2019/11/18/we-remember/?utm_source=feedburner&utm_medium=feed&utm_campaign=Feed%3A+tamuNewsHeadlines+%28www.tamu.edu+News+Headlines%29

Index

Al Jazeera 52–53, 55–58, 61–65
anger 204–205
anxiety 205–206
apology 47
Arab Spring 53, 55, 61, 64
artificial intelligence: automated information scanning 177–178; chatbots 177–181, 187–189; natural language processing 172–173; predictive analytics 178, 187; risk assessment 182

Black Press: background 7, 16–17, 26–27; COVID-19 7–8; health 14–16; internet video 17–28; video outlets 8
Blue Bell 33, 39–40, 42–43, 46–47

Chicago Cubs: rebuild 72–74; sell-off 72–73
Chipotle 33–34, 39, 42–43, 46–47
cloaking: defined 222; forgetting 226–227; narrative 227–228; public memory 222, 227–228, 231–232, 237–238; terministic screens 227–228
COVID-19 2–4, 7–8, 12–14, 124–125, 127–128, 136–137, 176, 195–196
crisis: accountability 223–226, 237; defined 11, 224; regenerative model 11–12; responsibility 223
crisis communication: adjusting information 8, 130, 133–134; defined 1, 224; instructing information 8, 130, 132–134, 175; link to risk communication 8, 11; medium 34, 38, 45–47; response strategies 34, 36–38, 175–176, 225–226; visual content 37–38, 45–46
crisis management: defined 11; stages 11, 173–174
cultural gatekeepers 21–24
cultural theory 8–9, 16, 28

discourse of renewal 227–232, 237
discrimination 210–211

efficacy 134–135
emotions 196, 198, 200–201, 204, 211–213
engagement 178–179
ethics: algorithmic biases 185–186; data privacy 184–185; human intervention 185–186
extended parallel process model 126–128, 136–137

fatigue 208–210
fear 206–208
FIFA World Cup: Denmark 90–98, 102–109; Germany 90–93, 98–109; human rights 81, 102; One Love 81, 92, 94, 102, 106; Qatar 81, 102, 108
framing: applications 53, 87–88, 107–108, 131, 227; conflict framing 56–57, 59–63; contests 88–89; news 53, 89–90; visual framing 53–56
fright 206–208

health communication 125–126

image restoration theory: applications 68, 86, 222–223; athletes 69–71; denial 71; differentiation 77–78
inductive content analysis 128–130
information dissemination 173–174, 176, 183
Integrated Crisis Mapping Model 199–201, 211–212

Kasperson 8

McLuhan 16
media and crises 1
memorials 231
message convergence theory 142, 144–148, 151–155, 158–163
misinformation: combating 180, 183; COVID-19 14, 26, 125, 127–128, 136, 195, 204; deepfake 179, 180, 183; detecting 179–180; problematic 174, 176, 178–179, 186, 188–189
multi-vocal 1, 142–144, 156

organizational secrecy 225
organization-public relationship 36, 40, 42–43

paranoid 208
perceived threat 134–135
PESO model 2
product harm crisis 34
product recall 33–34
public health crisis 127

racism 210
reputation 33, 222
rhetorical arena theory 82, 87, 142–144, 160–163
risk communication 8

SARF 8–10, 16, 23–24
sentiment analysis 174, 179, 181
situational crisis communication theory: applications 35, 86, 222–223; crisis response strategies 35–36; crisis types 35; relationship history 36
social media 147–148, 155–156, 158, 160–161, 179
sport: brand 71–72, 75–76; crisis 83, 86; intent to purchase 71–72, 74–77; intent to subscribe 74–77
sport activism 82, 85–86, 108–109

Texas A&M Bonfire: background 223–237; Bonfire Memorial 234–236; tragedy 234–235, 237
textual analysis 18, 201–202
Tuskegee Syphilis Study 24

warning message 4
weather communication 142–144, 147–149, 156, 161–163

Youtube apology 38–39, 46–47

FSC
www.fsc.org
MIX
Papier | Fördert gute Waldnutzung
FSC® C083411

Kolibri 360 GmbH
Ferdinand-Jühlke-Straße 7
99095 Erfurt, Deutschland
produktsicherheit@kolibri360.de